Life in the Political Machine

Life in the Political Machine

Dominant-Party Enclaves and the Citizens They Produce

JONATHAN T. HISKEY AND MASON W. MOSELEY

OXFORD
UNIVERSITY PRESS

OXFORD
UNIVERSITY PRESS

Oxford University Press is a department of the University of Oxford. It furthers
the University's objective of excellence in research, scholarship, and education
by publishing worldwide. Oxford is a registered trade mark of Oxford University
Press in the UK and certain other countries.

Published in the United States of America by Oxford University Press
198 Madison Avenue, New York, NY 10016, United States of America.

Library of Congress Cataloging-in-Publication Data
Names: Hiskey, Jonathan T., author. | Moseley, Mason Wallace, author.
Title: Life in the political machine : dominant-party enclaves and the
citizens they produce / Jonathan T. Hiskey, Mason W. Moseley.
Description: New York, NY : Oxford University Press, [2019] |
Includes bibliographical references and index.
Identifiers: LCCN 2019053609 (print) | LCCN 2019053610 (ebook) |
ISBN 9780197500408 (hardback) | ISBN 9780197500422 (epub) |
9780197500415 (updf) | 9780197500439 (online)
Subjects: LCSH: Dominant-party systems—Argentina—Provinces. |
Dominant-party systems—Mexico—States. | Subnational governments—Argentina. |
Subnational governments—Mexico. | Political culture—Argentina—Provinces. |
Political culture—Mexico—States. | Political participation—Argentina—Provinces. |
Political participation—Mexico—States.
Classification: LCC JL2098.A1 H57 2019 (print) | LCC JL2098.A1 (ebook) |
DDC 324.27200972/52—dc23
LC record available at https://lccn.loc.gov/2019053609
LC ebook record available at https://lccn.loc.gov/2019053610

1 3 5 7 9 8 6 4 2
Printed by Integrated Books International, United States of America

Contents

Acknowledgments

The roots of this project run deep and have been watered by many. With both of us growing up in a turbulent and rapidly changing U.S. South, the enduring impact of "subnational deviations" from national democratic institutions and procedures on the citizens living within those "deviations" has been something we have long recognized. When we saw our Americanist colleagues include a "South dummy" in their attitudinal and behavioral models, we knew all too well why such a control was necessary but also wondered why not much was done to figure out exactly what the "South dummy" was capturing. We wondered, too, why so few of our comparative colleagues seemed to pay much attention to the glaring heterogeneities that characterized the economic and political transitions occurring throughout the developing world during the 1980s and 1990s. When we read such award-winning books as *Democracy and Development* (Przeworski et al. 2000) and *Why Nations Fail* (Acemoglu and Robinson 2012), we found it striking how little attention was paid to the role intranational political and economic differences played in a country's development process.

Equally striking was the fact that most scholarly efforts to measure political regimes around the world seemed to ignore the clear subnational deviations that both of us knew so well. Indeed, in most of these measurement efforts, the United States received a perfect "full democracy" score throughout the 20th century (e.g., Polity between 1946 and 2000), despite the fact that close to one quarter of that country's subnational political systems were anything but democratic and, in fact, overtly violated the political, civil, and human rights of a significant percentage of their populations through at least the first half of the century. The genesis of this book, then, and our desire to understand how subnational deviations affect the political lives of individuals can be found in the fact that we both are products of just such a system.

As the reader will see in the following pages, we rely on and are deeply indebted to the handful of scholars over the years who did recognize the importance of intranational divides and provided us with guidance as we set out to explore the ways in which subnational deviations affect the political lives of citizens who live within them. Juan Linz and Amando de Miguel's seemingly forgotten volume on "within-nation differences and comparisons" (1966) served as our theoretical point of departure for thinking about how such intranational differences matter. V. O. Key's work on the one-party South (1949) proved invaluable in offering a highly nuanced treatment of the many different forms that a dominant-party enclave may take when embedded in a national-level democracy.

More recently, the work of Fox (1994), Nickson (1995), and O'Donnell (1993, 1998, 1999) on the highly uneven nature of Latin America's democratization processes during the 1980s and 1990s, along with the works of Mexican and Argentine scholars who were directly experiencing such unevenness, such as Gomez-Tagle (1997) and Wiñazki (1995), further laid the groundwork for our launch of this project. Finally, a tremendous debt is also owed to the small but growing community of scholars that over the past 20 years has made substantial contributions to our understanding of the origins and persistence of dominant-party enclaves around the world. These scholars include Gervasoni (2010b, 2015, 2018), Gibson (2005, 2013), Giraudy (2009, 2011, 2013, 2015), McMann (2006), and Snyder (2001) to name just a few. We are grateful for their work and for the opportunity to be a part of this community of scholars working on what we see as one of the defining characteristics of the many fledgling, and some established, democracies around the world today.

Moving beyond those whose research laid the foundation for this book, any project of this sort lends further support to the now certainly trite, but still very true, African proverb "It takes a village." And when sitting down to think about those who were part of that village for us, those to whom we are so deeply indebted, we are struck by how big the village is.

Over the course of working on this book, we have had the opportunity to present individual chapters and benefit from the insightful feedback of several colleagues. We would like to thank participants in panels at the 2015 and 2017 Latin American Studies Annual Congresses, the 2015 and 2016 American Political Science Association Annual Meetings, and the 2017 meeting of the Southeast Latin American Behavior Consortium (SeLAB). At the SeLAB meeting in particular, we received detailed comments from discussant Agustina Giraudy that greatly improved the manuscript, as well as from attendees including Fred Batista, Ryan Carlin, Mollie Cohen, Abby Córdova, Todd Eisenstadt, Greg Love, Noam Lupu, and Virginia Oliveros, among others. In addition, Rod Camp, Stephen Morris, Alejandro Díaz Domínguez, Shaun Bowler, and David Pion-Berlin all offered tremendous support for this project along the way. We appreciate their thoughtful suggestions for how we might refine the theoretical contribution and improve our research design.

Our colleagues and former mentors at Vanderbilt have also been so important in helping us move forward along the long and winding trail that led to this book. Beginning with Mitch Seligson, both of us have benefited in countless ways over the years by having Mitch in our corner—as a dissertation chair, the founder of LAPOP (Latin American Public Opinion Project), and a legend in his contributions to research on Latin American political behavior. Neal Tate, John Geer, Dave Lewis, and Alan Wiseman, among many others, have all been the source of sage advice and encouragement along the way. Also deserving of thanks is the wonderful community of Latin Americanists at Vanderbilt that helps make Vanderbilt such an intellectually stimulating place to study and work. Ted Fischer deserves special mention for his long stewardship of the Center for Latin American Studies and his ceaseless efforts to foster and support that community of scholars.

Special thanks must also go to Liz Zechmeister and the incredible team at the Latin American Public Opinion Project. Though Mitch founded LAPOP many years ago, Liz has now become synonymous with this research center. Indeed, just saying thank you to Liz, as well as to Daniel, Mariana, Georgina, Tonya, Nicole, Sebastian, and the many others who have helped establish LAPOP as the premier center for public opinion on Latin America, does not seem sufficient for all the help and support they have provided to this project over the years. Very clearly, this project would not have been possible without their tireless efforts. Further, Liz has taught us so much about so many aspects of this profession and never ceases to amaze in all of the tremendous contributions she makes to the department, our undergraduate and graduate students, the profession, and our understanding of Latin Americans' political attitudes and behaviors.

We would also like to thank all of the many former colleagues and graduate students whom we have worked with over the years at Vanderbilt. Though officially Hiskey's students, they quickly joined the ranks of the many teachers who have made such an impact on our lives and our understanding of Latin America, for which we are so deeply indebted. Among those who have taught us so much, and have become dear friends in the process, are Fernanda Boidi, Abby Córdova, Miguel Cruz, Alejandro Díaz-Domínguez, Juan Carlos Donoso, Brian Faughnan, Daniel Montalvo, Daniel Moreno, Diana Orcés, and Mariana Rodriguez. Thank you all.

At West Virginia University, we would like to thank participants in the comparative politics research workshops—notably, Erik Herron and Jay Krehbiel—for their valuable advice regarding the chapter on electoral accountability. We would also like to thank department chairs Scott Crichlow and John Kilwein, who each helped facilitate extended fieldwork in Argentina, with the support of the Eberly College of Arts and Sciences. We would also like to acknowledge the contributions of the Woolwine family, which has graciously funded multiple research trips for comparative faculty within the WVU Department of Political Science. Many of the interviews that are cited in the pages of this book were carried out in the spring of 2018, with that funding. We also would like to thank Maxwell Nimako for his excellent research assistance.

Also critical for the success of this project have been all of the many public servants, scholars, and everyday citizens in Argentina and Mexico who have helped us in countless ways during our many research trips over the years, from Hiskey's first field interview with an official from the Port of Veracruz in 1992, to those who helped with our research visits to D.F. (Mexico City) in 2017 and Buenos Aires and San Luis in 2018. In particular, we want to thank all of the many kind and gracious people throughout Buenos Aires, Jalisco, Mendoza, Michoacán, and San Luis who helped with our research in immeasurable ways dating back to the 1990s. Special thanks to Alfonso, Geo, Hector, and Pati in Zapopan, Brenda at CEDE, and the many public officials in Mexico who so graciously gave us their time and insights on this project. Also, Alejandro, Carlos, Maria Gabriela, Matias, and everyone at *Universidad Torcuato di Tella* were vital in assisting our work in Argentina. In addition, the organizations that made such research trips possible also must be mentioned, including the Inter-American Foundation, the Fulbright Commission, the National Science Foundation, and Vanderbilt's Research Scholar grant program.

We would be remiss if we failed to acknowledge the folks at Oxford University Press, notably Angela Chnapko, Alexcee Bechthold, and Shalini Balakrishnan for their outstanding work throughout this process. Angela was always quick to respond to whatever questions or concerns we had and did a wonderful job of selecting two anonymous reviewers who truly went above and beyond with their detailed recommendations for how to improve the manuscript. We thank her for her valuable insight on the content of this manuscript, and her professionalism throughout. We also appreciate that Alexcee and Shalini have been incredibly efficient and, when necessary, patient with us, during the production phase. In short, we could not have possibly had a better publication experience than what we had with OUP, and the quality of this book is undoubtedly much improved for having worked with them.

Finally, and most importantly, our families. Hiskey would like to thank his mom and dad, Kathy, Liz, Tim, Chuck, Christine, Sarah, Nathan, Mantha, and Nick, as well as Tom, Joyce, and Mac, all of whom helped with this project through their unconditional love and support. Thanks as well to Rod, Jay, and Gary, and the many other members of his extended Chapel Hill community of family and friends. Most importantly, an undertaking such as this would never have even seen the light of day if not for the love and support of his wife Lynn and their four beautiful, amazing kids, Caroline, Jessie, Eli, and Mason. Much love and thanks to you all for everything large and small you have given to this endeavor over the years.

Moseley would like to thank his parents for their constant support and irrational faith in him, his brother and friends (in Boone, Mendoza, Morgantown, and beyond) for companionship and needed distraction, and Natalia and Filipo, for their love and patience, and for providing him with a sense of purpose.

Dedicated to the memory of Richard and Kathy Hiskey

1

Welcome to the Machine[*]

On August 13, 2017, it appeared that the province of San Luis, Argentina, was on the verge of a political sea change. For more than three decades, the brothers Adolfo and Alberto Rodríguez-Saá had never lost a provincial election, trading off the governorship and one of the province's three seats in the National Senate seemingly at their own discretion. But on this day, the unthinkable happened—Adolfo lost the primary vote (Primarias, Abiertas, Simultáneas, y Obligatorias (PASO)) for national senator to former ally Claudio Poggi by a whopping 20-point margin. Alberto, the current governor, acknowledged the "adverse result" and vowed that his family's supporters would reverse the outcome in October (*La Nación* 2017a). Yet, in primaries that basically amount to glorified public opinion polls, which occur only weeks before the general election, 20 points seemed insurmountable, even for the once-invincible Rodríguez-Saá machine.

In the weeks that followed, the Rodríguez-Saá brothers proceeded to flex the political muscle that had allowed them to rule San Luis uninterrupted since the 1980s. And in the process, they offered a clear picture of the machinery that we view as essential to understanding why citizens in such dominant-party enclaves behave and think differently about politics than those living in competitive, multiparty systems. First, a judge appointed by Rodríguez-Saá declared that the opposition had acted illegally during the primaries, and banned Poggi from carrying out campaign activities—including having access to television, radio, and newspaper advertising—in the lead-up to the general election. When a federal judge finally intervened to lift the ban, there was only a week left before Election Day for the opposition to make their case to voters. While judicial allies pursued the disqualification of his competitors, Adolfo promised to "clean out all of the traitors" in a voice message leaked to the press, and Alberto fired his entire cabinet (Clarín 2017). The message was clear: If you are not with us, you are against us, and the consequences are severe.

Between August and October, the Rodríguez-Saá brothers wielded the carrot just as deftly as they did the stick. Following their defeat, the brothers

[*]Pink Floyd. (1975). "Welcome to the Machine." *Wish You Were Here*, Columbia Records. Vinyl LP.

Life in the Political Machine. Jonathan T. Hiskey and Mason W. Moseley, Oxford University Press (2020). © Oxford University Press.
DOI: 10.1093/oso/9780197500408.001.0001

pursued a massive public spending campaign in an effort to woo disenchanted primary voters. First, the brothers introduced a new social program that would provide basic foodstuffs for children at each of 5,000 locations throughout the province—what the provincial government called *merenderos*.[1] All of the locations would be staffed by Rodríguez-Saá operatives, and children were required to be accompanied by an adult to access their benefits, at which point loyal *militantes* could proselytize on behalf of the local machine. As rumors abounded that Adolfo was using publicly funded social programs to curry the favor of impoverished voters, his brother Alberto responded to the accusation by saying, "What is clientelism? It's called social assistance . . . (and) justice" (Torrez 2017; "Clientelismo y corrupción pre-electoral").

In perhaps the most egregious example of utilizing public funds for political purposes, Adolfo created a charity called Mujeres Puntanas in July, which would be run by his wife, Gisela Vartalitis, and was granted 20 million pesos by the provincial government. In August, after Adolfo's defeat in the primary, Vartalitis requested an additional 80 million pesos to fund a new program called Mujeres Emprendadoras, which was immediately provided by the governor and her brother-in-law, Alberto (Veneranda 2017). The newly formed organization used the money to purchase household appliances like ovens, microwaves, and washing machines, which were then raffled off to local women—ostensibly in exchange for their support in the election. The opposition leveled corruption charges against the provincial government, but to no avail in a province where virtually every local judge had been appointed by one of the Rodríguez-Saá brothers.

On October 21, 2017, Adolfo won reelection by a 12-point margin, representing roughly a 30-point turnaround from the primaries. In his triumphant victory speech, he called the turnaround an "epic poem" (Flores 2017, 1), fueled by the thousands of San Luis citizens who had trusted him with their fate on Election Day. He credited his willingness to listen to the concerns of *puntanos*,[2] and particularly the less fortunate, for his come-from-behind triumph, claiming "we were a legion of activists who were organized perfectly and embraced the less fortunate" to emerge victorious (Ybarra 2017, 3). As of 2017, the reign of the Rodríguez-Saá in San Luis was not dead yet.

***

[1] In Argentina, the *merienda* is a between-meal snack.
[2] The nickname for a denizen of San Luis, *puntano*, comes from the capital city's location at the foot of the Punta de los Venados mountain range in central-western Argentina (Bianchi 2013).

By all accounts, the June 4, 2017, gubernatorial elections in Mexico state (commonly referred to as Edomex) should have marked the end of the Institutional Revolutionary Party's (PRI's) nearly 90 years of control over the state's executive office. Approval ratings for the party's leader, former governor of Edomex and then president of Mexico, Enrique Peña Nieto, were close to single digits; the state's economy was stagnant; crime and violence had exploded in the years leading up to the election; and a nationwide rejection of status quo politics made Edomex, widely known as the "cradle of the PRI," a particularly ripe target for anti-incumbent sentiment among Mexican voters. Indeed, the PRI's gubernatorial candidate that year, Alfredo del Mazo, was the epitome of a machine politician: the son and grandson of former governors of Edomex, as well as a distant cousin of Peña Nieto. Further, his principal challenger, Delfina Gómez of the upstart, and decidedly anti–status quo, National Regeneration Movement (MORENA) party, was a relative newcomer to politics, spending most of her professional career as a primary school teacher. In sum, despite being one of the most entrenched dominant-party systems in the country, the PRI's political machine seemed primed for defeat heading into the June elections.

On the morning of Election Day, MORENA party officials at three separate locations arrived to their campaign offices to find a pile of severed pigs' heads on the sidewalk outside—a fitting testament to the depths to which the PRI and its supporters had sunk in order to keep their political machine running (Figure 1.1). If the pigs' heads were meant to intimidate MORENA workers, that was not the only such act of intimidation that day, or in the days leading up to the election. One election observer, for example, recounted reports that "numerous MORENA representatives had received phone calls on the eve of the election threatening violence against them and their families if they showed up on Election Day" (Thornton 2017, 17). Such efforts at intimidation as the election neared, however, were only one of the many tools of electoral malfeasance reportedly employed by the PRI during the 2017 campaign.

The most extensive account of the efforts put forth by the Edomex PRI machine comes from a team of international and domestic election observers from the organization Ni un Fraude Más, whose mission for the 2017 elections was to provide an outlet for citizens to report incidents of electoral fraud and intimidation. The final report of this organization offered a scathing indictment of the state's electoral process, concluding that in order to win, the PRI launched "the largest campaign of vote buying and coercion ever seen in Mexico's history" (Observatorio #NiUnFraudeMas 2017).

Figure 1.1. MORENA Campaign Office on Election Day in Estado de Mexico, June 4, 2017.
Source: Photograph by Betos Gy.

Categorizing the hundreds of violations reported to and investigated by the organization, the report found evidence for the following types of electoral dirty tricks:

1. Illegal use of government program funds to campaign and influence voters;
2. A "dirty war" against the MORENA candidate, Gómez, and her supporters, including acts of physical and psychological intimidation;
3. Campaign spending violations;
4. Pressure on government workers (teachers, public health workers, etc.) to campaign for the PRI;
5. Outright acts of vote buying and coercion;
6. Violation of the ban on campaign activities three days prior to the election;
7. Widespread irregularities with Election Day polling sites and vote counting; and
8. Gender-based political violence.

In total, the group received over 600 reports of election violations from citizens across the state, providing a comprehensive accounting of what incumbents in a dominant-party machine resort to when faced with a credible electoral challenge. Alas, del Mazo won by 3 percentage points over Gómez to continue the PRI's over 80-year dominance over Edomex politics through at least 2023.

Everyday Life in Dominant-Party Enclaves

We view Edomex and San Luis as dominant-party enclaves sustained by the ongoing operations of a political machine. In the following pages, we explore the political attitudes and behaviors of citizens who must interact with these machines on a daily basis. Though thousands of miles separate the two, the residents of Edomex and San Luis share the experience of living in a subnational political system, which, while nominally free and democratic, is dominated by a political machine that relies on a wide range of undemocratic tools to stay in power and keep its opponents at bay. While not overtly authoritarian, as they are embedded in national-level democratic regimes, these dominant-party enclaves clearly operate in ways that make them less than democratic.

For us, the essence of a dominant-party enclave—and the political machine that operates within it—is a single party's sustained hold on power through the maintenance of what we might call an "undemocratic incumbency advantage." The means through which dominant parties construct this advantage will differ within and across countries, but the end result is the same—a prolonged period of rule by a single party (or individual) achieved through legally questionable means. As Gervasoni (2018) points out, these are not the repressive, fully autocratic regimes of the past but, rather, fall in the "hybrid regime" category in which oftentimes subtle, and at times not-so-subtle, means of economic, political, and social "persuasion" take place, within a system that has all the trappings of a democracy.

Nearly 70 years ago, Key (1949) offered one of the first systematic assessments of a highly uneven democratic landscape in which dominant-party subnational political systems coexisted alongside, and within, a multiparty democratic regime. In examining the one-party systems of the U.S. South, Key highlighted the role that the "colorful demagogue" (106) played in organizing politics in such systems and noted that in such systems a "friends-and-neighbors appeal can assume overriding importance [and] issues are either nonexistent or blurred" (110). As Mickey (2015) notes in his work on these same political systems and their legacies, the one-party enclaves of the South "were effectively conflations of the state apparatus with those institutions regulating political ambitions" (5). In other words, while at the national level the United States had long been one of the world's beacons of liberal democracy, the "Solid South" remained the domain of entrenched political machines until the 1960s and bore little resemblance to what was going on in Washington, D.C., or other parts of the country.

Scholars of democracy working across the developing world in recent years have found a political landscape littered with similarly uneven regimes led by "colorful demagogues," in which politics are driven by "friends and favors" (Key 1949, 106). Whether in the former Soviet states, such as Kyrgyzstan, where many citizens are unable to "earn a living independent of the state" (McMann 2006, 28), or in Mexico and Argentina, which will be the focus of this book, we now have an international community of democracies in which many are dragged down by subnational dominant-party enclaves. These divided regimes, we contend, have important consequences for both the citizens that live within them and for broader efforts to deepen democratic rule and make it more durable.

The growing number of scholars exploring the roots of these subnational dominant-party enclaves (Behrend 2011; Cleary and Stokes 2006; Fox 1994; Gibson 2005, 2013; Gervasoni 2018, 2010b; Giraudy 2011, 2015; Lawson 2000) is indicative of their prevalence, and persistence, as a feature of today's young democracies. This regime unevenness is particularly notable in Latin America, where some citizens enjoy the near-universal acceptance of basic democratic institutions and procedures, while their neighbors live in systems in which dominant parties serve as "giant patronage systems that [often] give the citizens a vested interest in the perpetuation of the regime" (Magaloni and Kricheli 2015, 128). Though most of the region's national electoral processes now typically receive the international community's clean election stamp of approval, countless local- and provincial-level elections across the Americas continue to be plagued by significant issues of electoral malfeasance (e.g., Gervasoni 2018; Giraudy 2015). With such extreme divides running through many countries, it is imperative to recognize first that a regime label applied to a country as a whole may, in fact, mask important intranational variations in political systems, and second, that such divides can potentially have important consequences for the ways in which citizens of those countries think about and engage with their political world.

Indeed, while there is a vibrant academic literature that examines the day-to-day operations of political machines in Latin America, and the methods by which they perpetuate their power (e.g., Fagen and Tuohy 1972; Lawson and Greene 2014; Magaloni 2006; Oliveros 2016; Stokes 2005; Szwarcberg 2015; Weitz-Shapiro 2014), scant empirical research tackles machine politics from the perspective of the everyday citizens living within them.[3] As Auyero (1999, 299) notes, "Revolving around the same limited issues, they [studies of political machines] repeatedly leave certain subjects untouched. One of those unexplored subjects is . . . the different and competing views that 'clients' themselves hold of 'clientelist politics.'" In our view, life inside a political machine can affect all manner of ways in which citizens understand and engage in politics, from their attitudes toward democracy, to their willingness to hold politicians accountable, to the ways in which they participate in political life.

In sum, despite the many cases of uneven democracies we have seen across space and time, and the increased attention by scholars to the origins of that subnational unevenness, we know little about the consequences of these divided regimes for how citizens understand and participate in politics. Given the recent surge in public opinion research in the developing world, and the widely supported proposition that the political institutions and rules of the game under which one lives will shape to some extent her political attitudes and behaviors (e.g., Anderson et al. 2005; Machado et al. 2011; Carlin et al. 2015), the absence of such research becomes all the more conspicuous.

Further, there is considerable evidence that individuals' experiences with local politics can carry over to their evaluations of and interactions with national-level institutions and actors (Cleary and Stokes 2006; Hiskey and Seligson 2003; Hiskey and Bowler 2005; Key 1949; Seligson 2002; Shi 1997; Vetter 2002). We contend that citizens' views of politicians and political institutions that are shaped by their daily experiences with a dominant-party machine will also color their views toward democracy more generally and the electoral calculus they make when evaluating incumbent officials at both the provincial *and* national levels. We know from previous research, for example,

---

[3] A notable exception would be the work of Javier Auyero (1999, 2000, 2007) on machine politics in Argentina. In addition, Fagen and Tuohy's work on Xalapa (1972), Veracruz has long been viewed by many as one of the most extensive analyses of the daily lives of citizens living in Mexico's one-party system.

that an individual's direct experiences with street-level corruption—being asked for a bribe by local-level public officials—have a significant negative effect on her views of the legitimacy of the entire political system (Seligson 2002). We also have evidence that one's local electoral process—and whether it is perceived as free and fair—affects perceptions of and engagement with national elections (Hiskey and Bowler 2005). Similarly, Vetter's (2002) work on "the importance of the local level as a 'training ground' for democracy" (15) in the European context suggests that when the local/subnational level is *not democratic*, it might serve as a training ground for less-than-democratic political attitudes and behaviors. In short, if one learns how to play politics by following the rules of her subnational political game, it is perhaps likely that the characteristics of that subnational political system will also influence the way she engages with the national political game as well.

Getting to Know Dominant-Party Citizens

In this book, we explore the attitudinal and behavioral consequences of life in a dominant-party enclave. Through a comparative subnational analysis of the provinces and states of Argentina and Mexico, we find starkly divergent patterns of political attitudes and behaviors among citizens living in dominant-party enclaves and those living in competitive multiparty systems. For the latter, the prevailing political attitudes and behaviors approximate those found in established democracies. But for the former, we find political attitudes and behaviors that reflect, and, we argue, are a product of, political systems characterized by uneven electoral playing fields, pervasive corruption, and an overt conflation of the dominant party and the state.

How do dominant-party enclaves influence citizens' political attitudes and behaviors, and what are the consequences for national-level democracies? We view the prevalence of three key characteristics commonly found in these dominant-party enclaves—(1) the politicization of the rule of law, (2) a tilting of the electoral arena, and (3) a partisan deployment of state resources—as critical in shaping citizens' daily experiences with their political system, including their understanding of democratic principles, the ways in which they hold politicians accountable, and the nature of their participation in politics. These deleterious subnational influences on the ways citizens think about and engage with politics will not only affect the quality of democracy at the subnational level but also impede the larger project of deepening democracy for the country as a whole. Further, through our interviews with individuals living in dominant-party enclaves, as well as through our analyses of survey data, we find that a certain degree of tolerance of, if not acquiescence to, such systems can emerge among voters as electoral victories by the dominant party increasingly seem inevitable.

Through elevated exposure to vote buying and other corrupt practices, selective access to state resources, a political socialization into a system in which a single party controls the most powerful branch of government, and an electoral process that seems to provide little recourse for opponents of the incumbent party, we find that dominant-party citizens, when compared with their counterparts in multiparty regimes, tend to hold less democratic attitudes and are less willing to punish incumbents for poor performance, are less concerned about government corruption, and are more likely to participate in politics in ways that directly benefit the dominant party. Evidence for these distinct patterns of citizens' views of and engagement with their subnational political systems also emerges in the ways these same individuals evaluate and interact with their *national* elected officials.

Implications

Why do such dominant-party enclaves, and their attitudinal and behavioral consequences, matter? We contend first that they pose a potential threat to the further consolidation of national-level democratic systems around the world. By fostering a political culture characterized by tepid support for democracy, tolerance of such practices as corruption and vote buying, limited or distorted electoral accountability, and political participation patterns oriented toward maintaining the dominant-party status quo, these subnational enclaves can erode public support for democracy at the national level, particularly when the leaders of these dominant-party machines graduate to national-level office, as was the case with Presidents Néstor and Cristina Kirchner of Argentina and Enrique Peña Nieto of Mexico. These local strongholds of illiberalism in myriad ways thus provide added fuel to the recent global drift away from democracy (see Freedom House 2019; LAPOP 2016/2017; Gervasoni 2018).

Second, the dramatic differences that we find separating citizens living in subnational competitive multiparty systems from those living in dominant-party enclaves call into question a fundamental assumption found throughout much of comparative research that views the nation-state as the most appropriate unit of comparison when exploring patterns of political attitudes and behavior. With few exceptions, scholars have framed the comparative enterprise as one based on differences *between* countries (e.g., Inglehart and Welzel 2005). We contend that *within-country* differences can be just as, if not more, significant than those found across countries and can potentially confound conclusions based on national aggregations. While many scholars have recognized the significance of this subnational regime heterogeneity, there have been few systematic evaluations of the degree to which citizens of the same national polity engage in and think about politics differently based on the characteristics of their subnational political context.

Given the diverse set of political attitudinal and behavioral outcomes we examine (e.g., experiences with and attitudes toward democracy, exposure to corruption and clientelism, and various forms of political participation), and the many uneven democracies we know to exist around the world, our hope is to contribute to multiple research traditions in political science. Much as, for example, McMann's work on subnational regimes in Russia and Kyrgyzstan (2006) or Gervasoni's more recent work on Argentina (2018) hold important lessons for scholars of emerging democracies in other regions of the world, so, too, do we intend this study to appeal to regional specialists from around the world interested in the question of the behavioral and attitudinal consequences of uneven regimes. More broadly, a current area of concern for democratization scholars, international development organizations, and those involved in democracy promotion efforts is the increase in democratic "backsliding" or "decay" afflicting many of the world's emerging, and established, democracies. Our research speaks directly to these concerns and pushes forward our understanding of possible sources of such decay and what some of the consequences may be.

Finally, the subnational focus and findings from this book should also be of interest to the many scholars and students of Argentine and Mexican politics, from those focused on the democratization process in these two countries to those engaged in research on public opinion, elections, and political behavior. Indeed, as far as each regime has come since its national transition to democracy, the fact that millions of individuals in the two countries continue to dwell in less-than-democratic systems in 2020 merits a reckoning by the academic and policymaking communities of both countries. Simply put, we still know relatively little about what these dominant-party machines imply for efforts to move the democracy project forward in these countries.

While the attitudes and experiences of individuals in far-flung subnational regimes like Hidalgo, Mexico, and La Rioja, Argentina, are often relegated to the endnotes of national case studies or even ignored altogether, this study places the political lives of citizens in dominant-party enclaves as the focal point of its analysis.

A Roadmap

In the second chapter, we introduce in a more systematic fashion our concept of dominant-party enclaves and the theoretical avenues through which such systems potentially affect the political attitudes and behaviors of citizens living within them. Such jurisdictions frequently exhibit weak rule of law, high levels of corruption and clientelism, and an uneven electoral playing field, even decades after national-level transitions to democracy have occurred (Chavez 2004; Fox 1994; Gibson 2013; Key 1949; McMann 2006; Mickey 2015; O'Donnell 1998; Olson 1982). In some instances, these dominant-party enclaves have even served to help consolidate national-level political projects, as ambitious provincial politicians forge mutually beneficial relationships with national political leaders that, in turn, help to maintain, or even exacerbate, machine-style politics at the local level (Gibson 2013).

We argue that these distinct subnational political contexts influence the political attitudes and behaviors of citizens through multiple pathways. In particular, we focus our theory on three overlapping characteristics that we see as the driving force behind the distinct political profiles of citizenries living in dominant-party political contexts. The first is the politicized application of the rule of law. Whether through stamping out critical local media outlets, utilizing law enforcement to target opposition members, or packing the local judiciary with machine loyalists, the strategic perversion of institutional powers to benefit loyalists and punish dissidents will cultivate attitudes and behaviors aimed at survival rather than democratic expression.

The second such characteristic, grounded in what McMann refers to as "economic autonomy" (2006, 1), also serves to distinguish citizens living in multiparty states from those living in dominant-party enclaves and, theoretically, affects their political attitudes and behaviors in distinct ways. The overt use of state resources for partisan purposes commonly found in dominant-party enclaves (to varying degrees) will, we argue, have systematic effects on the ways in which citizens evaluate and engage with their political system.

In dominant-party enclaves, political machines seek to position the party as the embodiment of the provincial state, and sole vehicle for gaining access to much-desired social assistance programs, public jobs, and government contracts. Citizens thus equate the local machine with the state, viewing the party as the primary avenue for improving their well-being and advancing their careers.

The final feature of dominant-party enclaves that we view as a critical source of the differences in the political attitudinal and behavioral patterns of individuals living in multiparty and dominant-party contexts is the uneven electoral playing field that is decisively slanted in favor of the incumbent party. While incumbents the world over have a long history of pushing the envelope of the incumbency advantage, whether through the use of pork-barrel projects to reward supporters or attempts to construct barriers to voting for individuals living in opposition strongholds, the extent to which these practices are deployed in dominant-party enclaves often goes far beyond what is deemed permissible in free and fair electoral systems. Rather, in dominant-party enclaves, where such over-the-line practices have become the norm, we see limited degrees of electoral uncertainty, and rates of political efficacy (or the ability to understand and participate effectively in politics) grounded in the degree to which individuals support the all-powerful political machine. These trends in political efficacy, in turn, translate into distinct forms of political participation in dominant-party contexts. Though the *amount* of participation may be similar in dominant-party and multiparty regimes, we contend that the *motivations* behind such participation tend to be distinct. In dominant-party contexts, participation is often regime motivated, with "protests" just as likely to take the form of progovernment rallies as true protests against the incumbent machine, and voter turnout driven by a desire for private goods rather than by accountability concerns or standard socioeconomic predictors of participation.

We view these three dominant-party characteristics, and the ways in which they manifest themselves in the political lives of citizens forced to confront them on a daily basis, as critical in understanding differences in citizens' experiences with their political system, their views of democracy, their decision calculus when casting a vote, and the ways they engage with their political systems between elections. In subnational dominant-party enclaves, their attitudes and behaviors will reflect, and be driven by, these prevalent system characteristics that we argue are distinct in scope and degree from those associated with competitive multiparty systems. For largely instrumental reasons then, the modal citizen embedded in a dominant-party context will exhibit lower levels of support for democratic norms and processes, is less willing to hold politicians accountable for corrupt practices and poor performance, and participates in ways that tend to be conducive to the continuation of the system, rather than stir the pot in an effort to bring about change. In some cases, these divergent patterns represent conscious decisions by individuals attempting to maximize their self-interest in a less-than-democratic context. In others, this dominant-party political environment can permeate individuals' orientations toward politics in ways they might not even understand. Crucially, not only do these attitudinal and behavioral trends help sustain subnational dominant-party machines—*they also serve as a reservoir of support for undemocratic norms and processes at the national level in uneven political systems.*

Having presented our theory of political attitudes and behavior in uneven democracies in Chapter 2, we turn in the third chapter to a discussion of the two national cases we use to test our argument: Argentina and Mexico. We also introduce our concept and measure of dominant-party enclaves, which center on the admittedly post hoc assessment of a subnational political unit that has yet to experience that most fundamental moment in electorally democratic systems—alternation in power. As highlighted in the cases described at the beginning of this chapter, Argentina and Mexico represent prototypes of the uneven democracies that now characterize much of the developing world. With the ouster of Argentina's military junta in 1983 and the slow disintegration of Mexico's one-party system that culminated with the ruling party's exit from the presidency in 2000, both federal systems offer a group of subnational political machines that have successfully insulated themselves from these national-level political changes, as well as the many devastating economic and governance crises that have afflicted both countries, and have remained, as of 2020, dominant-party political enclaves that stand in contrast to their multiparty neighbors as well as their respective national political systems.

It is these pockets of dominant-party rule that drive our research. Just as the one-party South of the United States represented in many ways the antithesis of the democratic ideals on which that country's national system was based, so do these areas of dominant-party rule found within our two countries of interest. And just as the one-party South of the United States produced highly distinct patterns of civil and political engagement (Key 1949; Mickey 2015), so do we contend that the subnational systems of dominant-party rule scattered throughout Argentina and Mexico have consequences for how their citizens think about and engage with politics.

We then address the principal measurement challenge for our subnational comparative analysis: the identification and classification of dominant-party enclaves. Unlike at the country level, where political regime scores are published annually by an array of organizations (e.g., Polity, Freedom House, the V-Dem project), accessible, valid, and reliable regime indicators across time and space at the subnational level are rare. For this reason, students of subnational politics have had to craft their own measures of provincial regime characteristics—often in developing contexts in which reliable political data is hard to find. Typically, the best source for local political information that is accessible across subnational units and over time is electoral data (Wibbels 2005; Gervasoni 2010b, 2018; Giraudy 2013). While obtaining information regarding levels of press freedom, civil liberties, and judicial independence would be ideal for a full assessment of subnational regimes, such data is highly uneven across time and space and, thus, not ideal for our purposes.

Rather than focus on capturing the nuances of what might or might not constitute an authoritarian, hybrid, or democratic provincial political system, we opt for a measurement strategy that identifies those subnational political contexts that have been dominated by a single party to such an extent that even the most basic element of a democratic regime, alternation in power, is absent. Our measurement strategy then rests simply on the presence or absence of at least one peaceful transfer of control over the executive branch between parties. For any political system in the midst of a democratic transition, whether at the national or subnational level, a clear signal that such a transition is underway is the peaceful relinquishment of power. Just as the ouster of the PRI from the presidency in 2000 marked a critical point in Mexico's national democratic transition, for subnational units transitioning from an authoritarian past, the first alternation in partisan control of the governor's office offers an efficient, albeit blunt, marker for the presence of some degree of electoral uncertainty and competition between parties for control of subnational offices of power. Until that initial alternation in power takes place, the perception, if not the reality, will remain that the political system falls short of being a multiparty, electorally competitive regime, appearing, instead, to represent a hybrid system consisting of elements associated with the country's authoritarian past and democratic present.

Thus, our key metric of interest throughout this project is whether the Argentine province or Mexican state in question has experienced an alternation in the party of the governor—in Mexico since such alternation became a possibility in 1980s,[4] and in Argentina since the country transitioned to democracy in 1983. For Mexico, 9 of 31 states had yet to experience an alternation in power by early 2014 while in Argentina, 7 of 23 provinces had elected the same party to the governorship in every election since 1983. The chapter then explores these two categories of states and provinces in the two countries and offers an account of their socioeconomic and demographic characteristics, their similarities and differences, and their locations within their respective countries. We conclude with detailed case studies of the two subnational regimes we introduced at the beginning of this chapter, Edomex and San Luis, which for us offer examples of the potential range that dominant-party enclaves can have in terms of such features as economic and human development levels. These case studies draw on provincial-level data, survey data, and extensive fieldwork, which included in-depth interviews with prominent public officials and activists, in an effort to offer a detailed exploration of life in a dominant-party enclave through the eyes of those who live it every day.

The bulk of the data utilized in this book are drawn from the AmericasBarometer national surveys of Argentina and Mexico from 2008 to 2014—part of a larger regional survey project conducted by Vanderbilt University's Latin American Public Opinion Project (LAPOP) on a biennial basis throughout the Americas. Since 2004, these surveys have employed national probability samples of voting-age adults in dozens of countries throughout the Western hemisphere to gather data on citizens' political attitudes and behaviors. These surveys, carried out every two years, include close to 6,000 respondents in Argentina and more than 6,000 in Mexico for the period from 2008 to 2014. All samples are nationally representative, and the surveys were conducted using face-to-face interviews of voting age adults.[5]

---

[4] The Institutional Revolutionary Party (PRI) formed in 1929 as the National Revolutionary Party (PNR) and then changed to the Party of the Mexican Revolution (PRM) in 1938 before settling on the PRI in 1945. From 1929 to 1989 the PRI won every gubernatorial election, losing for the first time in Baja California in 1989.

[5] For more information on the LAPOP, its sources of funding, and the sampling methodology employed, please visit http://www.vanderbilt.edu/lapop/. The wording for all of the survey items used in the following analysis can be found in the Appendix.

In addition to this valuable survey data, we also bring to our analyses in the pages that follow information gathered by both authors in their collective fieldwork efforts over the past 20 years. Whether that work focused on the subnational dynamics of Mexico's antipoverty program of the early 1990s (*Solidaridad*) or on the underlying processes that make protest in Argentina one of the more common forms of political participation in that country, we have accumulated a wealth of interview and anecdotal data on the central theme of this study—dominant-party machines and their impact on individuals who must deal with them on a daily basis. Though less than systematic in terms of how we gathered such data, these accounts, nonetheless, have been critical in informing our theoretical and empirical investigation of how these machines shape the political lives of citizens who live within them.

In Chapter 4, we begin the empirical portion of the book. First, we evaluate the proposition that citizens in dominant-party subnational political systems are more likely to be exposed to and victimized by corruption and clientelism than their counterparts in multiparty systems. We then put forth the idea that because of this heightened exposure to these types of interactions with public officials, citizens in dominant-party enclaves will become desensitized to such activities when compared with their neighbors in multiparty contexts. Using survey data from a pooled sample of Argentine provinces and Mexican states, we test our theoretical expectation that a dominant-party electoral environment should facilitate a "business as usual" attitude toward corruption among government officials and citizens, while a multiparty electoral context may heighten citizens' awareness of corruption as a governance issue, even as their chances of being victimized by corrupt behavior is reduced. As efforts to deepen democracy and improve governance continue across the developing world, our findings highlight the real need to incorporate subnational political processes into efforts to understand and address such critical issues as corruption and its consequences.

As we highlight in Chapter 4, the daily political interactions and socialization experiences of citizens living in dominant-party enclaves are fundamentally distinct from those living in multiparty regimes, to the point where one's views toward democracy in general becomes shaped by those experiences. In Chapter 5, through analysis of data on citizens' democratic attitudes across the states and provinces of Mexico and Argentina, we find evidence for the existence of distinct subnational political cultures that, we argue, align with the basic contours of the subnational political system in which individuals live. Specifically, we utilize Carlin and Singer's (2011) approach to measuring "support for polyarchy" (1500) to gauge how the political culture of democracy varies by subnational regime type. Through multivariate analyses of democratic attitudes—including political tolerance, support for checks and balances, and preference for democracy as a system of government—we first find that individuals living in the multiparty provinces and states of Argentina and Mexico report average levels of democratic support similar to those found in the United States. Conversely, for those living in the dominant-party enclaves of these two countries, their levels of support approximate those found in such countries as Bolivia and Guatemala, two nations with decidedly less experience with democratic forms of government. These attitudinal gaps between citizens of the same country are roughly the equivalent of the cross-national gaps we find between such country pairs as the United States and Mexico or Chile and El Salvador, underscoring our point that *intranational* differences in political attitudes (and behaviors) can be equally, if not more, significant than cross-national differences.

Though constrained by the cross-sectional nature of the data, our findings speak not only to the need to deconstruct the concept of a national political culture, but also to an enduring debate on the causal nature of the regime type–political culture relationship. What such stark contrasts in subnational political culture suggest is that differences in terms of how individuals experience politics *within* countries shape their collective cultural orientations toward democracy at all levels. It is somewhat curious that such efforts at understanding the role subnational dynamics play in shaping citizens' political attitudes and behaviors are rare in comparative politics, yet in the subfield of American politics close attention to subnational differences and their import has spawned a cottage industry in the study of state politics and, more specifically, the many scholars devoted to the study of the politics of the U.S. South (e.g., Black and Black 1987; Hayes and McKee 2008; Kousser 2010). We view such efforts as all the more necessary in those emerging democracies that have such disparate subnational political landscapes.

Transitioning from an assessment of the general attitudinal contours of citizenries in dominant-party and multiparty subnational political contexts, in Chapter 6 we turn to an evaluation of differences in how citizens hold their elected officials accountable in these two distinct contexts. Specifically, we explore variations in performance-based voting and electoral accountability mechanisms among individuals living in these two political environments in Argentina and Mexico, and we find evidence for our basic proposition that the nature of one's subnational political system influences the degree to which perceived government performance plays a role in one's electoral evaluation of incumbent politicians. In subnational contexts in which competitive multiparty politics have taken hold, performance-based linkages such as those driving economic voting do, indeed, surface. However, in dominant-party enclaves, where clientelistic linkages between voters and political bosses tend to prevail, economic performance and other aspects of an incumbent's governance record appear less consequential for the voting calculus of citizens, in both provincial *and* national elections. By highlighting how subnational regime characteristics facilitate or undermine electoral accountability, we cast light on the very real representational consequences of dominant-party enclaves in Latin America.

In Chapter 7 we tackle the behavioral consequences of dominant-party machines, focusing on three key repertoires of political participation: voting, protest, and civic activism. The key distinction between multiparty and dominant-party systems that we highlight in this chapter is not the *amount* of participation but, rather, the political characteristics of *who* participates. Existing within nationally democratic regimes, dominant-party elites generally do not attempt to thwart participation altogether; rather, they exert tremendous effort to construct a "dominant-party citizenry" that actively participates in politics, but in ways dictated and incentivized by the regime itself. As such, we contend that through the development of clientelistic relationships between citizens and the state that are designed to ensure that loyal partisans are disproportionately represented at the ballot box and in the streets, coupled with the intimidation of machine opponents, dominant party elites encourage controlled, complicit participation on the part of a significant segment of society. In this environment we find, for example, that whereas demonstrators in multiparty systems tend to be critics of the incumbent government, demonstrators in dominant-party enclaves are just as likely to be supporters of the machine. Overall, while both protesters and conventional participants in multiparty contexts match standard profiles found in many democratic countries around the world, those most likely to protest and vote in authoritarian enclaves tend to directly challenge that conventional wisdom regarding the individual-level characteristics and attitudes commonly associated with political participation.

In the final chapter, we offer a discussion of the future of uneven democracy in Argentina and Mexico and consider the implications of dominant-party enclaves, and the citizens they produce, for democracies around the world. Whereas many of the dominant-party enclaves in Argentina have become less competitive and more entrenched in recent years, Mexico's dominant-party enclaves are fading, with the gubernatorial elections of June 2016 bringing about the demise of 3 of the remaining 7 dominant-party states. The factor that most distinguishes what we see happening in Argentina from what is occurring in Mexico seems to be the ability of machine opponents to put aside their ideological differences and join forces to dislodge the dominant party from power. We briefly explore how electoral coalitions between strange bedfellows have ousted the PRI in traditional dominant-party states, and how the rise of a national electoral alternative to Peronism in Argentina could facilitate a transition to more widespread democratic competition in Argentine provinces.

To conclude, we highlight the two principal contributions our work makes to research on political behavior and democratization. First, in order to fully understand the connection between the widespread adoption of democratic institutions and citizens' political attitudes and behavior around the world, we must shed our "whole-nation bias" (Rokkan 1970, 49; Snyder 2001) and work to systematically understand how an uneven subnational regime landscape shapes the way individuals understand and engage with their political system. We contend that the proliferation of electorally competitive, multiparty subnational systems across Latin America has contributed to and been supported by citizenries with attitudinal and behavioral profiles that approximate those of well-established democracies around the world. Conversely, within many of those same countries, there also exist to varying degrees dominant-party subnational political systems that foster decidedly less-than-democratic political attitudes and behaviors that reflect individuals' efforts to adapt to and survive in such systems. As a result, any effort to empirically evaluate, and understand, patterns of political attitudes and behavior across emerging democracies, if not established ones, needs to take into account these distinct subnational political environments.

Second, though most of the literature conceptualizes democratization as a country-level process (e.g., Huntington 1991), we argue that the deepening of democracy in emerging regimes depends in large part on the extent to which subnational politics mirrors the liberal norms and processes that have taken hold at the national level. Where uneven democracy persists, citizens nested within subnational dominant-party enclaves will continue to mold their political attitudes and behaviors to best survive under the local rules of the game, and their contribution to the national regime will reflect that divergent experience. For full democratic consolidation to occur, we argue that advocates of democracy everywhere need to look increasingly to the local level. Put another way, a country's democratic whole can only be understood by examining its least democratic parts.

Finally, though focused almost exclusively on the provinces and states of Argentina and Mexico, we bring the book to a close by discussing the implications of our findings for the many other uneven democratic landscapes that one can find in emerging and established democracies. While the cases of Argentina and Mexico certainly are unique in many ways, the phenomenon of central interest to us, dominant-party enclaves, is one from which no political system is fully immune (see Gervasoni 2018). Consequently, our exploration of the consequences of these subnational political systems in two countries can provide a baseline for future evaluations of other uneven regimes across the world. In this mixed-method study of how uneven regime landscapes beget drastically different experiences with and views of politics for citizens of the *same country*, we highlight the relevance of Tip O'Neill's well-known aphorism—"all politics is local" (1993)—for efforts to better understand patterns of public opinion and political behavior in an ever-changing global landscape.

2

Dominant-Party Citizens

> The machine is rather a non-ideological organization interested
> less in political principle than in securing and holding office for its
> leaders and distributing income to those who run it and work for it.
> (Scott 1969, 1144)

In its most recent report on the state of democracy in Latin America, the
Organization for Economic Cooperation and Development's (OECD) annual
Latin American Economic Outlook (2018) begins by noting "a growing disconnect between citizens and public institutions in recent years" and argues
that "reconnecting public institutions with citizens and better responding to
their demands is critical for well-being and the sustainable development of
the region" (15). Despite our shared perspective on the role of institutions in
shaping the attitudes and behaviors of citizens, a glaring omission in the 252-
page OECD report is any mention of subnational institutions and the critical
role they play in connecting citizens to the state. When a political machine
of the sort Scott described more than 50 years ago has gained monopolistic
control over those subnational institutions and exists within a national-level
democracy, it is the subnational machine, we argue, that will most influence
the ways in which citizens think about and engage with politics at all levels of
government.

As the OECD notes, and as many others have found through crossnational
research (e.g., Anderson 1995, 2000; Lewis-Beck 1988; Markus 1998; Whitten
and Palmer 1999), one's thoughts about and engagement with her political
system are driven at least in part by the underlying governing philosophy, the
institutions, and the rules of the game in the system in which she lives. The
critical question underlying this claim, however, is: Which offices and officials
most influence the ways in which citizens perceive and interact with their political system? Our answer, which we more fully develop in this chapter, focuses
on the provincial level of government, one that in federal systems, such as

Life in the Political Machine. Jonathan T. Hiskey and Mason W. Moseley, Oxford University Press (2020). © Oxford
University Press.
DOI: 10.1093/oso/9780197500408.001.0001

Argentina and Mexico, affects the daily lives of citizens in terms of the services they receive and the daily political practices they observe. Though central government institutions, the officials that occupy them, and the procedures they follow are certainly relevant as well in shaping the political lives of citizens, it is at the provincial level that politicians in many emerging democracies around the world have become increasingly empowered through decades of decentralization efforts,[1] and, as such, have begun to play an increasingly important role in how individuals view democracy, engage with politics, and evaluate the performance of their representatives.

In a relatively homogenous political system in which the governing philosophy and behavior of subnational officials align well with those of national institutions and officials, we might not see the impact of the subnational level on the general populace, as any systemic effects on attitudes and behavior may simply be assumed to be a product of the larger national system. Only when there exists a divergence in the institutions (both formal and informal) and behaviors of elected officials at the national and subnational levels will we be able to discern the role the subnational level plays in shaping the way one engages with and thinks about politics. In this chapter, we interrogate this assertion and detail the distinct mechanisms we see at work in dominant-party enclaves that should influence one's interactions with her political world.

We begin with a brief discussion of the ways in which the discipline's "whole-nation bias" (Rokkan 1970, 49; Snyder 2001) has impeded further understanding of these subnational drivers of citizens' political attitudes and behaviors. We move next to our theory that connects subnational dominant-party system characteristics to the political attitudes and behaviors of citizens living within them. Here we introduce three prevalent characteristics of dominant-party enclaves that we see as keys to understanding why citizens living in such systems might plausibly be expected to exhibit distinct attitudinal and behavioral patterns in their political lives when compared with their compatriots living in electorally competitive, multiparty subnational political systems. We then outline the dependent variables of our study—that is, the specific set of political attitudes and behaviors that we explore empirically in the following chapters. Finally, the chapter concludes with a discussion of the implications of our theory for *national* regimes and the deepening of democracy across the world.

---

[1] Recognizing that in recent years some of those same countries that invested so much time and resources in decentralization efforts have begun a process of recentralization in some areas (see, e.g., Eaton 2013).

Beneath the National Surface

Evidence abounds of the uneven nature of the many democratic transitions that have occurred across the world over the past 40 years (Fox 1994; Gervasoni 2018; Gibson 2013, 2005; Gibson and Calvo 2000; Giraudy 2015; Lawson 2000; McMann 2006; O'Donnell 1993; Nickson 1995; Snyder 2001). As Gibson notes, subnational authoritarian regimes "are a fact of life in most democracies in the developing and postcommunist world" (2005, 104). He goes further to argue that "with national democratization often came the consolidation of provincial authoritarianism. Democratic transitions, while transforming politics at the national level, create little pressure for subnational democratization. In fact, they often hinder it" (107). Such transition dynamics frequently get lost in the euphoria that surrounds a national regime change, only revealing themselves in dramatic fashion when the two worlds eventually collide in one way or another.

As this increasing number of uneven regime transitions has made clear, country-level aggregations can be misleading in various ways. Linz and de Miguel noted in their discussion of crossnational comparisons that "averages for very heterogeneous units might not be the best data to use, particularly if no account is taken of measures of dispersion" (1966, 268). Robert McNamara famously shifted the World Bank's focus away from macroeconomic growth indicators toward one targeting intranational disparities, declaring that "[economic] growth is not equitably reaching the poor. And the poor are not significantly contributing to growth. Despite a decade of unprecedented increase in the gross national product of the developing countries, the poorest segments of their population have received relatively little benefit."[2] More recently, O'Donnell highlighted the uneven nature of Latin America's democratization process, pointing out that:

> Current theories of the state often make an assumption that recurs in current theories of democracy: that of a high degree of homogeneity in the scope, both territorial and functional, of the state and of the social order it

---

[2] Robert McNamara, "Address to the Board of Governors." Nairobi, Kenya, September 24, 1973. Transcript of address available at: https://www.worldbank.org/en/about/archives/president-mcnamara-nairobi-speech-1973, (accessed February 2, 2020).

supports. It is not asked (and if it is, seldom problematized) if such order, and the orders issued by the state organizations, have similar effectiveness throughout the national territory and across the existing social stratification. (1993, 1358)

O'Donnell then asks a question that echoes one of our central objectives in this study, "What influences may this [intranational variation in state effectiveness] have on what kind of democracy may emerge?" (1993, 1358). As we have made clear throughout, we view the impact of subnational variations, whether in state effectiveness or the degree of dominant-party control, as considerable.

Though these concerns with state effectiveness and regime unevenness have a long lineage across many new and established democracies, we know very little about the lives of those individuals living on the wrong side of these intranational divides. V. O. Key's seminal research on the one-party system of the U.S. South is perhaps the most widely recognized work on how different a country's subnational parts can be from the nation as a whole, and the consequences of these differences. While the national regime of the United States moved along its democratic trajectory throughout the 19th and 20th centuries, Key identified in great detail the stunted democratization process of the U.S. South. Political bosses, systematic disenfranchisement, the violation of fundamental political and civil rights, personalism, clientelism, and the heavy-handed, arbitrary use of force all characterized the politics of the South described by Key. He then documented how these political defects in the U.S. political system manifested themselves in the social and economic development processes of the region.

A central concern of Key's was the extent to which the one-party political systems of the South helped sustain the status quo, noting that "the grand objective of the 'haves' is obstruction [and] organization is not always necessary to obstruct; it is essential, however, for the promotion of a sustained program in behalf of the 'have-nots'" (1949, 307). The implication behind this observation is that an existing political and economic status quo is likely to thrive in a political environment in which opponents have limited recourse to challenge those holding power. Key's work served as the point of departure for subsequent research on the implications of the one-party South beyond the watershed years of the 1960s, and the civil and political rights reforms that were presumed to have rid the region of those political obstacles to development (e.g., Mickey 2015).

What Key did for our understanding of the "American whole" through his analysis of the country's Southern parts, Linz and de Miguel (1966) did for the Spanish development process circa 1960. In an essay on "the eight Spains" Linz and de Miguel offered, in many important ways, a roadmap for how to systematically explore the question of the relation of the parts to the whole, laying out the fundamental problems with the "semideveloped societies" that O'Donnell would revisit more than 20 years later and that we seek to further explore in the following pages. We quote Linz and de Miguel here at length in part to highlight the relevance of this passage to our work (60 years after its publication) and in part to underscore the absence of analytical follow-up to their observations that remain so relevant for the emerging democracies of today:

> . . . it would seem that many societies we call semideveloped on the basis of a number of national indices are really a mixture of developed and underdeveloped sectors (or regions), and *that their peculiar problems result from that imbalance*. . . Overall inter-nation comparisons would not help much to clarify such problems. Studies not designed with *intra*-nation differences in mind but focused on overall national patterns might even altogether miss basic aspects of the problem of social change. (271, italics added)

The authors then posit that "many of the political tensions taking the forms of nationalism, separatism, and sectionalism have their origins in such differences of development . . ." (272). In raising these propositions with respect to Spain of the 1960s, Linz and de Miguel seem also to have provided an accurate portrayal of the challenges confronted by many Latin American countries during the course of their uneven regime transitions of the past 40 years.

Despite the continued relevance of these works, relatively few scholars since have pursued this agenda in a systematic way. The pervasive presence and inaccessibility of seemingly monolithic, highly centralized authoritarian regimes during the 1970s may help explain the paucity of subnational research on political development during this period.[3] And conversely, it is perhaps the glaring unevenness of the democratization process over the past 35 years that has sparked renewed interest in the political divides that lay beyond a country's capital. O'Donnell (1993) and Fox (1994) were among the first to recognize the uneven quality of the emerging Latin American

---

[3] Fagen and Tuohy's monograph *Politics and Privilege in a Mexican City* (1972) is one notable exception to the crossnational focus of most work during this period.

democracies of the early 1990s. O'Donnell's essay on what he termed the *blue, green,* and *brown* areas of Latin America and Fox's work on the growing import of local politics in Latin America and authoritarian enclaves in Mexico rightly stand as the forerunners to what became a growing trend toward analysis of the subnational parts as a means to understand the whole of a country's democratization process and prospects.

More recently, scholars such as Gervasoni (2010b, 2015, 2018), Gibson (2005, 2013), Giraudy (2015), McMann (2006), and Petersen (2018) have all advanced our understanding of why and how such subnational enclaves persist in the midst of a national democratization process, as well as the factors that may lead to their decline. McMann (2006), for example, offers an incisive analysis of the development of "hybrid" subnational regimes in Russia and Kyrgyzstan since the 1990s, citing reports in Russia where "opposition candidates in one region ran without negative repercussions, but those in another region lost their jobs [while] [j]ournalists in one province reported freely, but those in another censored their remarks" (6). In Latin America, scholars such as Fox, Gervasoni, Gibson, and Giraudy have all greatly advanced our understanding of where and why such authoritarian or hybrid subnational enclaves have persisted throughout the region's unprecedented era of democracy. Missing from much of this research on subnational enclaves, however, is work on the consequences for individuals living within them and the contours of their political experiences. It is this concern with the implications of dominant-party subnational systems for the everyday political lives of people within them that guides our work in the pages that follow.

What Are Dominant-Party Enclaves and How Do They Survive?

What is a dominant-party enclave?[4] For us, it is a subnational political system nested within a national-level democracy that has all the trappings of a democratic regime but lacks concrete evidence that those in power are willing to

---

[4] We chose the word *enclave* for the title of this book and section to clarify that our focus is *subnational* dominant-party systems that exist alongside multiparty subnational regimes *within* democratic countries. However, we use *system* and *enclave* interchangeably throughout the book, given that many of the defining characteristics we see as most important to dominant-party systems' impact on citizen attitudes and behaviors can be present at both the national and subnational levels.

relinquish that power and, conversely, offers every indication that they can and will employ a wide range of less-than-democratic techniques to ensure such a transfer of power does not occur. In contrast to "single-party regimes," in which viable opposition parties simply do not exist or are not allowed to participate in the electoral process, dominant-party systems are those that "permit the opposition to compete in multiparty elections [but] that usually do not allow alternation of political power" (Magaloni and Kricheli 2010, 123). This notion of a dominant-party system falls generally under the conceptual umbrella of Levitsky and Way's "competitive authoritarian regimes" in which "the state violates at least one of the three defining attributes of democracy: (1) free elections, (2) broad protection of civil liberties, and (3) a reasonably level playing field" (2010, 7). Yet, what sets it apart at the subnational level and makes it a decidedly hybrid system (Gervasoni 2018) is that it is embedded in a nationally democratic political system.

Despite this fundamental feature of being embedded in national-level democratic regimes, we can learn much about the operations of subnational dominant-party enclaves from the work done by scholars on national-level dominant-party systems that are characterized by many as "giant patronage systems that give the citizens a vested interest in the perpetuation of the regime" (Magaloni and Kricheli 2015, 128). Also consistent with what we find at the subnational level is the notion put forth by Arian and Barnes (1974) long ago that "[t]he dominant party mobilizes selectively and differentially ... It concentrates on groups that will make fewer demands than others or that will give a maximum political payoff for minimal effort . . . When joined with its centrist orientation, this selective strategy renders the task of opposition very difficult" (598). And if these selective strategies of political payoffs (and punishments) do not work, those in power can, and often do, resort to electoral fraud, economic sanctions, manipulation of the media, and/ or overt acts of repression (Petersen 2018).

Many of the characteristics highlighted in these works on national-level dominant-party systems also appear in mid–20th century accounts of the political machines found in U.S. cities during the late-1800s and early-1900s. Scott's comparative assessment of political machines (1966) identifies many of the same governing characteristics we have emphasized here. Gosnell (1933), in describing New York City's Tammany Hall machine, also pointed to the key elements we find as essential tools of governance in our dominant-party enclaves, including efforts by what he calls "grafting officeholders [and] gangster politicians . . . to manipulate the confused and apathetic voters by special favors, fraud, and force" (21). Though not often framed in such starkly derisive terms, the machine Gosnell describes is similar to those found in other U.S. cities (Wilson and Banfield 1965), Southern Italy (Chubb 1982), Mexico (Fox 1994), and Argentina (Auyero 2000). We, therefore, have an abundance of work drawn from two fairly distinct lines of inquiry—dominant-party systems at the national level and machine politics at the city level—which both highlight those characteristics and tools of governance that we see as essential to the dominant-party enclaves that serve as the focus of this study.

The basis for our claim that citizens in dominant-party enclaves will think and behave politically in ways that set them apart from their neighbors in multiparty systems is grounded in the ways in which incumbent officials in such systems tend to use the powers of government to remain in office, with state resources employed "to reward the loyal and punish the disloyal" (Magaloni and Krischeli 2010, 129). While officials in democratic systems the world over seek to maximize their incumbency advantage to stay in power, perhaps the defining characteristic of officials in dominant-party systems is their relatively unchecked power to construct an "undemocratic incumbency advantage" through reliance on such tools as the selective provision of what should be public goods to reward and punish the political behaviors of their constituents. Here, then, we are not simply referring to pork-barrel projects and constituency services but, rather, to overt manipulation of the levers of state power to reward loyal supporters and punish opponents in a variety of ways. In an effort to manage one's daily life under such a system, we posit that most citizens will eventually adapt their political behaviors and orientations in ways that allow them to successfully play this particular political game.

As noted above, a common thread that runs through the research on national dominant-party systems, local political machines, and the increasing number of works on the origins and persistence of dominant-party subnational systems around the world (e.g., Gervasoni 2018; Gibson 2005, 2013; Giraudy 2009, 2015; McMann 2006) are three governance strategies that characterize such systems: (1) the uneven, politically motivated application of the rule of law, (2) the politicization of state resources for partisan purposes (i.e., to reward supporters and punish opponents of the dominant party), and (3) efforts to tilt the electoral playing field in order to minimize the chances of defeat. It is these three overlapping tools of dominant-party rule that we view as the key sources for the distinct patterns of political attitudes and behaviors that we expect to find among citizens living in these systems.

Figure 2.1 offers a depiction of what we see as the core dynamics linking these common characteristics of dominant-party enclaves with the political attitudes and behaviors of citizens living within them.

As should be clear, the key theoretical assumption we make, and one we contend is essential to understanding the impact subnational systems can have on individuals around the world, is that citizens will think about and engage with politics in ways that reflect and are in response to the political rules of the game they are confronted with on a daily basis. While such rules in some countries may emanate most powerfully from the national level, as in the case of North Korea where the authoritarian rules of the game presumably prevail throughout the country, in many countries with uneven regime landscapes we see the subnational level as one at which many relevant, and impactful, political rules and norms will be found.

With few exceptions (e.g., Fox, 1994; Gervasoni 2018; Gibson 2005, 2013; Giraudy 2009, 2015; McMann 2005), much of what we know about dominant-party systems in emerging democracies comes from work at the national level. A clear and significant difference between national-level dominant-party systems and those that persist at the subnational level within a democratic system is that the latter are constrained to some extent by national-level institutions, officials, and oversight mechanisms. As such, the degree to which officials in these subnational systems can veer from nationally established democratic norms and procedures will be similarly constrained. In other words, ruthlessly violent repression of opposition movements and individuals, while not unheard of (e.g., the U.S. South

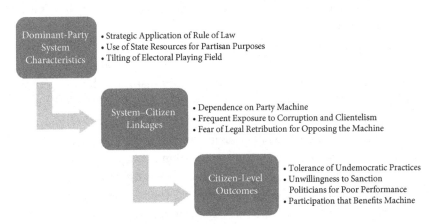

Figure 2.1. How dominant-party enclaves shape attitudes and behavior.

throughout much of the 20th century), are relatively rare in these cases of "regime juxtaposition" (Gibson 2005, 2013).

Rather, the most effective tools that subnational dominant-party officials have available to them are those that tilt the economic and electoral playing fields in favor of supporters of the status quo and, conversely, make more difficult the economic and political lives of opponents, while not straying too far away from the democratic governing norms and procedures found at the national level. As noted above, such techniques typically fall into the general categories of how and when the rule of law is enforced, efforts to equate the dominant party with the state through the overtly partisan use of state resources, and the distortion of the electoral process to the extent possible (while maintaining a semblance of free and fair elections) with the aim of increasing the degree of ex ante electoral certainty of a ruling party victory (Alvarez et al. 1996). We offer below a brief examination of each of these three overlapping characteristics common to dominant-party enclaves and discuss how they might influence citizens' political attitudes and behaviors.

Strategic Application of the Rule of Law

The observation that the "initial construction of the rule of law requires the balanced dispersal of institutional power" and that "[t]he rule of law is in part a product of a balance of power between at least two political parties, neither of which sustains monolithic control [over the various branches of government]" helps us understand how the absence of such conditions allows officials in a dominant-party system to strategically employ the law as a reliable tool for the continuation of the system (Chavez 2004, 15). Whether manifested in the form of corrupt bidding practices for state-funded projects or police harassment of pro-opposition organizations and individuals, the result of such a system likely will be a citizenry that learns how to play the dominant-party system's political game in order to survive, if not thrive. In the process, clear violations of the principle of the equal application of the rule of law become business as usual for citizens in such systems—simply a feature of the rules of the game underlying a dominant-party system.

The Mexican state of Puebla during the 1990s offers but one example of how officials in a dominant-party enclave deploy this strategy in a way that achieves the intended effect of undermining political opponents while not resorting to overt authoritarian rule. In the face of growing electoral opposition at the municipal level, Manuel Bartlett, governor of Puebla from 1992 to 1998, engineered passage of the *ley Bartlett* (Bartlett law) that sought to fiscally punish opposition-controlled local governments in his state and reward those most loyal to the PRI, the state's long-dominant party, through selective distribution of state resources. As Giraudy notes in her description of this case, such practices "enable rulers to appropriate state resources (such as power, money, information, and material goods) for themselves, and to exercise authority in ways that benefit some groups and citizens over others" (2013, 73). Central to our conceptualization of dominant-party systems then is the regular use of such techniques by incumbent officials in order to engender acquiescence, if not outright support, for their continuation in power on the part of citizens and economic interests.

We expect, then, this general tendency prevalent among dominant-party systems to influence the ways citizens view their nominally democratic system and evaluate the officials who run it. In such a context, corruption scandals, for example, that may spark citizen outrage in a competitive, multiparty system may raise few eyebrows in dominant-party systems or may never be uncovered in the first place. Similarly, whereas violations of political and civil rights would likely bring about calls for trials and sanctions in a multiparty system, in dominant-party systems we might expect only the most egregious of violations to carry with them any consequences for the perpetrators. The majority of citizens living in such contexts are likely to grow accustomed to such behavior by state officials and adapt their behavior accordingly. The end result is that in such a context in which violations of the law by state officials become routine, despite occurring within a nominally democratic framework, support for democratic principles and active engagement in politics by citizens may become less tenable, creating a political culture that, in turn, becomes more tolerant of continued dominant-party rule. Certainly we will always be able to find within these systems those individuals steadfastly committed to the principles of democracy and opposed to the political practices and customs they must endure while living inside a machine, but these individuals will likely be outnumbered by those individuals simply finding ways to make it through another day.

We also expect that the strategic application of the rule of law will manifest itself in efforts to skew electoral contests in favor of dominant-party officials by improperly rewarding citizens for proincumbent political behavior and punishing, or disincentivizing, anti-incumbent behavior. In a competitive, multiparty electoral system, an individual's decision to vote should theoretically be only marginally related to whether or not she supports the incumbent. While efforts to increase (or decrease) voter turnout often constitute a strategy of a particular political candidate or party in even the most democratic of systems, we should not find consistent differences in voter turnout or other forms of participation between incumbent supporters and opponents across time and space in such systems. In dominant-party enclaves, however, political officials will frequently engage in "turnout buying" and/or "abstention buying" (Gans-Morse et al. 2014, 417), incentivizing political participation by loyalists while placing hurdles to participation in the paths of potential opponents. The illegal measures taken by dominant-party elites in the U.S. South to prevent African-Americans from exercising their right to vote is an obvious example of this. Threatening phone calls, questionable legal hurdles put in place prior to Election Day, and unannounced changes in polling sites are just a few of the ways in which dominant parties influence which citizens turn out to participate in politics.

Accounts of similar, and sometimes even more egregious, efforts at voter intimidation can be found across the democratizing world, from Eastern Europe (McMann 2006) to the many emerging democracies of Africa. Rauschenbach and Paula (2019), for example, find in their study of seven, marginally democratic African countries that "voters living in incumbent strongholds are most likely to report having been bribed in elections, whereas those living in opposition strongholds are most fearful of violent intimidation" (13). Across all of these examples, the common thread is the targeted, legally questionable nature of the efforts to either encourage or discourage a person from participating in politics. In other words, these are not simply "get out the vote" campaigns but, rather, strategies that explicitly dangle a carrot or wave a stick in front of specific voters in order to bring about or prevent certain political behaviors.

Further, evidence from Argentina suggests that these efforts extend far beyond the ballot box and can affect both the quantity *and* motivations for street manifestations that emerge across that country's 23 provinces and autonomous capital (Moseley 2018). Whereas minimally competitive, multiparty subnational regimes are characterized by higher rates of street activism, such expressions of political voice are often punished in dominant-party enclave systems through the withdrawal of social programs, termination of employment, and, in keeping with our emphasis on the strategic application of the rule of law, outright repression by a politicized law enforcement. Such efforts serve to make protest costlier and less common in these contexts. When it does occur, it is equally, if not more, likely that "protesters" will in fact be proincumbent sympathizers who have been mobilized by government officials to take to the streets either in favor of a particular government action or in response to some controversy that has put the regime in a bad light. Thus, rather than street protests representing strident opposition to the incumbent government's actions, as conventionally viewed, in dominant-party enclaves, protests often serve, paradoxically, as a form of regime support.

Politicizing the State to Serve the Party

A second, and very much related, feature of dominant-party governance involves efforts to deploy the resources and powers of the state in ways designed to serve the dominant party. In the process, citizens are either rewarded or punished materially based on their relationship with the dominant party (McMann 2006). It is this tool of governance that most harkens back to the political machine described by Scott at the beginning of this chapter. Evidence of such machine-like efforts can be found at all levels of the dominant-party enclave—from the local patron on whom citizen clients depend for bank loans, employment opportunities, and myriad other necessities of everyday life to the privileged access some businesses are granted to government contracts. In every corner of such a system dominant-party officials will incessantly seek to position the party, through its control of state resources, as the source of economic prosperity or poverty for citizens. Going along to get along becomes the norm. This is not to suggest that such dynamics can be found only in dominant-party enclaves. We know this is not the case. Rather, our contention is simply that all else equal, such behavior will be more prevalent in subnational systems in which a single party faces limited opposition or oversight in its deployment of the powers of the state for the purpose of staying in power. Further, though we contend that virtually all dominant-party enclaves attempt to politicize state resources to some degree, we also recognize the great deal of variability that will exist with respect to a dominant-party's ability to capture state resources and use them for partisan purposes.

At the societal level, this mechanism, described by Diaz-Cayeros et al. (2001) as one of "tragic brilliance" whereby "the party can remain in power without sustained economic prosperity . . . wherein the party distributes rents to citizens who remain loyal and withdraws them from those who defect," serves to lock "poor voters into supporting the [regime] because their livelihood depends on state transfers" (Magaloni and Kricheli 2010, 128). Individuals or companies seeking to resist such efforts and create for themselves a degree of economic autonomy are often confronted with obstacles constructed by government officials through their strategic, selective application of the law. Moreover, in many dominant-party enclaves, the provincial state itself is the largest employer, meaning that the dominant party has immense influence in determining who has access to stable employment and benefits (Gervasoni 2010b). Across dominant-party systems, we argue that the machine seeks to positions itself as the embodiment of the provincial state, and the only avenue for obtaining economic assistance and career advancement.

When one's "ability to earn a living independent of the state" (McMann 2006, 28) is limited, this should, in turn, shape the ways in which she engages with her political system. The most likely manifestation of this heightened economic vulnerability will be that individuals in dominant-party enclaves will be less likely to overtly challenge the political status quo (Magaloni 2006; McMann 2006; Morgenstern and Zechmeister 2001). This general risk aversion in the realm of politics that is a byproduct of low levels of economic autonomy translates, for us, into another mechanism that should produce distinct attitudinal and behavioral profiles in dominant-party and multiparty systems. For example, citizens' electoral evaluations of the dominant-party incumbent will be driven less by standard performance metrics (e.g., economy, crime), and participation in "proincumbent" street marches should be more common than in multiparty contexts. More generally, in such a system in which public spending serves as a tool for government officials to reward supporters and punish opponents, we can see the basis for the dominant party's "ability to make identification with the political system and support for the party interchangeable ... [mobilizing] support in unobtrusive ways by blurring the distinction between themselves and the state" (Arian and Barnes 1974, 608, 611).

Electoral Malfeasance

Electoral "contestation entails three features: (1) ex-ante uncertainty, (2) ex-post irreversibility, and (3) repeatability" (Przeworski et al. 1991, 16). While outright reversals or cancellation of elections risk raising red flags for national-level officials, holding elections with a minimal risk of losing is the sine qua non of incumbent officials in a subnational dominant-party system. Indeed, this goal of reducing the degree of electoral "ex ante uncertainty" about the outcome—an uncertainty that is essential to democratic rule— guides much of the behavior of elected officials in dominant-party enclaves. And, not surprisingly, it is when the outcome of an election does become somewhat uncertain that we tend to see most clearly evidence of the electoral manipulation tools available to incumbents in a dominant-party system.

As we noted in the opening chapter, when the 80-year reign of power for the PRI in the state of Mexico (Edomex) looked vulnerable in the face of a challenge by a MORENA party candidate in the 2017 gubernatorial elections, the state's ruling party reportedly doubled down on efforts to buy or coerce a favorable outcome (Thornton 2017). Similarly, in the Argentine province of San Luis, after being soundly defeated in the initial PASO vote in the summer of 2017, the Rodríguez-Saá political machine resorted to a wide range of tactics in its bag of tricks to eventually claim a double-digit win in the general election two months later. These are just two of countless examples of subnational incumbents around the world employing whatever tools necessary to fend off an opposition threat to their grip on power. Whether in the provincial systems of Russia and Kyrgyzstan in which McMann (2006) found that "[o]pposition candidates in one region ran without negative repercussions, but those in another region lost their jobs" (6) or in the one-party regime of the U.S. South, where the voting rights movement of the 1950s and 1960s led to highly violent retaliatory measures by system proponents, we can most clearly see the undemocratic tendencies of these subnational systems when they are threatened by viable electoral challenges to the status quo.

A close election in a dominant-party enclave, then, is a sign that the various tools used between elections to strengthen the party's grip on power have not worked as expected. These tools of dominant-party governance, such as those discussed above, involve the somewhat subtler strategies of patronage, economic cooptation, and clientelism, which are intended to dampen credible opposition threats before they get started. As Magaloni and Kricheli (2010) note in their description of national dominant-party systems, "If the population overwhelmingly supports the party and the party controls the distribution of power, positions, and rents, potential elite rivals have no chance to gain power and spoils by competing outside the party" (128). And as we have learned from various scholars studying these machine dynamics at both the national and subnational levels, a key to their survival is elite cohesion. If "elite fracture, defection of groups from the authoritarian elite to the opposition, and opposition unification" occur, the tenure of the dominant-party's hold on power is put in jeopardy no matter how advantageous the electoral playing field may be (Petersen 2018, 36). The message of electoral certainty, then, is one sent to both elites and the mass public that the dominant party is the only game in town, and incumbent officials are the ones that make the rules for that game (within reason). As such, citizens and elites must learn to play by these rules, rather than fight to change them, in order to have any measure of success. They learn, in other words, to go along to get along.

Before moving to a brief overview of the specific attitudes and behaviors that we expect to be most affected by such a system, and that serve as the dependent variables of our study, it is worth touching on an issue here that we will revisit throughout the pages of this book: causality. Do dominant-party systems shape the attitudes and behaviors of citizens, as we contend, or might it be the attitudes and behaviors of certain subsets of a nation's citizenry that allow dominant-party enclaves to emerge and persist? While this question is difficult to answer definitively one way or the other, we hope to convince the reader throughout this book that a far more compelling theoretical and empirical case exists in support of the idea that political systems have more influence on attitudes and behaviors than vice versa.

Though dominant-party systems ultimately depend at least in part on the support, or at least resigned acceptance, of a sizable segment of the mass public, and though we thus would expect a recursive relationship will emerge between the two, the responsibility for the day-to-day operations of the dominant-party machine falls largely on the shoulders of party elites. For it is these officials who target certain individuals, groups, and businesses in society with rewards and punishments. It is these officials who either condone or reprimand acts of corruption. It is these officials who politicize state resources in order to generate support and deter opposition to the machine. And, it is these officials who must commit to unity in an effort to avoid the cracks that give hope to opposition movements. If they fail at these tasks, we might see widespread calls for a truly democratic opening from society. What this suggests is that many citizens will adapt to a dominant-party system for largely instrumental reasons, but if their Faustian bargain with dominant-party elites falls apart, they typically will not hesitate to call for democratic change.

The role of elites in dominant-party system maintenance is worth empha-sizing at this point as we turn to an overview of our expectations regarding the ways in which such systems shape citizen attitudes and behaviors. This predominant role of elites, and the very intentional way they seek to incen-tivize citizens to at least tolerate their continued rule, suggests that with re-spect to the "chicken-or-egg" question, dominant-party systems come prior to an acquiescent, if not supportive, civil society. Though it is difficult to em-pirically establish such a causal relationship, we endeavor to offer support for it in the following chapters. For now, though, we turn to a brief overview of how in our view dominant-party systems shape citizens' attitudes and behaviors in ways that have significant consequences for local and national regimes.

Dominant-Party Attitudes and Behaviors

In many ways, the core theoretical inspiration for this study is quite simple—having established that stark differences exist in the nature of local politics *within* the same national regimes, we suspect that individuals will think about and engage with politics in ways that, in part, reflect the characteris-tics of the subnational system in which they find themselves. Where electoral accountability exists—that is, in systems in which the bums can be thrown out—voting behavior should, in part, be driven by this feature of the system. Conversely, if showing up at a political rally is rewarded with material goods, and the failure to attend is punished through the withholding of such goods, then it stands to reason that individuals may be more inclined to attend such rallies. The influence of a dominant-party system on the political attitudes and behaviors of its citizenry emanates in large part from the ways in which such systems, and the officials that run them, engage and incentivize citizens to interact with their political world.

Clientelism and Corruption in Dominant-Party Systems

If we are correct that incumbent officials in dominant-party enclaves are more likely to rely on corrupt and clientelistic practices than their counterparts in multiparty systems, then citizens who live in dominant-party systems should have more experience with such practices than their counterparts in multiparty systems. We explore this possibility in Chapter 4 and find clear and robust evidence that in both Argentina and Mexico, an individual living in a dominant-party context is significantly more likely to be familiar with, if not actively participate in, a relationship with elected officials that rests on the "sale" of her political voice in exchange for private goods of some sort. As these types of relationships persist, largely unchallenged with the absence of a viable political opposition, citizens view these interactions as the only way through which one can extract goods from the state, and such exchanges thus also become the basis on which individuals evaluate the performance of their elected officials (see, for example, Magaloni 2006).

These variations in the degree to which clientelistic exchanges characterize relationships between citizens and their provincial government officials provide one source for the differences that we see between citizens of dominant-party and multiparty systems. As Gandhi and Lust-Okar (2009) point out in their overview of research on participation in authoritarian regimes, "patronage distribution and control over resources" (408) serve as essential tools for incumbents in such systems, and the normalization of these tools seems likely to generate distinct attitudinal and behavioral profiles among citizens living in these systems.

Similarly, the normalization of corruption, particularly those street-level forms of corruption with which many citizens have direct experience, constitutes a second governing tool that should also color citizens' views of how the political game must be played. Though certainly an act that engenders distaste, if not disgust, among many, it is also one, when practiced enough, to which people will grow accustomed. Whether in the form of bribing a police officer to avoid a ticket or being required to pay "a fee" to schedule an appointment at a government-run hospital, such extralegal acts, when pervasive enough, become a part of one's daily life. Wrong's (2009) account of corruption in Kenya highlights this tendency toward the normalization of such practices:

> Western analysts have remarked on Africans' "astonishing ambivalence" towards corruption, but it is not so surprising. Under the colonial occupiers and the . . . "black *wazungas*" who replaced them, the citizen had learnt to expect little from his government but harassment and extortion. "Anyone who followed the straight path died a poor man," a community worker in Kisumu once told me. "So Kenyans had no option but to glorify corruption." (55)

A similar, more concise reflection of this toleration of corruption comes in the form of the widely recognized saying in Mexico during the heyday of the PRI's one-party regime that a politician who is poor is a poor politician (*un político pobre es un pobre político*). Once normalization, and toleration, of corruption becomes widespread, citizens find themselves playing the dominant-party political game out of necessity and thus are less likely to see corruption as a problem or use it as an issue on which to evaluate the incumbent government. From the perspective of dominant-party officials, corruption then becomes yet another tool with which to "reward" followers (even if they have to pay for it) and punish opponents.

A final, potential consequence of the ongoing efforts in dominant-party systems to tilt the electoral playing field in favor of the incumbent officials and their supporters is low levels of political efficacy among much of the electorate, particularly those not willing to play the dominant-party political game. In a system with limited opportunities to effectively exercise one's political voice, in which political submissiveness is rewarded and outspokenness punished, it should be no surprise to find citizens who express doubts as to how much they can influence politics. Such a citizenry, for dominant-party elites, is precisely the type of society the system is designed to produce, as acquiescence and dependence are central to most forms of citizen engagement with the state. In such a context, many citizens will participate in political rallies or turn out to vote, but only when they are told to and receive rewards for doing so. From this dynamic emerges a robust dominant-party status quo in which incumbents remain in power and supporters receive some reward for their role in the process, all under the guise of an electoral democracy. It should be no surprise then to find in these systems a citizenry with a jaded, highly instrumentalist view of democracy and how it functions.

Attitudes toward Democracy

Having first looked at the extent to which dominant-party citizens experience the corruption and clientelism that are so essential to the operation of the political machine in which they live, we next turn to an assessment of these citizens' views of democracy. We focus in Chapter 5 on the ways in which citizens think about politics, and democracy more generally, with the expectation that citizens in dominant-party systems will have a more cynical view of the virtues of democracy. With this expectation then, we again are siding with the "institutions first" position in the regime type–democratic culture chicken-and-egg debate. Given the socioeconomic and ethnic diversity of the dominant-party states and provinces across Mexico and Argentina (explored in Chapter 3), we view it as unlikely that any similarities in attitudes toward democracy among citizens living in these provinces will be due to a common political culture formed prior to the onset of democracy in the two countries. Whereas Putnam (1993) may have viewed the differences in the quality of governments in Northern and Southern Italy as a product of centuries-old differences in the cultures of the two regions, we see the differences in the modus operandi of dominant-party and multiparty systems as the driver of attitudinal and behavioral differences we find across and within Mexico and Argentina.

This position finds support in recent crossnational work on cultural characteristics of countries and their prospects for democracy. Dahlum and Knutsen find "no support for any causal effect of self-expression values on democracy" (2017, 437). Instead, these authors conclude that democracy may, in fact, bring about "the learning of self-expression values within [a] population" (437). At the subnational level, it is even more likely, given the cultural traits shared by citizens of a single country, that distinct patterns of democratic attitudes and behaviors would be the result of differences in a country's subnational political systems. Put more bluntly, we see the uneven democratic landscapes of these two countries not as products of subnational cultural differences but, rather, as critical sources of the gaps in democratic attitudes and behaviors we find evidence for across the two countries. That said, and as we noted above, we also recognize the ways in which such attitudes and behaviors can, in turn, reinforce the prevailing "rules of the game" in a system.

Work on the concept of a democratic political culture has recently focused primarily on the extent to which individuals support key components of liberal democracy like tolerance and inclusive participation, limits on executive authority, and institutional checks and balances (Carlin 2011; Carlin and Singer 2011). In drawing on Dahl's (1971) conceptualization of "polyarchy," Carlin and Singer explore how Latin American citizens fit into different support profiles, based not only on long-term explanatory factors like wealth and education, but also short-term predictors related to economic performance and corruption victimization. Ostensibly, the prevalence of democratic values would be explained by not only individual-level factors like education and age, but also the context in which citizens operate and the extent to which they are imbued with the values and norms that predominate in a particular setting.

We argue that being nested within a certain type of local political environment should influence how citizens view these democratic principles. If we think of one's attitudes toward politics as being shaped by the political game she plays or at least observes being played by political elites, then it does not require much of a leap to posit systematic differences in the degree to which citizens embrace democratic principles between those living in a dominant-party provincial system characterized by clientelism and corruption and those living in multiparty systems that are likely to have considerably lower levels of both, and to at least pay lip service to a political ethos in which such practices are deemed unsavory, if not illegal.

This proposition rests on the idea that individuals who spend their lives in less-than-democratic local political environments are shaped fundamentally by that experience. These individuals have never witnessed the governor's party lose an election, they are far more likely to have been targeted for vote buying and other corrupt practices, and they have only borne witness to dominant executives with a history of running roughshod over the institutions designed to check them. Moreover, these individuals live in environments where opposing views are discouraged, if not repressed. In this context, many, though not all, individuals will tend to adapt and adjust their attitudinal profiles in ways that will allow them to navigate this particular type of system.

Just as Mattes and Bratton (2007) speak of "democratic learning" in African countries, where the embrace of democratic principles comes with the experiences one has with democracy, here we posit that citizens will experience the opposite—a process of dominant-party learning within regimes that have at the national level already democratized. This argument is grounded in research on how national-level democratization processes shape orientations toward democratic politics. Similar to the finding of Peffley and Rohrschneider (2003) that political tolerance tends to increase in democracies over the course of time, and Rohrschneider's (1994, 1996) analysis of the attitudinal consequences of institutional variation between East and West Germany, we argue that many individuals in dominant-party provinces and states have not yet experienced democratic governance to the degree that country-level measures of democracy would indicate. With this expectation, we should find that a less-than-democratic political culture prevails in these dominant-party subnational systems, producing a vicious cycle wherein individuals in such systems fail to embrace the norms of democratic politics that help nascent democracies thrive and, instead, adopt political principles, such as support for a dominant executive and skepticism about basic individual rights, that are necessary for success in the one-party system.

Electoral Accountability Mechanisms

Turning to the ways in which voters evaluate incumbents in dominant-party systems, we expect a decidedly distinct set of evaluatory criteria to guide them when compared with their compatriots living in multiparty systems. For the latter group, where at least minimally competitive elections have taken hold, and citizens have evidence that peaceful alternation in power can happen, we should find voters behaving in ways consistent with those found in work on performance-based voting in more established democracies. This extensive body of research, focused in large part on economic voting, rests on the core assumption that voters are willing and able to hold incumbents accountable for their performance in office, economic and otherwise. Though debate continues about the basis for such retrospective evaluations, and how closely they map across individuals to objective conditions (e.g., Achen and Bartels 2017), we have fairly consistent support from research across Europe and the United States for the role a voter's evaluations of economic conditions play in the decision she makes at the ballot box.

On the other hand, where no concrete evidence exists that those in power will ever relinquish that power, this core assumption of the performance-based voting literature will *not necessarily hold*. In Chapter 6, we pursue this line of argument. Several features of such dominant-party systems suggest that rather than rely on standard performance-based metrics on which to base their evaluations of incumbent governments, citizens will, instead, be driven by the clientelistic linkages that tend to prevail in such contexts, the conflation of the incumbent party with the state more generally (e.g., Gervasoni 2010b; Magaloni 2006; McMann 2005), and the risk-aversive behavior that officials in such systems often seek to propagate among the citizenry (Morganstern and Zechmeister 2001).

All of these characteristics prevail in dominant-party systems in which the chances of the electoral ouster of the incumbent are minimal, thus rendering performance-based voting ineffective as a mechanism of accountability. If an individual sees no chance of "throwing the bums out" with her vote, one alternative becomes toleration of, if not participation in, the game of dominant-party politics in which selling one's vote, pursuing economic gains through the state, and "going along to get along" become a strategy of survival, if not prosperity. Recalling the work of Key once again (1949), "the one-party system both contributes to low levels of citizen interest and in turn perhaps is perpetuated in part by citizen disinterest" (489). Simply put, our expectation is that when an individual's provincial political system does not provide or allow for democratic linkages between citizen and state, the mechanisms driving the performance-based voting thesis will falter, leaving one's vote choice, if, indeed, she chooses to vote, influenced by other factors such as the incumbent's selective provision of supposedly public goods as a way to reward and punish voting behavior.

When individuals are embedded in distributive networks, view the provincial state and incumbent party as essentially one in the same, and understand politics as a fundamentally clientelistic, rather than programmatic, game, these norms and behaviors can seep into the ways in which they engage with and evaluate their national-level politicians. Whereas potential heuristics regarding the current state of the economy, the quality of public services, or levels of insecurity weigh heavily on the minds of individuals who see the connection between party platforms and policy outcomes on a day-to-day basis, such cues might be left out of the voting calculus of citizens situated in less democratic contexts. Further, if accountability mechanisms between constituents and politicians are distorted in dominant-party enclaves at the subnational level, these distortions may then also affect how citizens evaluate their national-level institutions and actors (Cleary and Stokes 2006; Vetter 2002). We explore this possibility as well in the chapters that follow.

Political Participation in Dominant-Party Systems

The theoretical mechanisms discussed above hold two notable implications in terms of who is most likely to participate in politics in dominant-party enclaves versus multiparty systems, which is the focus of Chapter 7. First, classic socioeconomic-status (SES) models of participation from the literature on developed democracies *will not necessarily apply* to participation patterns in dominant-party systems. In particular, the relationship between education and political participation seems likely to function quite differently in dominant-party systems when compared with its conventional role in participation models for established democracies. Whether seen as a proxy for "other factors that catalyze political participation" (Kam and Palmer 2008, 626) or as a causal influence in and of itself (Hillygus 2005), higher levels of education have long been associated with higher levels of political engagement. We expect, however, that in dominant-party systems individuals with advanced levels of education, who are the most keenly aware of the less-than-democratic inner workings of the local machine, will be less likely to engage in politics than educated citizens in more democratic contexts.

Given the reliance of political officials in dominant-party systems on the selective provision of public goods, clientelist-based relationships with their constituents, and the overt use of the state for partisan purposes, we expect those with high levels of education to be more likely to reject such strategies of governance and disengage from politics (as much as possible) as a form of protest or, at a minimum, to avoid as much as possible playing a role in its legitimation. While we recognize the possibility that some highly educated individuals will be willing and, arguably, most able to benefit from the system in which they live, regardless of how democratic or not it might be, we posit that in general, higher levels of education will increase the likelihood of an individual rejecting the game of politics as it is played in a dominant-party system.

Evidence for an admittedly extreme version of this proposition comes from the former Soviet Union, where Karklins (1986) found that the "demographic profile of nonvoters tends to support the proposition that nonvoting in the Soviet Union is a political act qualitatively similar to voting in democratic systems" (455). A more recent, and perhaps more relevant, example comes from the work of Croke et al. (2015), who find evidence from their work in Zimbabwe that in a context of "limited liberalization," where "[t]he formal adoption of electoral institutions allows the regime to claim democratic credentials," more educated citizens, who also tend to be more critical of such regimes, are left with "two suboptimal options: play the 'democratic' game in which they are assured to lose while legitimizing the regime, or withdraw from politics altogether" (598). Though most work on this question has been carried out at the national level, we contend that we should find evidence of this negative relationship between education and political participation occurring in dominant-party systems at the subnational level as well.

Second, and most central to our argument, we expect that government sympathizers are the more likely participants in the political life of dominant-party systems, as they engage in a variety of behaviors designed to serve the incumbent machine. For example, in great contrast to multiparty systems, in which participants in street marches tend to be critics of the incumbent government (see Beaulieu 2014; Boulding 2014; Moseley 2018; Silva 2009), we expect many demonstrators in dominant-party enclaves to, in fact, be supporters of those in power, with their street-level participation simply being one manifestation of that support, driven by expected rewards from the government. Overall, while voters, protesters, and community activists in multiparty states should match the standard profiles found in many democratic countries around the world, we anticipate that those most likely to participate in dominant party enclaves will challenge the conventional wisdom regarding the determinants of political participation.

Similarly, we expect the distinctive characteristics of dominant-party systems to also influence which citizens engage in politics directly through contacting political officials in order to solve a problem. This form of participation in many ways captures a defining element of a system based on clientelistic relationships. Just as citizens in such a system are available to "take to the streets" when called upon by political elites, so, too, do those political elites make themselves available to citizen/clients in order to solve specific problems. Emblematic of this personalist approach to politics that characterizes dominant-party systems is the late Venezuelan president Hugo Chávez's radio call-in show *Alo Presidente*, in which Chávez would respond directly to citizen grievances, simultaneously inculcating tremendous loyalty among his core constituency and demonizing his opponents. In such a political context, it is no surprise that those citizens most likely to engage in these types of personal contacts with elected officials will be regime supporters, while such access will likely be limited, if not denied, to opponents of the incumbent government. Conversely, in less personalist, more established democratic systems, one's views toward the incumbent should be far less decisive in identifying those citizens who seek out help from public officials. Though certainly not immune from partisan bias in the degree of responsiveness of local officials, citizens in such systems will likely not view their own relationship with the ruling party as a reason to either seek help or not. Once again, this expectation is grounded in a fundamental quality of dominant-party systems: citizen-incumbent relations built on the private provision of rewards for loyal supporters and punishments for opponents.

While such displays of support and selective engagement with public officials are commonly associated with extreme forms of authoritarianism, such as the near 100 percent voter turnout reports from North Korea and proregime demonstrations in Venezuela, attention to these regime effects on the political behavior of citizens at the subnational level in largely democratic countries is limited. What these gaps in subnational democracy suggest is that citizens within the same country, just as African-Americans living in the U.S. South throughout much of that country's history, have fundamentally different relationships with and access to their political representatives. Further, studies of political behavior and democratization that do not take into account the subnational divides that characterize many emerging democracies will not capture these distinct relationships that citizens have with their political system. If one of the core set of questions guiding the study of politics around the world remains "who gets what, when, and how?" (Lasswell 1936), then knowing the role that subnational political divides play in answering those questions seems a vital step for comparative scholars of many emerging (and some established) democracies the world over.

Implications for National Regimes

Democracy is on the decline worldwide. In 2017, 71 countries experienced declines in political rights and civil liberties, marking the 12th consecutive year that more countries have suffered declines in freedom than gains (Freedom House 2017). Perhaps most troubling, rather than just the "usual suspects," the past decade has seen significant democratic recession in some of the world's most established democracies, including the United States (V-Dem 2017). Eastern European countries like Hungary and Poland appear to have transitioned to illiberal rule, and several Southern European countries like Greece, Italy, and Spain have witnessed the emergence of illiberal parties on both ends of the ideological spectrum. Further, recent elections in France, Germany, and Great Britain demonstrate that not even Western European powers are immune to the appeal of authoritarian populism.

Latin America is no exception to this global drift toward less democratic forms of government. Eleven countries in the region were classified as either "partially free" or "not free" in 2018—including such regional powers as Colombia, Mexico, and Venezuela (Freedom House 2018). Over the past half-decade, Venezuela has completed its transition to full-scale authoritarianism under Nicolás Maduro, cemented by recent sham elections that were boycotted by most of the opposition. Mexico remains plagued by high levels of crime and corruption and continues to be one of the most dangerous places in the world for journalists.[5] And in Brazil, the region's largest country, which experienced a heated presidential impeachment process in 2016 amid a massive corruption scandal, a far-right ex-military officer and authoritarian nostalgist, Jair Bolsonaro, entered office on January 1, 2019.

These worrisome trends are reflected in public opinion. According to the 2016–2017 round of the AmericasBarometer survey, only 58 percent of Latin Americans believe democracy is, in spite of its flaws, the best system of government—a decline of nearly 10 percent compared with responses in 2014 (LAPOP 2017). Perhaps most alarming, a significant number of Latin American citizens appear to support military coups under conditions of high crime or corruption, even in some of the region's most stable democracies (e.g., 53 percent in Costa Rica and 33 percent in Chile). Public support for the executive shutting down the legislature during hard times also spiked in the most recent round of regional surveys, and trust in elections is now lower in Latin America than at any time since the AmericasBarometer launched in 2004 (LAPOP 2017).

In our view, one element behind these broader trends can be found at the subnational level. Beyond having significant consequences for how individuals interact with their local political system, we posit that the distorted nature of politics that prevails in subnational dominant-party enclaves will shape their interaction with *national* political institutions and government officials as well. If democratic subnational political systems can serve as a "'training ground' for democracy" (Vetter 2002, 15), then so, too, can a less-than-fully-democratic subnational system distort the ways in which citizens think about and engage with their national-level regime. Cleary and Stokes (2006), comparing political attitudes among citizens of selected Argentine provinces and Mexican states, find that "people in less democratized regions identified the character of politicians, and not institutional constraints, as the chief determinant of government responsiveness [and] were more prone to clientelism . . . [and] were less inclined to voice unconditional support for the rule of law" (178). The personalistic nature of dominant-party enclaves can thus become so engrained in individuals that they translate those lessons to their evaluations of national-level institutions and actors as well.

---

[5] See, for example, the chapter, "Edited by Drug Lords," by Elisabeth Malkin in the Committee to Protect Journalists' 2017 report *Attacks on the Press* (https://cpj.org/2017/04/edited-by-drug-lords.php)

If, for example, individuals nested in dominant-party systems are more likely to have firsthand experience with corruption, the country-level consequences could be substantial. Seligson (2002) finds that experience with corruption has a significant effect on regime legitimacy, as corruption victims tend to hold more negative views of central national regime institutions. He also provides evidence that experience with corruption has a negative impact on interpersonal trust, which has been posited by many to have numerous downstream effects on such areas as social capital (e.g., Putnam 1993) and democratic governance (Inglehart 1999). If individuals' day-to-day interactions with corrupt dominant-party officials reflect poorly on the national regime itself, the continued presence of less-than-democratic subnational institutions could contribute to the hollowing out of democratic system support throughout Latin America.

When it comes to broader components of democratic public opinion, we also see the experience of living in a dominant-party system as crucial to understanding individual-level variation in support for key democratic regime institutions and processes. Just as Hiskey and Bowler (2005) find that fraudulent elections at the local level influence how citizens view their national electoral system, so, too, do we expect that citizens in dominant-party systems will translate their experiences with provincial politics to their views of and engagement with national politics. When governors change the provincial constitution to allow for indefinite reelection, as has happened in Argentine provinces like Formosa, San Luis, and Santa Cruz, citizens of those provinces might assume that similar machinations at the national level are normal, and even necessary. When critical voices are censored in local media by the dominant-party machine in the name of the "greater good," individuals living in such contexts might absorb the "lesson" that such measures are necessary to maintain order at the provincial *and* national levels. We find significant support for these ideas in Chapter 5's focus on political culture in dominant-party systems.

The regime unevenness, then, that we explore in this work and that characterizes many emerging democracies can influence not only provincial politics, but national politics as well. If correct, these subnational political divides will have important implications for the direction taken by democracies around the world moving forward. Though certainly not the only reason the current global political landscape seems best characterized by democratic backsliding, the persistence of subnational dominant-party enclaves represents an important obstacle that we see as impeding efforts to reverse that trend.

Conclusion

In this chapter, we have presented our theory of dominant-party enclaves and the citizens they produce, outlining the mechanisms by which subnational political machines fundamentally alter the political attitudes and behaviors of individuals nested within them. While an abundance of social scientific research has explored the nexus between political institutions and behavior, this literature has, like other areas of scholarly inquiry, been driven by a "whole-nation bias," (Rokkan 1970; Snyder 2001) with an almost exclusive focus on crossnational analyses and national-level institutions. Here we offer a new direction for this research in seeking to understand how local political context matters in shaping citizen attitudes and participation. Building on a newly vibrant body of research on the origin and continuation of subnational authoritarianism (e.g., Fox 1994; Gervasoni 2018; Gibson 2013; Giraudy 2015), our research represents an effort to propel the conversation toward the *consequences* of such regime unevenness.

In our view, there are three principal mechanisms that link dominant-party system characteristics with the attitudinal and behavioral patterns of citizens living within them. First, we argue that dominant-party systems' tendency to manipulate the rule of law for political gain warps individuals' understanding of how democratic political institutions should operate and thwarts any potential impetus to disturb the status quo. Second, the seemingly ongoing efforts by dominant-party officials to conflate the ruling party and the state in the minds of citizens, allowing for the former to wield the resources of the latter in ways designed to reinforce the status quo, lead to the normalization of corrupt and clientelistic behaviors to the point where citizens tend to no longer view such behaviors as problematic. Third, we expect that the highly uneven electoral playing field that is a product, in part, of these first two dominant-party traits, along with the oftentimes overt manipulation of the electoral environment, will lower feelings of political efficacy among citizens, disincentivizing them from pursuing change, and contributing to the entrenchment of the dominant-party machine as the only game in town. These mechanisms shape the ways in which individuals think about and engage with politics as they try to manage life in the machine.

3

Conceptualizing and Measuring
Dominant-Party Enclaves

Having presented our theory of how dominant-party enclaves undermine democracy through their influence on the ways in which citizens think about and engage with politics, in this chapter we outline our approach to conceptualizing and measuring these subnational dominant-party systems. After reviewing extant approaches to this task, with an eye toward relevant points of intersection and divergence with our own conceptualization of subnational regime type, we introduce and discuss our measure of dominant-party systems as those that have never experienced an alternation in the party of the governor since the onset of democracy at the country level.

We conclude the chapter by returning to the two cases of dominant-party enclaves we introduced in Chapter 1—Estado de Mexico (Edomex), Mexico, and San Luis, Argentina—in an effort to further highlight the key characteristics of these political systems that we see as critical to understanding patterns of political attitudes and behaviors within them. While these two cases differ on a number of important economic, cultural, and political variables and are separated by over 4,000 miles, they share the three characteristics of dominant-party systems that we argue shape the political attitudes and behaviors of citizens residing within their borders. These case studies are based on extensive fieldwork and survey data in Argentina and Mexico; draw on dozens of interviews with local politicians, activists, and academics conducted over the years; and, we hope, serve as compelling portraits of everyday life in subnational systems in which the incumbent political party deals "in *particularistic, material rewards* to maintain and extend its control over its personnel" (Scott 1969, 1144) and exerts ongoing efforts to tilt the electoral playing field in its favor.

Life in the Political Machine. Jonathan T. Hiskey and Mason W. Moseley, Oxford University Press (2020). © Oxford University Press.
DOI: 10.1093/oso/9780197500408.001.0001

Measuring Subnational Regime Type

Unlike at the country level, where placement of the world's regimes on an authoritarianism–democracy scale has a long and well-established tradition (e.g., Polity; Freedom House; V-Dem; see Collier and Levitsky 1997),[1] accessible and reliable regime-type measures across time and space at the subnational level are rare.[2] For this reason, students of subnational politics have had to craft their own measures of provincial regime characteristics—often in developing contexts in which political data is harder to find. Typically, the best source for local political information that is accessible across subnational units and over time is electoral data (Cleary and Stokes 2006; Gervasoni 2010b; Giraudy 2013, 2015; Wibbels 2005). Indeed, while obtaining more direct measures of the standard operating procedures of a subnational system would be ideal, whether in levels of press freedom, the pervasiveness of vote buying, or documented incidents of Election Day malfeasance, such data are rarely available equally over time and across subnational units from two countries, thus limiting scholars' ability to fully test their propositions at the subnational level.

In looking at the burgeoning literature on subnational authoritarianism, some of the more prominent measurement efforts offer sophisticated strategies to measure the *degree of democracy* at the subnational level, rather than our more modest goal of establishing the presence or absence of a dominant-party enclave. Gervasoni (2010a, 2018) and Giraudy (2015) offer two recent examples of this strategy, with Gervasoni providing dual measurement approaches for gauging subnational democracy that employ electoral data and elite surveys, respectively, to evaluate electoral competitiveness across Argentine provinces. For Giraudy, the data demands are even greater as she evaluates both the electoral dimension of subnational systems (e.g., clean elections, turnover, and competitiveness) and a dimension that she refers to as the "exercise of power" that distinguishes between "patrimonial" (undemocratic) and "bureaucratic" (democratic) administration styles. Both of these efforts represent important steps forward in understanding the particular points of variation across subnational political systems and are certain to be reference points for future research in this area.

---

[1] More information on these sources can be found at the following sites: http://www.systemicpeace.org/polityproject.html; https://freedomhouse.org/; https://www.v-dem.net/en/

[2] With notable exceptions being Gervasoni (2018) and Giraudy (2015).

Gervasoni's recent work (2018) goes a step further in developing a "Comparative Subnational Democracy Index" that is designed to be "comparable across countries and historical periods" (234). The index includes only "objective indicators of contestation" (234) and thus resolves some of the concerns we have expressed regarding the availability of data across time and space. Despite the foundational contribution this work provides to current and future scholars of subnational political processes, it is less applicable to our efforts here for the reasons previously discussed, primarily that our concern is with a dominant-party system that often reveals itself most when confronted with a viable electoral challenge, meaning that a measure based, in part, on electoral competitiveness will not adequately capture the core concept we are seeking to capture—a system in which parties do not lose elections, no matter how close they may be. In this sense, then, we align ourselves more closely with the crossnational measurement strategy employed by Alvarez et al. (1996), who classify systems as democratic or not based on whether there are elections for the executive and legislative offices, whether there is an opposition (one or more political parties allowed to compete for elections), and, critically, if all other criteria are met, whether the incumbent party has "continuously held office" (Alvarez et al. 1996, 14). This last criterion, what these authors refer to as their "Type II Error" rule, is a recognition of those systems that have all the trappings of democracy yet lack concrete evidence that a peaceful transfer of power can occur between two opposing political forces. Departing from these efforts to identify democratic regimes, we instead use the *absence of alternation* as our decision rule to identify dominant-party systems.

Here we also agree with Schedler that "until alternation actually happens we can never know for sure whether a ruling party would be willing to hand over power in the case of electoral defeat. We can only make informed guesses" (2013, 184). This critical first alternation in power does not necessarily mean the state suddenly becomes fully democratic, nor that it will forever be immune to political malfeasance or succumb to a new era of dominant-party rule under another (or the same) political party. What the initial ousting of an incumbent party does tell us, however, is that the citizens of this particular political system have managed to effectively exert some form of electoral accountability by bringing about a change in government. This simple fact, we argue, is vitally important in identifying those subnational systems that we refer to as dominant-party enclaves. In short, though a first alternation does not tell us much about the *quality* of democracy that follows, the absence of a first alternation, we contend, provides a powerful proxy for capturing our concept of interest consistently across time and space.

Further, as noted above, efforts to craft a continuous measure of the degree of democracy for a subnational unit become vulnerable to short-term changes in such dimensions as the competitiveness of elections, even when there is a low probability of an actual alternation in power. For example, if in a province like San Luis, Argentina, there is a momentary narrowing of the gap between the dominant party and the opposition like there was in 2017, that shift would bring about a corresponding increase in the province's "democratic quality" score according to some measures. And while a highly competitive election that is still won by the dominant-party may, indeed, be a harbinger of a subsequent political opening, it would not mean the system at that moment had become more democratic. Indeed, the occasional close election in a dominant-party enclave typically brings out the worst that system has to offer in terms of voter intimidation, vote-buying efforts, and other forms of manipulation of the electoral process. The relatively close elections in San Luis and Edomex in 2017 did not make those systems more democratic—rather, they shone a light on the degree to which the dominant party held a decidedly undemocratic incumbency advantage. Once a peaceful alternation in power becomes a reality, the competitiveness of elections perhaps can provide insight into the partisan dynamics of a particular province or state, but not until all concerned have concrete evidence that election outcomes will be definitive in the determination of who rules. In dominant-party enclaves, with no such alternation having occurred, this is unlikely to be the case.

This discussion of categorical versus continuous measures of subnational regime type is also relevant to the mechanisms we outline in Chapter 2. According to our theoretical approach, the experience of living within a dominant-party enclave is one that accumulates over time—that is, the flip side of what Rohrschneider (1999) calls "democratic learning." A fleeting moment of competitiveness in a dominant-party system does not inoculate citizens against the accrued experience associated with residing in a province devoid of meaningful "institutionaliz[ed] uncertainty" (Przeworski 1991, 14). The circumstance that we contend does have a more immediate impact on the way citizens view the game of politics being played in their daily lives is when a dominant party loses an election and actually cedes power to its opponent. Though this singular event does not guarantee that a high-quality democracy will ensue, it does demonstrate that elections have consequences and that those once deemed "dominant" can be ousted. Measures tabulated based on yearly shifts in competitiveness, therefore, underappreciate the notion that the only way to begin to diminish the attitudinal and behavioral consequences of dominant-party rule is through the electoral defeat of the provincial machine.

Our Approach

Because our concern in this book is the impact that dominant-party enclaves have on the attitudes and behaviors of individuals living within these political systems, we focus our measurement strategy on what for many is the essence of an electorally competitive system: alternation in power. As we have mentioned previously, for any political system in the midst of a democratic transition, whether at the national or subnational level, a clear signal that such a transition is underway is the peaceful relinquishment of power from one party to another. Just as the ouster of the PRI from the presidency in 2000 marked a critical point in Mexico's national democratic transition, we view as equally critical a subnational unit's first experience with alternation in partisan control of the governor's office. Until that initial alternation in power takes place, the perception, and, more often than not, the reality, will remain that the political system falls short of being fully democratic, instead, approximating a continuation of its authoritarian past.

The paths toward democracy taken by Mexico and Argentina are quite different, with that of the former characterized by a decades-long erosion of a dominant-party system that culminated with the party's defeat in the 2000 presidential elections, while that of the latter being one of a relatively quick ouster of a military junta in 1983. Despite these different routes toward national-level democracy, however, the two countries have shared similarly uneven subnational political landscapes since the 1980s, with some provinces and states being early leaders in their country's democratization process while others, even today, remaining grounded in largely undemocratic norms and practices.

For Mexico, driven by an increasingly strong opposition movement challenging the PRI's dominance in the 1980s that was capped off by the PAN's electoral victory in Baja California's 1989 gubernatorial contest, and, more importantly, the subsequent peaceful transfer of power, the country's move toward a multiparty democracy was as much a subnational process as it was a national one (Loaza 2000). The fact, though, that opposition efforts at both the state and local level were able to push forward in efforts to pry power from the PRI also served to widen the gap between these areas and those where the PRI's decades-long grip on power continued well into the 21st century. In this latter group of municipalities and states, the PRI's one-party machine became more entrenched even as, or perhaps because, the national-level democratization project was underway around them.

While unique in many ways, Mexico's highly uneven democratization process finds parallels in many other emerging democracies. O'Donnell's assessment of the South American cases, for example, highlights the uneven nature of the regime transitions those countries, including Argentina, went through, Foweraker and Krznaric (2002) found in Guatemala that "the rural oligarchy's traditional political dominance has continued through the period of democratic transitions" (43). They also point to Brazil and Colombia as prime examples of what they refer to as "uneven democratic performance." In Mexico, these transition divides have remained evident well beyond the national-level democratization process that culminated in 2000 with the successful ouster of the PRI from the presidency. We are now close to two decades into this country's new era of democratic politics, and there remain several states that have yet to witness the PRI lose control of the governor's office.

Whereas Mexico's transition entailed a decades-long erosion of "the perfect dictatorship,"[3] Argentine politics have never been characterized by such stability. After several years of economic stagnation and brutal state repression, the country's military junta finally carried out one boondoggle too many with its failed invasion of the Falkland (*Malvinas*) Islands in 1982. With the ineptitude of the military regime on full display, Argentina quickly pivoted in the direction of democracy and, despite numerous economic, political, and institutional challenges, it remains intact nearly 40 years later (Levitsky and Murillo 2005). Yet if Argentina's national political history has been one marked by volatility, one area of relative stasis has been the continued presence of provincial political machines. In cases like the Juarez dynasty in Santiago del Estero and the Rodríguez-Saá in San Luis, individual

---

[3] *Perfect dictatorship* is a term coined by Mario Vargas Llosa in describing the Mexican one-party system of the 20th century—one that had all the trappings of a democracy but was decidedly undemocratic in the way it worked. As such, despite staying in power for more than seven decades of uninterrupted rule, it rarely had to rely on the overt authoritarian practices that other, more imperfect, dictatorships would typically employ.

families have dominated the politics of certain provinces for over a half-century, no matter which national-level regime was in place. During the current democratic era, in extreme circumstances the federal government has intervened to dislodge these bastions of subnational authoritarianism—like in the case of Santiago del Estero (Gibson 2005, 2013)—but they have mostly been allowed to coexist with national-level democracy and even see their governors elected to the presidency (e.g., Menem from La Rioja and the Kirchners from Santa Cruz).

In both countries, then, the ouster of the incumbent party from the subnational executive office has proven essential to moving that subnational political system beyond its authoritarian past. As we have noted above, a single occurrence of alternation in gubernatorial power tells us very little about the *quality* of democracy that prevails in the years that follow. Indeed, there are likely cases in which alternation in power has occurred but only resulted in the establishment of a new cadre of authoritarian-minded rulers. It is this scenario, in fact, that led Huntington to put forth his "two-turnover test" for democracy (1991). Our approach, however, is to concern ourselves first with those subnational systems that have offered *no evidence* of being systems in which citizens can "throw the bums out."

An important element of this focus on single-party control of the provincial executive office in Argentina and Mexico is the duration of uninterrupted rule *combined with* a prevalence of undemocratic measures used to stay in power. This combination of characteristics allows us to distinguish our category of dominant-party systems from those well-known national-level cases of extended single-party rule in industrial democracies (e.g., Japan and Sweden) where a well-established democratic system simply rewards a popular and successful political party with continued reelection to office. With two decades or more of singular control over the executive branch, combined with evidence of decidedly less-than-democratic practices, as determined both from our years of collective fieldwork experiences and secondary research from both countries (e.g., Alonso 1992, 1995; Bailón Corres 1999; Beer 2006; Benton 2012, 2016; Bianchi 2013; Chavez 2004; Cornelius et al. 1999; de Remes 2000; Díaz-Cayeros et al. 2009; Eisenstadt 2004; Gervasoni 2010a; 2010b; Gomez-Tagle 1997; Guillén Lopéz 1996; Herrmann 2010; Langston 2017; Loaza 2000; Magaloni 2006; Petersen 2018; Rodríguez and Ward 1995; Ziccardi 1995), we view our dominant-party category as one that captures a distinct political context from what exists in provinces and states that have experienced alternation within the past 25 years. This temporal threshold exceeds that used by Sartori (1976) to identify those systems dominated by a single party and is consistent with Bogaards's (2004) basic view of dominant-party systems as more categorical than continuous. Further, it maps onto the understanding of national-level dominant-party regimes put forth by Magaloni and Kricheli (2010) as systems that "permit the opposition to compete in multiparty elections that usually do not allow alternation of political power" (124). Finally, this approach finds support in the regime measurement strategy put forth by Alvarez et al. (1996) and Przeworski et al. (2000), which rests in large part on the availability of concrete evidence (i.e., actual alternation) that the incumbent can and will cede power through the electoral process. In later work on the substantive import of a system's first alternation, Przeworski (2015) concludes that "the first experience of election in which the incumbent rulers subject themselves to the verdict of the people, lose, and peacefully leave office has a powerful effect . . . It almost doubles the probability that peaceful electoral competition will continue indefinitely" (121). In examining subnational systems in which a single party or individual has held the most powerful political office for more than 25 years, then, we feel on safe ground in positing that the political context of these cases will differ substantially from those in which even a single alternation has occurred.

By relying on such a blunt measure to distinguish between "dominant-party" and "multiparty" subnational units, then, we are far more confident in the former category than the latter. Given our extensive research in both countries, and what we know about the 22 dominant-party states and provinces (as of 2008) we have identified through our measurement strategy, it is unlikely, though certainly not impossible, that we have included in this category a state or province that is, in fact, simply a multiparty system in which the incumbent party has enjoyed an unusually long run of electoral success. As noted previously, we have little doubt that the vast majority, if not all, of the cases we categorize as dominant-party belong in that category. Conversely, our "multiparty" category may be tainted by the inclusion of some provinces and states with political contexts that are more dominant party than multiparty, despite having had at least one alternation in power. We would rather err on this side, however, in order to ensure that our collection of dominant-party cases across time and space is as close to our concept as possible. Further, while our dichotomous measure sacrifices nuance in terms of short-term shifts in electoral politics, it is the long-term impact of life in a dominant-party machine on individuals' attitudes and behaviors that we seek to evaluate.

As with any dichotomous categorization of political systems, we fully recognize also the likelihood that there is considerable within-category variation across a range of factors for both our dominant-party and multiparty categories that we are unable to capture (Giraudy 2015). Clientelism, for example, may be far more pervasive in some states and provinces than others. Similarly, the partisan use of state resources may be more evident in some cases than others. Likewise, in our dominant-party category, even though alternation has not taken place, there is quite a bit of variation in how vibrant, and viable, the electoral opposition to the dominant party is. Recognizing this intracategory variation, we maintain that for understanding the consequences of uneven subnational political regime landscapes, distinguishing subnational systems on the basis of whether or not alternation has occurred is a good place to begin. Further, in the models we look at in subsequent empirical chapters, we include several variables designed to control for these intracategorical differences, including one for the level of electoral competitiveness within each state and province (which approximates measures utilized by Gervasoni (2018) and Giraudy (2015)), in order to account for any impact variations in competition may have on our dependent variables of interest.

As noted previously, we certainly do not see multiparty systems as immune to all of the mechanisms or characteristics we associate with dominant-party enclaves. Indeed, there is an abundance of evidence that clientelism, corruption, and the selective provision of what should be public goods prevail in even the most democratic of systems. Stepping outside the region of Latin America, one need only look at the political machines found in many U.S. cities to appreciate that no democratic system is fully immune to power-hungry individuals who seek ways to distort and undermine the tenets of democratic rule.

Nor do we view dominant-party contexts as completely void of individuals and organizations that refuse to play the dominant-party game and, instead, continue vigorously fighting against the controlling party's uninterrupted hold on power. Indeed, one of the most striking, and inspiring, elements of our research efforts in dominant-party systems in both Argentina and Mexico have been conversations with opposition leaders in dominant-party systems during which the courage, persistence, and tenacity of these individuals becomes clear. Rather, our contention is simply that in the dominant-party political contexts that are the focus of this research, where no alternation in power has occurred, we have good reason to believe that the mechanisms discussed in Chapter 2 are far more prevalent than in multiparty regimes and, thus, will serve to drive systematic differences in the political attitudes and behaviors of citizens living in these distinct political environs.

Case Selection: The Uneven Regimes of Argentina and Mexico

We chose to conduct our analysis of the attitudinal and behavioral consequences of uneven democracy in Argentina and Mexico for several reasons. First, these two countries are among the most well-documented and researched cases of uneven democracy in the literature on the topic, dating back to the early 1990s (e.g., Fox 1994; Gervasoni 2015, 2018; Gibson 2013; Giraudy 2015; O'Donnell 1993). By exploring the attitudinal and behavioral consequences of uneven democracy in Argentina and Mexico, then, we are building upon a wealth of research on the origins of this unevenness and pushing that research forward by beginning to look at its implications for two of the "crucial cases" in extant research (Eckstein 1975; Gerring 2004).

While both have made considerable advances toward liberal democracy, the two countries' politics have historically been dominated by similarly hegemonic parties in the form of Argentina's Peronist party (Partido Justicialista [PJ]) and Mexico's PRI, each of which has relied on clientelism and other such "governance tools" to construct broad, nonideological electoral coalitions that have all the trappings of the political machines long studied in United States (e.g., Scott 1966). Despite having suffered defeat at the national level, the grip on power by these parties in some provinces and states, where they have not relinquished power in decades, is emblematic of the dominant-party systems we wish to better understand. The relatively nonprogrammatic traditions and machine-like qualities of the PRI and PJ are important when it comes to differentiating between dominant-party systems (e.g., San Luis, Argentina, or Estado de Mexico, Mexico) and subnational governments that win consecutive reelections simply because they are closer to the median voter (e.g., the Republican Party in Utah, United States). In the face of numerous economic crises, corruption scandals, and other assorted political crises suffered by the national parties, the PJ and PRI have persisted in retaining power in many subnational units for decades by using governing tools that have little to do with representation or good governance. We provide evidence for this assertion below.

Important for this study as well, both countries in recent decades have witnessed a considerable devolution of power to the provincial level (Falleti 2010; Rodríguez 1997), making the impact of the subnational political context, and the power that dominant-party executives have in those systems, all the more significant in terms of their impact on the daily lives of citizens. Whereas in past decades, the provincial level of politics in both Mexico and Argentina was largely structured to serve the interests of relevant national-level officials, since the onset of democratic politics and the market-based economic reforms initiated by both countries in the 1980s and 1990s, the political and fiscal empowerment of provincial governors in particular has accelerated. As part of this decentralization strategy, governors have been given control over a variety of government purse strings, allowing for the even more overtly political use of such funds when left unchecked by a viable opposition presence (e.g., Acemoglu et al. 2014; Eaton 2004; Falleti 2010; Mattingly 2016; Rodríguez 1997).

Alongside these similarities, however, we also recognize and incorporate into our analysis several important differences between the two countries. Argentina, for example, generally enforces the compulsory voting law it has in place, while Mexico does not.[4] Conversely, Mexico, until recently, did not allow any elected official to be re-elected, making for a party-based system of accountability rather than one centered around individual politicians. Argentina, on the other hand, is characterized by significant cross-provincial variation in terms of reelection laws, spanning from provinces that ban reelection in all circumstances (e.g., Mendoza and Santa Fé) to provinces with indefinite reelection (e.g., Formosa or San Luis). Further, whereas Argentina's co-participation scheme creates stark differences in terms of the fiscal resources at the disposal of provincial governments (Gervasoni 2018, 2010b), federal transfers to Mexican states are somewhat less decisive in creating "rentier" subnational regimes. In addition to these

---

[4] See the International Institute for Democracy and Electoral Assistance website for a complete crossnational compilation of compulsory voting laws: https://www.idea.int/data-tools/data/voter-turnout/compulsory-voting

institutional differences both across and within our two countries of interest, there are also myriad differences among the 55 provinces and states in terms of such factors as the economic and human development levels, the types of economic activities, and region-specific historical and cultural features.

Despite these differences, we expect to find similar dynamics at play in the dominant-party subnational systems in both countries in terms of the mechanisms by which they inculcate certain values and behaviors in their citizens. Driving this expectation is the notion that the dominant-party characteristics introduced in Chapter 2, which are common to varying degrees across all of our dominant-party cases in both countries, will be far more influential than any differences that may exist among those cases. And though the national governments still clearly play an important role in the lives of citizens in both countries, the prominence of governors in the states and provinces of Mexico and Argentina has increased substantially. These two countries, and their 55 states and provinces, thus provide ideal laboratories for testing our argument.

Our key independent variable of interest is thus whether the Argentine province or Mexican state has experienced an alternation in the party of the governor—in Mexico since the emergence of viable and sustained subnational electoral opposition in 1982,[5] and in Argentina since the country transitioned to democracy in 1983. In 2008, the first year for which we have data for both countries, there were 14 of 31 states in Mexico that had not witnessed an alternation in power since at least 1982. By 2014, the last year of our data, this number had dropped to 9. In Argentina, of the country's 23 provinces, 8 had not experienced alternation as of 2008. This number dropped to 7 by 2014 with the defeat of the dominant-party candidate in Rio Negro in 2011 (see Table 3.1 for a list of provinces and

---

[5] Though the starting point for Mexico's democratic transition is up for debate among scholars, with hindsight we can point to 1982 as a significant early marker point in the country's regime transition, as that year witnessed the beginning of a prolonged economic crisis, signs of a growing electoral challenge from the center-right Partido Acción Nacional (PAN), the rise of the technocratic wing of the PRI that ultimately led to the splintering of the dominant party by 1988 and the first defeat of the PRI in a gubernatorial election in 1989 with the victory of the PAN's Ernesto Ruffo Appel in the state of Baja California. This first-time defeat for the PRI at the state level came on the heels of the hotly contested and widely disputed presidential election of 1988 in which Carlos Salinas de Gortari was declared the winner following a "mysterious" breakdown of the computer system used to count the votes. Salinas's principal challenger in that election came from former PRI leader and governor of Michoacan, Cuauhtémoc Cardenas, the candidate for the National Democratic Front (FDN), a loose coalition of center-left opposition and PRI dissidents that later would become the principal left-of-center party in Mexican politics, the Party of the Democratic Revolution (PRD).

Table 3.1. Argentine Provinces and Mexican States by Subnational Regime Category (circa 2014 with Transition Years when Applicable)

	Multiparty Provinces/States	Dominant-Party Provinces/States
Argentina	Buenos Aires, Catamarca, Chaco, Chubut, Cordoba, Corrientes, Entre Rios, Mendoza, Misiones, Rio Negro (2011), Salta, Santa Fe, Santiago del Estero, San Juan, Tucuman, Tierra del Fuego	Formosa, Jujuy, La Pampa, La Rioja, Neuquen, San Luis, Santa Cruz
Mexico	Aguascalientes, Baja California, Baja California, Chiapas, Chihuahua, Durango, Guanajuato, Guerrero, Jalisco, Michoacán, Morelos, Nayarit, Nuevo Leon, Oaxaca (2010), Puebla (2010), Queretaro, San Luis Potosi, Sinaloa (2010), Sonora (2009), Tabasco (2012), Tlaxcala, Yucatan, Zacatecas	Campeche, Coahuila, Colima, Durango, Hidalgo, Mexico, Quintana Roo, Tamaulipas, Veracruz

states by subnational regime type).[6] In total, the 16 dominant-party states and provinces of Mexico and Argentina in 2014 were home to close to 30 percent of the two countries' total population. Nearly 40 percent of Mexican citizens and about 1 in 7 Argentines live in a dominant-party enclave, which reinforces the importance of understanding how such political contexts shape the political attitudes and behaviors of the citizens who live within them.

From just a glance at the two maps in Figure 3.1, we can see that there is a degree of geographic heterogeneity in terms of where we find our dominant-party enclaves. Though a number of these systems in Mexico are found along the country's east coast, we also have the cases of Colima and Edomex in the central-western part of the country and several in the northern region. In the case of Argentina, we see that the eight dominant-party provinces (in 2008) are fairly evenly distributed across the country, from Jujuy in the north to Santa Cruz in Patagonia. This geographic distribution of the cases in both

---

[6] Our categorization of respondents into either dominant-party or multiparty states was done based on the status of their provincial political system at the time of the survey, reflecting the fact that we include survey data collected in 2008, 2010, 2012, and 2014.

Figure 3.1. Multiparty and dominant-party systems in Argentina (Panel A) and Mexico (Panel B) (2008).

countries suggests that we need not worry about geography as a potentially endogenous factor that could perhaps explain why citizens living within these dominant-party systems may exhibit common patterns of political attitudes and behaviors within each country, much less across Argentina and Mexico, two countries that are quite distinct in terms of their populations and cultural characteristics. Though such a concern would be valid for a case like the United States in the 1950s, where all of the dominant-party systems

(b)

Figure 3.1. Continued.

in that country shared a common Southern heritage and culture, we do not face that issue with our cases of interest in Argentina and Mexico.

To further examine the possibility that some factor other than the dominant-party system itself may be driving any distinct attitudinal and behavioral patterns we may find in these 22 states and provinces with un-interrupted partisan control of the executive branch (in 2008), Table 3.2 offers a cursory comparison of the average levels of development between the dominant-party and multiparty cases in our analysis. Evident from this comparison is that whether we look at the gross state product (GSP) per capita or literacy rates, neither group within either country is substantively distinct from the other. Indeed, as we will see in this chapter, such dominant-party cases as Edomex in Mexico, despite having a relatively low GSP per capita, is, in fact, more developed along many indicators than neighboring multiparty states such as Querétaro. Once again, this should reassure the reader that any distinct patterns of political attitudes and behaviors that we find in our dominant-party cases are not the product of, for example, uniformly low levels of economic or human development in that category of cases.

Table 3.2. Socioeconomic Statistics by Subnational Regime Category in Argentina and Mexico

	Gross Provincial/State Product/Cap (2007 US$)	Literacy Rate (%) (2010)	Manufacturing Sector (%) (2010)
Mexico Multiparty	9,582	92.26	28.9
Mexico Dominant-Party	10,414	92.33	25.5
Argentina Multiparty	7,372	97.52	14.77
Argentina Dominant-Party	10,177	97.68	14.55

Source: For Mexico data, INEGI website (http://www.beta.inegi.org.mx/datos/); INDEC for Argentina.

Data

Throughout the following chapters, we rely primarily on the extensive survey data collection of the Latin American Public Opinion Project (LAPOP), housed at Vanderbilt University. LAPOP conducts the AmericasBarometer surveys on a biennial basis throughout the Americas and is the preeminent source for information on citizen attitudes and behaviors in the region. Since 2004, these surveys have employed national probability samples in dozens of countries throughout the Western hemisphere to gather data on citizens' attitudes toward democracy, patterns of political participation, and other relevant socioeconomic and demographic data. These surveys include around 6,000 respondents in both Argentina and Mexico when we pool the samples from the national surveys of each country from 2008 to 2014.

The greatest advantage to using AmericasBarometer is the diversity of survey items included that map onto our theoretical perspective. As far as the mechanisms associated with dominant-party enclaves go, the AmericasBarometer surveys ask about experiences with both clientelism and corruption, in addition to citizens' perspectives on the prevalence of such underhanded tactics within their countries. The surveys also boast numerous batteries that explore citizens' support for democratic norms and processes (i.e., "polyarchy": Dahl 1971; Carlin and Singer 2011), which are crucial for us to understand how local context affects fundamental attitudes regarding what democracy is and how it should operate. Finally, the AmericasBarometer instrument also asks numerous questions about citizens' participation in politics, including presidential and gubernatorial vote choice, civic participation, and protest activity. Altogether, there is no better source for investigating how uneven democracy shapes political behavior in Latin America.

While our data are not representative by state or province, both country samples are nationally representative, and the surveys were conducted using face-to-face interviews of voting age adults.[7] Approximately 25 percent of individuals interviewed in Argentina and Mexico from 2008 to 2014 lived in dominant-party systems—which approximates the actual number of citizens living in those systems (~30 percent) across the two countries. In addition to these data, we also incorporate findings from open-ended interviews conducted in both countries over the past 10 years, partially funded by a grant from the National Science Foundation. Finally, for the in-depth look at Edomex and Queretaro, two neighboring states in central Mexico, which we present in this chapter, we leverage the *National Values Survey*, an extensive data collection effort that offers representative samples for each of Mexico's 31 states, as well as the Federal District. The survey was conducted in 2010 under the direction of *La Fundación Este País* and BANAMEX.

Everyday Politics in Two Dominant-Party Systems

Before proceeding to our analysis of specific dimensions of political attitudes and behavior in Argentina and Mexico in coming chapters, we conclude this chapter with a return, more in-depth visit to the two dominant-party cases we introduced in Chapter 1, San Luis, Argentina, and Estado de Mexico (Edomex), Mexico. Though analysis of these two cases does not provide a fully representative picture of such systems or the citizens they produce, we believe they capture the essence of dominant-party enclaves, illustrating the ways in which political life in dominant-party enclaves is distinct from multiparty contexts, and how citizens' daily experiences with a political machine shape their attitudes and participation.

---

[7] For more information on the LAPOP, its sources of funding, and the sampling methodology employed, please visit http://www.vanderbilt.edu/lapop/. The wording for all of the survey items used in the following analysis can be found in the Appendix.

San Luis, Otro País

San Luis is a small province in the Cuyo region of Argentina, located in the central-western part of the country. Unlike neighboring provinces— Mendoza to the west or Córdoba to the east—San Luis is sparsely populated and lacks the fertile soil necessary for large-scale agriculture. As of the 2010 national census, the total population of the province was less than 500,000, with about half of the province's inhabitants residing in the capital city or surrounding area. Though San Luis possesses a few notable tourist destinations—Merlo's mountains and casinos, in particular, attract thousands of visitors from Argentina's more populous eastern cities every year—the province lacks any obvious claim to fame, that is, aside from the Rodríguez-Saá brothers, who have run provincial politics for nearly 40 years.

Since Argentina transitioned to democracy in 1983, either Adolfo or Alberto Rodríguez-Saá has held the governorship for all but six years, and their party has never lost control of the provincial legislature or the governor's office.[8] In most cases, as exemplified by the 2003 gubernatorial election in which Alberto won 90 percent of the vote, provincial elections have not been competitive. In 1987, Adolfo was able to reform the provincial constitution to allow indefinite reelection of the governor, making San Luis one of the few provinces in Argentina characterized by such a law. Further, when one brother has resided in the governor's mansion, the other has typically represented San Luis in the National Senate, and during Argentina's famous economic and political crisis in December 2001, Adolfo was president for a week.

Explanations of the origins of the Rodríguez-Saá brothers' political fiefdom are varied but mostly revolve around the provincial government's relative economic power vis-à-vis other more populous provinces. San Luis fits Gervasoni's (2010b) conceptualization of a "rentier" province, but not in the conventional way. Rather than build political strength through the deployment of rents from some major extractive industry like petroleum or minerals, the Rodríguez-Saá have managed to use transfers from the federal government as their own personal piggy bank. Argentina's coparticipation scheme, originally established in 1934, redistributes far more federal tax

---

[8] According to Bianchi (2013), the Rodríguez-Saá dynasty goes back much further, to when the first Saá was elected governor of San Luis in 1860. Overall, five governors have come from the Rodríguez-Saá family tree, underlining the personalistic, familial nature of politics in San Luis.

revenue per capita to smaller provinces than to more populous ones—and by one local academic's estimation, San Luis received in 1989 roughly the same amount of federal revenue as Santa Fé province, which has a population seven times larger than that of San Luis (Guiñazú 2003). To this day, San Luis receives more than twice as much funding from fiscal transfers as its population would warrant in a truly proportional system.

The other critical factor underlying the Rodríguez-Saá brothers' economic dominance in San Luis has been the Industrial Promotion Law, which was put into effect under President Raúl Alfonsín in the 1980s as reparation for the western provinces' (Catamarca, La Rioja, San Juan, and San Luis) sacrifices during the war for independence (Samper 2006). The law essentially granted massive tax exemptions to companies that relocated some phase of production to one of the preferred provinces, and it delegated enormous powers to provincial governments both in granting decrees to businesses and reaping the economic (and electoral) rewards of rapid industrialization (Bianchi 2013). While certain scholars have pointed to San Luis's relatively high levels of industrialization and low public employment as a symptom of bureaucratic professionalism (e.g., Giraudy 2011), Bianchi argues that the Rodríguez-Saá used the industrial promotion law as a means of consolidating their grip on economic power, given that many of the supposed benefits of provincial industrialization never materialized, and most of the newly arrived industries left San Luis once the tax exemptions were eliminated years later.

One key example of the political nature of the industrial promotion law is that the provincial government has traditionally shared little revenue with municipalities in San Luis, which results in mayors throughout the province being dependent on the Rodríguez-Saá for basic funding—even in the 1980s and 1990s when provincial tax revenue was at an all-time high thanks to the unprecedented influx of industrial activity (Bianchi 2013). Furthermore, public works projects during this time were largely allocated to municipalities governed by loyalists, and construction contracts were typically granted to political allies with long-standing business ties to the Rodríguez-Saá (Wiñazki 1995). Rather than demonstrate the professionalism of the Rodríguez-Saá bureaucracy, the government's management of the industrial promotion law underlined its talent for naked political opportunism.

The brothers' vice grip on the provincial state has extended beyond its ability to hire and fire public employees or control the rollout of the industrialization policy and disbursement of provincial tax revenues. According to Bianchi (2013), the brothers constructed over 40,000 public homes in the

1980s and 1990s in a province of only about 400,000 people. These homes range from low-cost apartments to spacious suburban housing and require minimal down payments and dirt-cheap mortgage payments. The political utility of these public housing programs is compounded by the fact that, since the mid-1980s, the brothers have maintained control over most major local media outlets, including the two provincial newspapers and the local public television channel (Wiñazki 1995; Behrend 2011). The provincial government advertises heavily in these news outlets, which include a weekly rundown of ongoing housing projects and write-ups about specific families that receive new homes, accompanied by photographs of them with one of the Rodríguez-Saá brothers. One anti-Rodríguez-Saá activist recounted the story of how when she was chosen to receive a house, she refused to participate in the ceremonial handing over of the keys that would serve as positive PR for the provincial government. She was later informed that she would not be receiving a home and was sent on her way (interview with author, March 2013).

In San Luis, all three of the primary mechanisms linking provincial politics and citizen behavior are clearly present. The provincial government wields a great deal of power over individuals' livelihoods through disproportionate access to fiscal resources vis-à-vis more populous provinces, and the Rodríguez-Saá brothers have deployed those resources to great political effect. One opposition leader shared his frustration with the uneven playing field he and his fellow party members faced, and the resulting disincentive to engage in politics among many San Luis citizens:

> There are some provinces that possess a high population density and relatively low levels of revenue flowing from the federal government. San Luis, on the other hand, is one of the provinces that receives the highest fiscal transfers per capita via the national co-participation scheme and the industrial promotion law . . . which means the provincial government can fund public services without charging citizens additional taxes. This has produced a break in the fiscal contract that has allowed the provincial government to reap the electoral benefits of public spending without the political costs associated with taxation, and [thus] consolidated a patrimonial regime . . . and with it, a level of concentrated power in the same political force for decades, which produces dejection and fear in civil society.[9]

---

[9] Interview with author in 2014; our translation.

The rule of law in San Luis is highly politicized. In Chavez's (2004, 2006) study of Mendoza and San Luis, she argues that economic diversification and political competition are crucial to forging judicial independence—and thus, the rule of law. Mendoza province, lying just to the west of San Luis, is characterized by a relatively diverse economy, with a vibrant agricultural sector, mineral extraction, and tourism. The wine industry in particular, which for geographic and climactic reasons has long encouraged small-scale production rather than the emergence of major conglomerates, has served as an equalizing force in terms of economic power, as thousands of small-scale local vineyards compete in domestic and international markets (Chavez 2004). In Chavez's view, this level of economic fragmentation, in turn, fueled the dispersal of political power among multiple competing factions in Mendoza—indeed, unlike most Argentina provinces, Mendoza is home to a vibrant three-party system including the PJ, Radical Civic Union (UCR), and Democratic Party (PD), which is a center-right party found only in Mendoza. This degree of power-sharing between multiple parties has thus produced a legal system characterized by high levels of professionalism and low levels of partisan meddling.

San Luis, on the other hand, has long been characterized by a relatively weak private sector (except via the Industrial Promotion Law, which is largely managed by the Rodríguez-Saá) and minimal party competition. Given the consolidation of power in the hands of one dominant party—that is, in the absence of "institutionalized uncertainty" (Przeworski 1991)—governors in San Luis have encountered little resistance in their efforts to "dismantle countervailing power centers" (Chavez 2004, 424). This has meant that the Rodríguez-Saá brothers have handpicked judges and violated judicial tenure when necessary, resulting in a provincial court system that rarely decides against the government (Chavez 2004). Citizens of San Luis thus encounter a legal system that treats them differently depending on whether or not they are aligned with the provincial government. In an interview, an opposition leader told of reports that upon entering office, provincial Supreme Court justices were required to submit signed, undated letters of resignation to the governor's office, in the event that Alberto was displeased with their performance (authors' interview, March 2018).

The politicization of the rule of law was especially apparent during the only real episode of citizen unrest in San Luis since 1983—the *multisectorial* protests of 2004–2005. For the most part, the Rodríguez-Saá have been successful in suppressing the formation of significant social movements, primarily through cooptation. But when a controversial attempt at strategic redistricting—or to use U.S. vernacular, "gerrymandering"—incurred the wrath of multiple sectors of society, including university faculty and students, they took to the central plaza demanding that Alberto walk back his effort to isolate opposition voters in one district of the greater San Luis area. The government's response was swift and violent, featuring tear gas and nightstick-wielding police officers, and resulted in dozens of injuries and the imprisonment of more than 100 protestors.

Yet, the Rodríguez-Saá-directed police crackdown on protestors was only part of the story. According to multiple interviewees, including movement organizers and an opposition party leader, the Rodríguez-Saá also deployed recipients of social inclusion plans to conduct counterdemonstrations by threatening them with the revocation of their benefits. As we argue in Chapter 2, only in a society in which large swaths of citizens depend on the provincial state for their livelihood would such a strategy be viable. Thus, two of our three "pillars" of dominant-party rule have combined to produce a province characterized by some of the lowest rates of protest participation in Argentina—a country that at the national level registers one of the highest levels of contention in Latin America (Moseley 2018).

There is also evidence that performance-based linkages between the citizenry and the government operate differently in San Luis. In late 2001, Argentina lurched into one of the most severe economic crises in recent Latin American history. After initiating the largest sovereign debt default on record in December, the Argentine economy contracted by more than 10 percent in 2002, with over 20 percent unemployment (INDEC [Instituto Nacional de Estadístico y Censos; National Statistics and Censuses Institute]). Citizens responded by staging mass protests in Buenos Aires, which escalated into violent riots in certain neighborhoods and eventually led to the resignations of two presidents in the span of two weeks (Auyero 2007). When a new presidential election was finally held in 2003, Argentines elected Peronist Néstor Kirchner—a little-known governor who had no connection to the government in power at the time of the crisis. So, the well-established literature on economic voting would seem to have found a textbook national case to support the argument that performance-based considerations weigh heavily on voters' minds when they enter the voting booth, as Argentine voters dispensed with the incumbent Fernando de la Rúa administration and its allies by supporting Kirchner.

Yet in San Luis, there was no electoral reckoning for the Rodríguez-Saá, despite the fact that unemployment reached its highest level in decades in

2002 (and was higher than the national average), and the Gross Provincial Product (PBG) per capita had fallen from over $9000 (USD) in 1997 to $7000 in 2003 (INDEC). The Rodríguez-Saá won over 60 percent of the vote in the 2001 provincial legislative elections, and Alberto managed to garner 90 percent of the vote in the 2003 gubernatorial election (amid high levels of invalid voting). Despite a national economic crisis of epic proportions, the brothers were able to largely insulate themselves from what was happening nationally through an expansion of the provincial Social Inclusion Plan and their tight control of local media and, if anything, further consolidated their control of provincial politics in the subsequent gubernatorial and legislative contests. In our view, the seeming lack of performance-based voting is a consequence of severed representational linkages in dominant-party systems, abetted by high levels of citizen dependence on the provincial state and the absence of realistic alternatives in the context of a steeply tilted playing field.

Individuals in San Luis bear the markings of a citizenry that has endured nearly four decades of dominant-party rule. Compared with multiparty provinces, they protest less often, and they seem reluctant to punish the incumbent government, even under circumstances as extreme as the 2001–2002 economic crisis, which, if anything, hit San Luis *worse* than it did the whole of Argentina. We argue that these trends are the consequence of the extent to which the Rodríguez-Saá machine had positioned itself as the embodiment of the provincial state, politicizing the rule of law and disbursing public funds for partisan purposes. The first two mechanisms, in particular, have produced a society that is hesitant to oppose the Rodríguez-Saá machine for fear of losing access to material benefits or incurring the wrath of a biased judicial system. In subsequent chapters, we look at this relationship between the pillars of dominant-party rule and the political attitudes and behaviors of citizens who live within such systems. But first, we take a brief look at the state of Mexico, one that on the surface could not be more different from the province of San Luis but, as we will see, looks strikingly similar to San Luis in terms of the way the game of politics is played.

Estado de Mexico: Un Político Pobre Es un Pobre Político

In terms of population size, urbanization, and almost any other socioeconomic variable one might wish to consider, Edomex stands in stark contrast to the province of San Luis. Edomex is the most populous state in Mexico, with over 16 million citizens calling it home in 2015, representing over 13 percent of the country's population. As the state wraps around Mexico's Federal District on the latter's western, northern, and eastern borders, its population has grown rapidly from the 1950s onward as a byproduct of Mexico City's urbanization, with millions of Mexicans migrating to the lure of relatively well-paying jobs in the Federal District area. Not surprisingly, the state is also a significant contributor to the country's total economic output, providing close to 10 percent of total gross domestic product, and ranking second in industrial output behind the state of Nuevo León (INEGI 2019).

Though certainly not the most developed state in Mexico with respect to standard socioeconomic indicators such as education levels and basic service provision, the state is by no means among the country's least developed. In comparing this state with the province of San Luis in Argentina, then, it is clear that they differ quite a bit. In that sense then we have a classic most-different-systems design at work—two subnational units in different countries, with different cultures, histories, economies, and peoples. Such a design, however, rests on two such highly disparate cases sharing one theoretically important characteristic that helps to explain a similar outcome on a variable of interest (Przeworski and Teune 1970). As the reader knows by now, the shared characteristic that we see as critical in shaping individuals' political attitudes and behaviors across these two distinct cases is the fact that both of these subnational units, separated by over 4,000 miles, have in place dominant-party political systems.

If one were interested in learning more about the core characteristics of these dominant-party systems that we have discussed above, Edomex would be a fine place to start. Since the beginning of the PRI's one-party system in 1929, the state has been ruled by the PRI,[10] with a reported "political fraternity" (Camp 2017) established in the municipality of Atlacomulco, located to the northwest of Mexico City, which has produced 7 of the state's past 16 governors. Despite the fact that those linked to it have long denied its existence, the Atlacomulco group (Grupo Atlacomulco) is reportedly the engine of the state's political machine, with "Atlacomulco governors [running] the state like little chieftains, accumulating power and wealth" (Quiñones 2017).

So extensive and widely accepted were the nefarious practices of governors in this state that even fellow PRI governors from other states have long viewed the Atlacomulco Group as the "model" for dominant-party rule.

---

[10] The original name of the PRI was the National Revolutionary Party (PNR), then the Party of the Mexican Revolution (PRM) before adopting its current name in 1946.

The former governor of nearby Tlaxcala, for example, who won his 1992 race for governor with 85.7 percent of the vote, noted that "Mexico's clientelism . . . was created in Atlacomulco . . . It's a system that uses political resources to hugely enrich a few while slightly corrupting millions" (Montes and de Córdoba 2017, 8). Indeed, we, too, see the strategy of enriching oneself (and perhaps a few others) while "slightly corrupting millions" as the essence of the dominant-party playbook—distributing enough goodies among a sufficiently large segment of the general public to ensure electoral dominance while also continuously padding one's bank account. If operated effectively, much of the citizenry becomes at some level a part of the machine, thereby influencing the types of political attitudes and behaviors that tend to prevail. Even nested within a nationally democratic system, such dominant-party subnational systems should produce widespread tolerance, if not acceptance, of a now famous Mexican political saying attributed to former Edomex governor, and multimillionaire, Carlos Hank González—"Un político pobre es un pobre político" ("a politician who is poor is a poor politician") (Montes and de Córdoba 2018).

For nearly 80 years then, the Atlacomulco political machine has, with few exceptions, ruled unchallenged in Edomex. As can be seen in Figure 3.2, while the PRI's electoral grip over the state's executive branch has been steadily declining since the 1980s, there have been only two "close" elections in the state since that time, with the hotly contested, and widely disputed, election of 2017 discussed in Chapter 1 being the most recent. These trends stand in contrast to the electoral trends of the neighboring state of Querétaro that borders Edomex to the north. Figure 3.3 reveals the development of a competitive two-party system between the PRI and the PAN, with the PRI ousted in 1997, only to return to power in 2009 and subsequently lose in 2015. As opposed to what happened in Edomex then, in Querétaro it seems clear that once that first alternation occurred, a level of electoral competitiveness between the PAN and PRI emerged and has become the norm over the past 20 years.

In Edomex, following that first instance of truly competitive elections in 1999, the dominance of the PRI quickly reemerged, with the party winning the next two gubernatorial elections by an average of over 30 percentage points. It remains to be seen whether the dominant-party machine can again rebound following its razor-thin, and highly contested, victory in 2017. Interestingly, it is these two "close calls" in 1999 and 2017 that help shine an even brighter light on the workings of

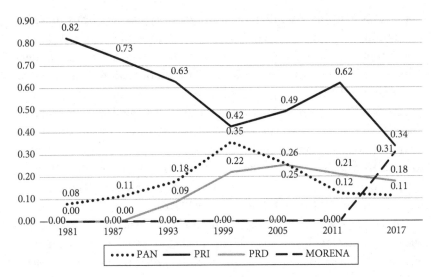

Figure 3.2. Edomex gubernatorial election results, 1981–2017.

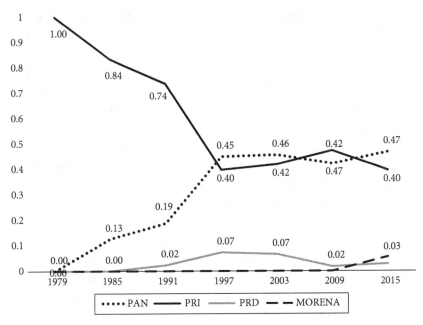

Figure 3.3. Querétaro gubernatorial election results, 1979–2015.

the machine in this state than do those more typical elections in which the dominant party makes clear its electoral dominance. In a *New York Times* report on the 1999 election, long-time Mexican correspondent Julia Preston noted that "With a full-bore mobilization of its political machine, the [PRI] managed to carry Arturo Montiel Rojas . . . a candidate described even by his own party as undistinguished and inarticulate, to the statehouse" (Preston 1999, 3). She went on to report that "[t]hroughout the campaign, PRI party workers used a variety of tactics to pressure voters or reward them for their vote, from a massive drive to get photocopies of voter credentials to Election-Day food handouts and outright payments to voters" (Preston 1999, 16).

Similarly, as we noted in the opening chapter, the 2017 election was widely disputed, with "the president's cousin . . . declared the victor amid widespread allegations of voter intimidation, vote buying, and misuse of public resources" (Lakhani 2017, 1). In one account of the election, one state government employee described his election "assignment:" "Our job was to ensure people vote for the PRI, or don't vote at all . . . The tactics we're forced to use are illegal but working for the government means we're forced to work for the party" (Lakhani 2017). Once again, we see the three governing tools of dominant-party rule in action, with the strategic application of the rule of law and the partisan use of state resources, including government workers, as keys in incumbent efforts to further slant the electoral playing field in their favor. We also see in the above quote an indication of the ways in which life in such a system may affect how one views politics and engages with her elected officials. But for a more empirical look at this question, we now turn to a brief survey-based profile of the political attitudes and behaviors of citizens living in the dominant-party enclave of Edomex and compare them with those of citizens living in the neighboring state of Querétaro.

Though we will explore in subsequent chapters the merits of the propositions we have put forth through extensive analysis of AmericasBarometer data across both Mexico and Argentina, we turn now to a rather unique collection of data drawn from Mexico's 31 states and Federal District in the fall of 2010 in order to offer a survey-based snapshot of the political attitudes and behaviors of the citizens of Edomex on the eve of that state's 2011 gubernatorial elections. The National Values Survey (ENVUD), funded by BANAMEX and *La Fundación Este País*, gathered representative samples from each of Mexico's states, with close to 16,000 interviews carried out across the country.[11] We are thus able to offer a fairly accurate picture of similarities and differences in patterns of political attitudes and behavior across distinct states, at least for one particular moment in time. The obvious limitation is that the data does only offer a snapshot of what Mexicans were thinking and doing in 2010, but this will allow us an opportunity to glimpse into the political lives of *Mexiquenses* and see how they compare with their neighbors to the north living in the multiparty political system of Querétaro.

As noted previously, this data was collected in 2010, eight months prior to Edomex's 2011 gubernatorial election that was won handily by the PRI candidate, Eruviel Ávila, with a nearly 40-point margin of victory. As with past (and future) elections, this one also was tainted by charges of widespread vote buying and intimidation, with one woman reporting that she "had been promised a $50 monthly subsidy," noting that "[e] ven though they don't tell you openly to vote for the PRI, I mean if you are going to keep the aid, well, you vote for the PRI, right?" (Malkin 2011). In this election, Ávila "kicked off his campaign with a promise to give cars to party operatives who could deliver him the most votes . . ." (Malkin 2011, 22–23). As previously discussed, these techniques used to increase the degree of *electoral certainty* were perhaps not as noteworthy or publicized in this landslide election as they have been in the two relatively close elections held in Edomex, but the fact that Ávila continued to employ them in an electoral contest he was almost certain to win underscores the importance of not just retaining power for dominant-party officials, but also doing so with overwhelming electoral "strength" when possible.

The question we explore in this chapter is the degree to which the attitudinal and behavioral profile of citizens in this state, on the eve of a landslide electoral victory in 2011, map to our expectations we have outlined in previous chapters. To answer this, we turn to the ENVUD data. In each of the following graphs, we offer simple bivariate aggregate comparisons between respondents from the state of Mexico and the state of Querétaro. As noted, the two states share a border and, as Figures 3.4, 3.5, and 3.6 reveal, are largely similar in the socioeconomic makeup of their citizenries, with respondents from Edomex recording slightly higher aggregate scores across most of these indicators. A key difference in the two states, as we have already noted, is that Querétaro in 2010 stood as the epitome of a competitive, multiparty political

---

[11] For more information on the methodology employed for the ENVUD survey, see "ENVUD-Apendice metodológico" (Moreno 2011).

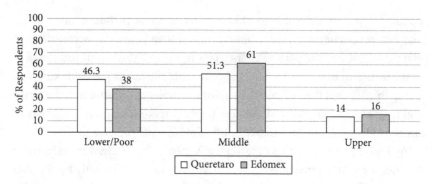

Figure 3.4. Development level of respondents' neighborhoods in Edomex and Querétaro (%).

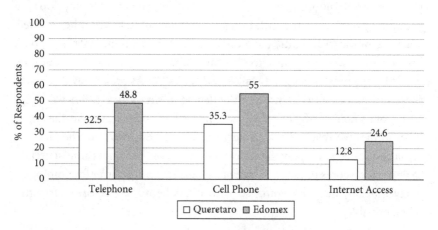

Figure 3.5. Access to communication technologies in Edomex and Querétaro (%).

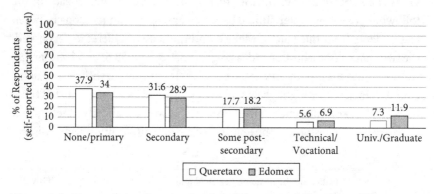

Figure 3.6. Respondent education levels in Edomex and Querétaro (%).

environment, with partisan alternation in the gubernatorial office occurring two times since the 1990s, including the July 2009 election that saw the incumbent PAN party candidate defeated by the PRI's candidate in a close, but widely accepted, election. Indeed, there were very few public accusations of electoral fraud or malfeasance during that electoral campaign, and a peaceful transfer of power took place in October of that year. In sum, all of the most prominent features of a dominant-party system that we have described in the preceding pages have been largely absent from Querétaro politics for at least the past 25 years.

In looking at Figures 3.4–3.6, we see that Edomex respondents tended, on average, to live in more developed neighborhoods and to have greater access to both landline and cell phones, as well as the Internet, and recorded similar education levels to respondents from Querétaro. Thus, with at least similar, if not slightly higher, socioeconomic development and education levels, along with greater access to communication technologies, and a gubernatorial election around the corner, we might expect indicators of political interest and involvement to be higher in Edomex than in Querétaro. Yet we find something very different. As our theory would suggest, many citizens of Edomex in 2010 seem to have disengaged from politics, talking about politics less than their neighbors to the north, reporting higher levels of distrust in their political system, and in general offering a profile of a citizenry with little interest in their political system.

Our first look at the potential impact a dominant-party system can have on citizens' engagement with politics is in the area of one's interest in politics. If one lives in a political system characterized by a long history of electoral certainty, economic dependence on the state, and a daily vulnerability to the strategic application of the rule of law, we should expect interest in politics to be less than for those individuals living in a competitive multiparty environment in which elections, and one's political voice, matter. In looking at the ENVUD survey data collected in Edomex and Querétaro in 2010, this is precisely what we find. Taking standard political interest survey items such as "How much do you talk about politics with others?," "How interested are you in politics?," and "How much do you participate in politics?," we can see from the charts displayed here (Figures 3.7, 3.8, and 3.9) that across the board, citizens in Edomex tend to be far less engaged than their counterparts in Querétaro.

We see from these results that a substantial portion of the Edomex citizenry appears to have largely disengaged from a political game that gave

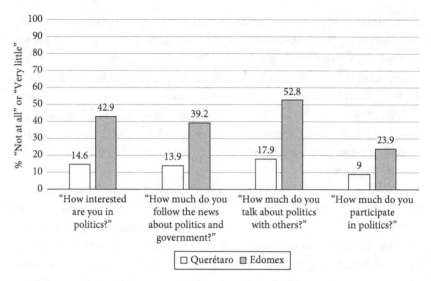

Figure 3.7. Political disengagement in Edomex and Querétaro.

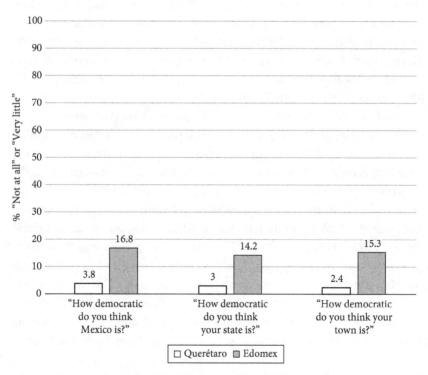

Figure 3.8. Citizen views of democracy in Edomex and Querétaro.

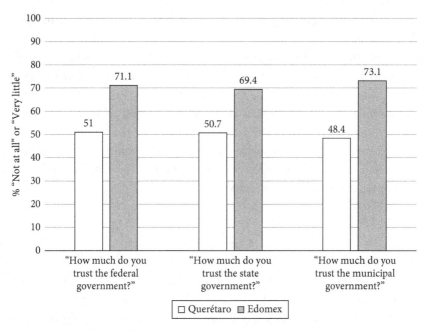

Figure 3.9. Citizen levels of trust in government in Edomex and Querétaro.

them no legitimate voice but, rather, only a passive role to play in the maintenance of the system. Though the results presented in Figure 3.6 are merely aggregate comparisons across two states, the strikingly high levels of disengagement in Edomex suggest a civil society that, in 2010, exhibited many of the characteristics we have highlighted in the preceding pages. This impression is reinforced when we look at results in Figures 3.7 and 3.8 from survey items that ask respondents their views of democracy in their country/state/ town and their levels of trust in those three levels of government. Once again, we see the citizens of Edomex offering a far more negative assessment of both than respondents in Querétaro.

Though certainly not an exhaustive analysis of individuals' political attitudes in these two states, the comparisons presented here are certainly suggestive of a citizenry in Edomex that is fundamentally distinct from that found in its neighbor. The fact that eight months later, the PRI's gubernatorial candidate won a landslide victory would seem strange and in stark contrast to the voter distrust and disinterest we see in these figures. This apparent contradiction, though, is consistent with what our theory would expect in a dominant-party state—electoral certainty amid an electorate that is largely disengaged from politics, participating only when called upon by the machine operators.

In both this brief look at two neighboring states in Mexico and the in-depth discussion of the province of San Luis, we have taken our first step in establishing support for the fundamental claim in this book—that the implications of a dominant-party system go far beyond policy decisions and electoral outcomes in that they fundamentally shape the ways in which citizens of these systems think about and engage with politics at both the provincial and national levels. In the coming chapters, we take further, and more comprehensive, steps in this direction.

Conclusion

Having presented our theory of political attitudes and behavior in uneven democracies in Chapter 2, here we began our discussion of the two national cases we draw on to test our argument: Argentina and Mexico. Most importantly, we have also introduced our concept and measure of subnational dominant-party enclaves, a type of subnational political system that has survived, and in some cases thrived, during an era of national-level democratization.

In this book, we rely on a simple, but effective, measurement strategy that allows us to distinguish between "dominant-party enclaves" and "multiparty systems": alternation in the party of the governor. Just as the defeat of the PRI in the 2000 presidential election marked a decisive moment in Mexico's national democratic transition, for subnational units transitioning from an authoritarian past, the first alternation in partisan control of the governor's office provides an efficient marker for the presence of some degree of uncertainty over electoral outcomes and competition between parties for control of subnational offices of power. Until that initial alternation in power takes place, however, the perception will remain that the political system falls short of being fully democratic—even if, as was the case in San Luis and Edomex in 2017, a momentary challenge to the incumbent machine emerges. In presenting this measurement approach, we also explore what dominant-party systems look like in Argentina and Mexico, in comparison with multiparty states, and offer initial evidence supporting our basic measurement premise—that is, that the primary difference between the political attitudes and behaviors of citizens of dominant-party and multiparty systems is a result, rather than a cause, of the antidemocratic mechanisms associated with dominant-party enclaves.

We conclude the chapter with two case studies that serve to further validate our measurement approach. Edomex and San Luis are, on the surface, two subnational units that differ significantly on numerous economic and cultural indicators. However, citizens of these two regimes share the common experience of living for decades under the same dominant party machine. Our contention, that we probe in a variety of ways in the following chapters, is that this key similarity shared by citizens of San Luis and Edomex, along with the other dominant-party enclaves in Argentina and Mexico, will overwhelm whatever cultural, economic, social, or ideological differences may exist among citizens of these states and provinces, and it will produce a pattern of political attitudes and behaviors that are quite distinct from those found in multiparty systems.

4

Tilling the Soil of an Uneven Landscape

Dirty Politics in Dominant-Party Enclaves

> Now the elections make me crazy. They know I have lots of resources.
> Everyone comes and requests and I fulfill. There is a funeral and they
> come looking for me. They need money, El Tigre. They need zinc
> sheets, El Tigre. They need food handouts, El Tigre. Everything is
> El Tigre. (Argentine political broker as quoted in Nichter and Peress
> 2017, 1092)

In this chapter, we explore the parts of the machine that play a central role
in shaping the poltical attitudes and behaviors of citizens – clientelism and
corruption. The lament of El Tigre offers one glimpse into how these parts
work and the impact they have on citizens, and a story told to us more than
once over the years of doing research on local development in Mexico offers
another.

Weeks before an election, so the story goes, in towns long ruled by the PRI
but threatened by a growing electoral opposition, government officials would
announce a much-needed and long-demanded public works project in a
neighborhood known to be an area of opposition party sympathies (typically
for the left-leaning PRD). In one account told to us, the project was street re-
pair, with extensive street closures and construction carried out in the weeks
leading up to an election. A week prior to Election Day, however, the workers
and equipment disappeared, sending what seemed to many to be a very clear
signal—"Vote the way we want you to vote, and your streets will be better
than new after the election. Vote for the opposition and they will remain in
disrepair." Aside from these anecdotal accounts, we were not able to ascertain
whether or not this type of collective, coercive use of public works projects as
an electoral "motivational tool" was, indeed, employed by the PRI. The fact,
though, that the story persists is emblematic of how citizens view the PRI's

Life in the Political Machine. Jonathan T. Hiskey and Mason W. Moseley, Oxford University Press (2020). © Oxford
University Press.
DOI: 10.1093/oso/9780197500408.001.0001

time in power and the no-win situation many individuals perceived them-selves to be in with respect to playing the PRI's game of machine politics. As Magaloni noted in her work *Voting for Autocracy*, electoral support for the opposition in a dominant-party setting is made difficult for individuals "because their choices are constrained by a series of strategic dilemmas that compel them to support the autocrat, even if reluctantly" (2006, 271).

Indeed, a prototype of the dominant-party machine that stands at the center of this study was that crafted by Mexico's PRI between 1929 and 2000, where "[c]orruption [was] not a characteristic of the system . . . it [was] the system" (De Palma as quoted in Morris 2009, 1). With the 2000 ouster of the PRI from the presidency, the national-level machine that had endured countless political and economic crises in the previous 70 years at last had failed in its essential purpose of delivering an electoral victory for the party to continue its hold on the country's most powerful office. Alternation in control of the nation's highest office had occurred.

But in a number of Mexican states, alternation remained only a dream of the opposition. The PRI continued its decades-long reign in power despite pervasive economic volatility, repeated episodes of official malfeasance, and a woefully spotty record of delivering even the most basic of services. The political machines in these states kept churning well into the 21st century, while in some neighboring states the PRI had become an electoral also-ran. The result of these various electoral dynamics has been a "patchwork" na-tional system, in which "a reformed electoral regime guarantees free and fair competition at the national level, but corruption, bossism, and other lega-cies of authoritarian rule constrain and delimit democratic accountability" at the subnational level (Lawson 2000, 286). While citizens of certain Mexican states have continued to move beyond the PRI's machine politics of the past, others still find themselves subject to the old, dominant-party rules of the game.

A key component of the theory presented in this book is that individ-uals in dominant-party enclaves, where incumbent governments seek to thwart potential challengers through tilting the electoral playing field in their favor and conflating the dominant party with the state, are more likely to be exposed to the seedy underbelly of machine politics—specifically, clientelism and corruption. Individuals' experiences with such practices thus warp their conceptualization of "everyday politics," in a sense normalizing these illegal uses of public monies and power, and in the process, incentivizing attitudes and behaviors that, while conducive to survival in a local context where the political game is rigged, can have lasting deleterious effects on the development of a democratic political culture.

In this chapter, we begin to probe the observable implications of our argument regarding the linkages between dominant-party systems and citizens' daily encounters with the state, and their resultant political attitudes and behaviors, focusing in particular on (1) individuals' likelihood of being exposed to corruption and clientelism by subnational regime type, and (2) their views regarding the acceptability of such practices. Our core expectation is that citizens in dominant-party enclaves will be more likely to have firsthand experience with corruption and clientelism, but less likely to view such tactics as problematic, given their ubiquity in local politics.

Scholars of corruption know well that perceptions of and even experiences with corruption and clientelism can be highly subjective and shaped by a variety of individual and contextual factors (see, for example, Bailey and Paras 2006; Morris 2008; Morris and Blake 2010). What one person sees as corruption, another might see as "getting things done." What might clearly be seen as overt vote buying in one setting may simply be seen as politicians delivering the goods in another. We know less, however, about the source of these variations in citizens' understandings of corruption and clientelism. The two general factors most commonly invoked in efforts to answer this question are culture and institutions. A society may be plagued with a "culture of corruption," political institutions (both formal and informal) that are conducive to corrupt behavior or, most commonly, both. That is, countries with particularly acute corruption problems often are seen as having both a culture and a set of institutions that lend themselves to widespread incidents of corruption.

One theme of recent work on both clientelism and corruption concerns the impact the introduction of national-level democratic institutions has had on levels of illicit political activity and on the culture of graft and vote buying that is thought to exist in many developing countries (e.g., Gerring and Thacker 2004; Rock 2009; Seligson 2001). The highly uneven nature of democratic change across the subnational political landscapes of many of these emerging democracies offers an opportunity to further explore the extent to which such institutional change does in fact matter. Through explicit examination of these subnational variations in political systems we can begin to more fully understand the relationship between political institutions, a culture of clientelism and corruption, and citizens' attitudes toward and experiences with dirty politics in an era of national democracy.

Here, we leverage the uneven institutional contexts found across the provinces and states of Argentina and Mexico to better understand the role of subnational political systems in shaping citizens' experiences with and views of clientelism and corruption. Though national-level democratization processes may heighten citizen awareness of the corrupt and clientelistic practices of their elected officials in the capital city, we view citizens' attitudes toward and experiences with corruption and clientelism as partially driven by subnational dynamics, where citizens must interact with state and local officials on a far more regular basis than they do with national officials. Thus, until an individual's subnational political system can move beyond the dominant-party enclaves we have described in this book, she is likely to continue to view corruption and clientelism as standard operating procedures rather than acts that warrant electoral retribution. This toleration, if not tacit acceptance, of machine politics, may, in turn, color the ways in which those individuals engage with their national system as well. In our view, the continued prevalence of such less-than-democratic practices in dominant-party enclaves thus becomes crucial to understanding how such political systems contribute to distinct political cultures within a single country.

For Argentina and Mexico, then, we should expect to see evidence of corruption and clientelism much more clearly in those states where dominant-party control of the provincial/state government remains intact than in those subnational systems where multiparty competition has been established. With the tools of governance in dominant-party systems employed to keep the electoral uncertainty of more democratic systems at bay, and forged from the illicit use of state power and resources to reward supporters and quiet opponents, we expect citizens living within such systems to become accustomed to these practices and be less likely to punish incumbents associated with them.

Crossnational Research on Clientelism and Corruption

Clientelism and corruption are conceptually distinct, but linked, phenomena that tend to thrive "in the same kinds of countries—polities with high levels of poverty, weak democratic institutions, short democratic histories, and a large state economic presence" (Singer 2009, 2). In this section, we briefly review work on the two phenomena in turn, focusing on lessons gleaned from crossnational analyses as to where these behaviors are most likely to occur and what their consequences might be in terms of citizens' views of and interactions with their political system.

For our purposes, the vast literature on the causes and consequences of corruption over the years and across many disciplines can be distilled into a few key propositions. In terms of the factors most directly linked to variations in levels of corruption around the world, scholars have settled on a society's culture and/or its political institutions as the primary suspects. For the former, Morris and Blake (2010) note that there are quite a few "cross-national empirical studies [that] . . . pinpoint the statistical significance of a range of cultural factors" (16), pointing to works such as Catterberg and Moreno (2006) and Blake and Martin (2006) as just a few of the many examples of this type of work (see also Morris 2003; 2008). Triesman (2007) too offers a comprehensive cataloging and assessment of those cross-national works that offer some degree of support for the culture-corruption connection.

Similarly, there is an abundance of work on the institutional factors related to corruption, much of which focuses on the different types of democratic institutions that have arisen across the world over the past four decades. Gerring and Thacker (2004), for example, look at institutional differences in the vertical and horizontal dispersion of power within democratic systems, focusing specifically on the unitary/federal and presidential/parliamentary dimensions, as important determinants of a country's level of corruption. Conversely, Montinola and Jackman (2002) find evidence of a nonlinear, inverted-U relationship between the degree of democracy present in a country and its level of corruption, finding that both established dictatorships and democracies tend to exhibit lower levels of corruption than those systems transitioning from the former to the latter. Homing in on one of those emerging democracies, Morris (2009) offers an in-depth analysis of the case of Mexico and the degree to which its democratization process had affected corruption in the country during the first decade of the 21st century. These are but a few examples of the many works on this topic that, again, tend to focus either on a country's culture or its political institutions as the main explanatory factor behind levels of corruption.

One underlying assumption shared by most of this work is that corruption itself, and its possible causes, are best studied at the national level. From this perspective, it is a country that is more or less corrupt, and it is the country's culture and/or national political institutions that best explain how corrupt that country is. As should be clear to the reader by this point, we take issue with this type of "mean-spirited analysis" (Snyder 2001, 98), positing instead that corruption, and its possible cultural and institutional causes, should also be explored at the subnational level in countries where significant variations in all of these factors can persist well into the consolidation of a democratic regime at the national level.

The story for clientelism—or, "the proffering of material goods in return for electoral support" (Stokes 2007, 605)—is similar to that of corruption. While much literature attempts to explain variation in levels of vote trafficking across national contexts, and which individuals make the most likely targets for clientelistic exchange (see Carlin and Moseley 2015), little research has explored such variation across subnational regimes. At the national level, evidence suggests clientelism is common in developing countries where large portions of society are impoverished, enabling politicians to get "more bang for their buck" by preying on individuals for whom small material rewards might make a big difference (Kitschelt and Wilkinson 2007; Calvo and Murillo 2004). While early studies viewed clientelism as a relic of premodern society (Scott 1972), empirical research since the initiation of the most recent era of democratization has found that it often thrives in democracies, albeit ones characterized by fragmented party systems lacking in real programmatic competition (Geddes 1991; Keefer 2006; Kitschelt et al. 2010). In sum, while clientelism is a near-universal phenomenon, it appears to be particularly widespread and consequential in emerging democracies characterized by underdeveloped party systems and high levels of economic inequality.

Argentina is one country that has received considerable scholarly attention in studies of clientelism—and particularly its famously effective Peronist machine (e.g., Calvo and Murillo 2004; Carlin and Moseley 2015; Stokes 2005; Nichter 2008; Stokes et al. 2013; Weitz-Shapiro 2014). Research addressing the dyadic nature of clientelistic exchange in Argentina has uncovered a number of potentially important determinants of which individuals get targeted. Most agree poverty is the strongest predictor of vote selling (e.g., Auyero 2005), but others have posited that one's status as a "core" or "swing" voter (see the exchange between Stokes 2005 and Nichter 2008), their connectedness to partisan networks (Szwarcberg 2015), and their commitment to democratic norms and processes (Carlin and Moseley 2015) might also play a role in determining whether or not an individual is approached with a vote-buying offer. Yet little research has examined the possibility that local political context affects individuals' likelihood of entering into clientelistic arrangements.

One exception is Weitz-Shapiro's (2014) study of clientelism at the municipal level in Argentina. As opposed to most major empirical studies on the topic, rather than attempt to explain where clientelism does occur, Weitz-Shapiro instead asks where politicians *opt out* of vote trafficking. Her answer rests on the interaction between competitiveness and socioeconomic characteristics of municipalities—that is, when elections are competitive and constituents are largely poor, clientelism becomes an attractive option for Argentine mayors. Where a significant middle class exists, such illicit support-buying tactics become costly given more affluent citizens' distaste for clientelism. Though we cast our analytical lens at the provincial level, we share this emphasis on political context as an important part of the answer to the question of where such vote-buying behavior is most likely to occur.

As we have argued to this point, rarely will a country with a long authoritarian past become democratic overnight. Though elections for national office may become relatively free and fair in a short amount of time, subnational electoral processes may be resistant to such change. As O'Donnell (1999) pointed out more than two decades ago, national-level democratization processes often are characterized by "[p]rovinces peripheral to the national center [that] create (or reinforce) systems of local power which tend to reach extremes of violent, personalistic rule open to all sorts of violent and arbitrary practices" (138). In dominant-party enclaves we cannot expect changes in national-level institutions to have much impact on the more common forms of street-level illicit tactics that many encounter in their daily lives, such as police officers demanding "donations" to help with neighborhood security or partisan "brokers" paying buses full of voters to support their candidate on Election Day. We view this behavior as much more influenced by local and provincial-level political norms and institutions than by the national political system.

Certainly, a widely publicized scandal involving prominent national-level politicians will have an impact on citizens' perceptions of corruption, as would a prominent, national anticorruption or anti–vote selling public information campaign. But just as all politics is local, so, too, are the most common forms of corruption and clientelism (see, e.g., Seligson 2006). And it is these daily acts of dirty politics, we argue, that are most likely to survive in subnational political systems that have withstood national-level democratic change.

Dirty Politics in Dominant-Party Enclaves

In those subnational political units in which elements of the old regime survive and oftentimes thrive, during an era of democracy, why do we also suspect clientelism and corruption to continue as well? As we outlined in Chapter 2, both tend to serve the overarching goal of dominant-party machines to continue their grip on power behind a facade of democracy. In the context of a province or state where a dominant party, despite multiple economic crises and governance disasters, has yet to be dislodged from the executive office, it should be expected that local public officials (and thus, citizens) continue operating under the old rules of the game regardless of what may have occurred at the national level. In many ways, this argument is consistent with Olson's thesis in his seminal *Rise and Decline of Nations* (1982), in which he argues that the longer a political system remains intact, the more likely it will fall prey to "distributional coalitions" intent on rent seeking. Only with some type of exogenous shock to the system can such entrenched interests be dislodged. In the case of Mexico and Argentina, we see the decades-long, uninterrupted control of provincial dominant parties as a classic example of systems captured by entrenched interests bent on rent-seeking behavior. The watershed electoral ouster of a party from a state's executive branch can greatly increase (but not guarantee) the chances that such entrenched interests will be, at least temporarily, dislodged. Only when this occurs do overt forms of vote buying and corruption become behaviors deemed by many as truly outside the scope of the acceptable political rules of the game.

Returning to the Southern region of the United States, we have one notable example of the persistence of such interests in distinct subnational political systems that contrasted significantly with the country's larger democratization process. The one-party South developed its own set of political norms and institutions that in many respects ran counter to the democratic ideals, if not institutions, of the country as a whole. These distinct, and decidedly undemocratic, political environments produced a wide array of subtle and not-so-subtle consequences in terms of the quality of governance, citizens' quality of life, and the relationship between citizens and their elected public officials (Key 1949). For these states of the U.S. South, then, just as with dominant-party enclaves in Argentina and Mexico, the decades-long rule of a single organization or group of elites allowed for the creation of an informal, and sometimes formal, institutional framework founded on rent seeking by a privileged class of people. It is the strength of these vested interests in maintaining corruption and clientelism as "business as usual" that we see as so critical in understanding systematic differences in corruption experiences and attitudes across subnational units.

As noted in Chapter 3, by 2014,[1] the PRI continued its 80-year grip on the executive branch of government in nine states, and in Argentina, 7 of 23 governorships remained under the control of the same party that first took power in 1983 as the country emerged from its period of military rule. In such systems, we argue, manipulation of the electoral playing field is routine, and members of the dominant party exercise a great deal of control over rule-of-law institutions, which they leverage to punish opponents and reward allies. As a consequence, we expect more citizens within dominant-party enclaves to report experiences with corruption and clientelism, but perhaps have a more jaded view of the extent to which this sort of behavior is a problem. That is, when the baseline is one of high levels of corruption and clientelism, as in the political machines of Mexico and Argentina, we suspect that citizens embedded in those regimes will be less likely to recognize such tactics as problematic.

No matter how democratic the national systems have become in these two countries, we view the persistence of these forms of elite behavior, and citizen acquiescence, as far more likely in these states and provinces where architects of this style of governance have never left power. Suggestive evidence in support of this proposition comes from two complementary perspectives. First, the proposition implies that with the ouster of the dominant party, and the rejection of old-style, dominant-party politics, we should see a decline in the pervasiveness of vote-buying and corruption. This is precisely what Sharafutdinova (2010) finds in an analysis of Russia's regions, where greater electoral competition was, in fact, associated with heightened citizen perceptions of corruption as a problem (see also, Grzymala-Busse 2007).

Second, in situations in which citizens lack experience with any other type of provincial regime, they will continue to interact with their political system in ways that have worked for them in the past. For example, if elections typically come with the distribution of goods and/or payments, individuals may come to expect these in the future. Similarly, if an individual starting a business knows that payments to certain public officials will expedite, or

---

[1] 2014 is the final year of data for our subsequent analysis of citizens' corruption attitudes and experiences.

even allow, the permitting process, these payments simply become part of the costs of doing business. In systems in which these practices are common, and we argue they are in dominant-party enclaves, citizens will continue to behave in ways consistent with what they know to work—they go along to get along.

Studies have shown that firsthand experience with clientelism and corruption can have other deleterious downstream consequences besides just generalized ambivalence regarding less-than-democratic practices. Seligson (2002) demonstrates persuasively that corruption victimization can undermine democratic legitimacy, in that citizens who experience the shady side of politics tend to demonstrate less faith in core democratic institutions and practices. Cohen et al. (n.d.) uncover a similar effect for being targeted for vote buying, as individuals who are proffered some kind of material reward in exchange for their vote demonstrate lower confidence in elections. It is our view that local experiences can thus shape attitudes regarding broader institutional norms and processes—that is, citizens nested in dominant-party enclaves, who interact more frequently with corrupt politicians, might begin to question the legitimacy of *national* political institutions as well.

Conversely, with the initial election of an opposition party and successful ouster of the dominant party from power, the latter's ability to maintain its partisan control over the machinery of government is eroded. With this loss of control, the long-standing culture of vote buying and corruption may be more likely to erode as well. Further, with a new political party taking control of the governor's office, anticorruption rhetoric and attention to a releveling of the electoral playing field may become more prevalent than in those states and provinces still controlled by the dominant party. Individuals living through these initial opposition governments then should exhibit more sensitivity to acts of corruption and efforts to buy votes and thus may be more inclined to hold their government officials accountable in the fight to reduce these types of elite behaviors. Will such behavior be eliminated completely with the ouster of a dominant-party machine? Clearly not. But we do posit that in dominant-party enclaves, where corruption and clientelism continue to play a central role in the incumbent officials' governing repertoire, citizens will likely have more experience with such tools of governance but be less likely to use such experiences as a metric on which they evaluate the incumbent government.

Data and Methods

To investigate citizen interactions with corruption and clientelism in dominant-party enclaves, we utilize data from the 2010–2014 rounds of the AmericasBarometer surveys carried out in Argentina and Mexico by the Latin American Public Opinion Project (LAPOP) at Vanderbilt University.[2] We combine these three rounds of surveys into one pool of data with over 9,000 observations (each round in each country included around 1,500 respondents) in order to maximize the number of respondents from dominant-party and multiparty provinces and states.[3] All three rounds of surveys were carried out with similar sampling frames and survey items.[4] From these data, we find that roughly 25 percent of respondents lived in dominant-party states and provinces at the time of the survey in question, while the remaining 75 percent lived in states and provinces that had experienced alternation. Our expectation after controlling for an assortment of relevant individual-level factors is that those respondents living in dominant-party enclaves in the two countries will report attitudes toward and experiences with corruption and vote buying that will be distinct from their neighbors living in multiparty states and provinces and reflect the nature of life in a political machine.

In our individual-level analysis we examine four dimensions of corruption and clientelism tapped by AmericasBarometer survey items—experiences with corruption, receipt of a vote-buying offer, attitudes about the extent of corruption in society, and views of the government's effectiveness in fighting corruption. All variables are recoded 0–100 for ease of interpretation. We measure our dependent variables as follows:

1. *"Street-level" corruption involvement in the previous 12 months:* A series of items that ask respondents whether in the past 12 months they have been asked for a bribe or illegal payment by a variety of public officials (e.g., schools, health officials, police).

---

[2] The results presented below are from the 2010, 2012, and 2014 data because several key variables, including our measure of whether or not citizens had received a vote-buying offer, were not added to the AmericasBarometer until 2010. Results from reduced models of corruption victimization and perceptions that include the 2008 data are consistent with the results presented in this chapter.

[3] For respondents living in states that transitioned from dominant-party to multiparty between 2010 and 2014, we recategorize them for the survey data collected after their state's transition.

[4] We include in all of the analyses fixed effects for survey year and country.

2. *Receipt of a vote-buying offer:* "In recent years and thinking about election campaigns, has a candidate or someone from a political party offered you something, like a favor, food, or any other benefit or thing in return for your vote or support? Has this happened often, sometimes or never?"

3. *Perceived extent of corruption in the political system:* "Taking into account your experience or what you have heard, is corruption by public officials very common, somewhat common, a little common or not common?"

4. *Evaluations of effectiveness of government anticorruption campaign:* "Using a seven point scale that goes from 1 which means none to seven which means a lot [could you please tell me] . . . to what point would you say the current government is combating corruption within the government?"

As we have laid out previously, we expect to find street-level forms of corruption and clientelism significantly more likely to occur in those states and provinces where the incumbent machine has never lost power, allowing its culture of clientelism and corruption to remain intact.[5] Figures 4.1 and 4.2 offer support for that expectation, as individuals in dominant-party enclaves appear significantly more likely than those living in multiparty contexts to have experience with such practices. However, these simple descriptive statistics do not control for important individual- and provincial-level factors that might also influence who is targeted for corruption or vote buying. We take this next step in the multivariate analyses in this chapter.

We utilize the third and fourth variables to explore our proposition that the "business as usual" view of corruption in dominant-party systems will make citizens less likely to see corruption as a problem and less critical of their government's fight against corruption than individuals living in multiparty states. Here again, this expectation rests on the idea that citizens living in states where the incumbent party has never left power will view corruption as a necessary evil, and perhaps more positively as a way of getting things done, and so will be less inclined to see it as a problem or blame their government for its persistence. This speaks to the fundamental differences we see in terms

---

[5] See Seligson (2006) for a full description of the corruption items included in the LAPOP instrument.

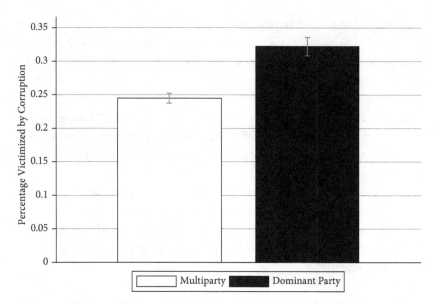

Figure 4.1. Corruption victimization by subnational regime type.

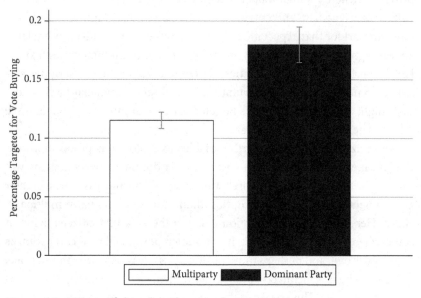

Figure 4.2. Vote trafficking by subnational regime type.

of system–citizen linkages in dominant-party enclaves vis-à-vis subnational regimes in which some degree of political competition has taken hold.

All models employ a standard set of variables that offer appropriate controls with which we can explore the independent contextual effect of a state's electoral environment on corruption attitudes and behaviors. Our controls seek to account for possible alternative determinants of citizens' experiences with vote buying and corruption and their views regarding the prevalence of these "dirty politics" behaviors. Fortunately, we have a well-established body of research from which we can identify theoretically important control variables (e.g., Seligson 2006; Morris 2009). The first such control is a respondent's level of wealth, a factor long viewed as being positively associated with one's probability of being exposed to corruption, and negatively associated with being targeted for clientelism. Given that the LAPOP data are constructed to offer comparable socioeconomic measures across multiple country settings, we employ a "level of wealth index" that consists of responses to a series of questions asking individuals if they possess certain household items, including indoor bathrooms, televisions, vehicles, and washing machines (Córdova 2009).[6] As the number of items a person owns increases, so, too, does their score on this wealth index.

We also include other standard socioeconomic and demographic controls such as years of education and age, and a categorical measure of the respondent's place of residence in order to capture the potential impact that town population size may have on exposure to corruption. For all of these, previous research suggests clear expectations with respect to their impact on one's potential for being involved in corruption and, in turn, influencing attitudes toward corruption. Generally, we expect more educated, wealthy, urban respondents to be more likely to report involvement in corrupt behavior than their counterparts. With respect to age, the typical relationship to corruption involvement is nonlinear, with those falling in the middle age range most likely to be exposed to corruption. We also include a control for gender, as males have been shown to be more likely victims of corruption, as well as variables to control for the year of the survey, the country in which individuals live, and the relative level of economic development in their state or province[7] (Seligson 2006). Finally, we include a control for skin color,

---

[6] For a complete list of those items included in the wealth index, see the Appendix.

[7] The level of development variable captures whether citizens live in a lower, middle, or high-income state or province, relative to the other states and provinces in her country. These data are drawn from official government statistics regarding per capita income by province or state in Argentina and Mexico, as referenced in Chapter 2.

given evidence that racial and ethnic minorities are more likely to be victimized by corruption (Singer et al. 2014).

Moving to our attitudinal and behavioral controls, we first include measures of both interest in politics and civic participation. These variables were coded 0–100, with a value of 100 being assigned to respondents who reported high levels of political interest or community activism during the past year. The expectation here is that those respondents more involved in the civic and political life of their communities will be more likely to come into contact with a corrupt public official and, as a result, likely have distinct views regarding the pervasiveness of corruption. In the models of exposure to vote buying, we also include a control for democratic support, given its importance as a predictor of who is targeted by clientelistic brokers (Carlin and Moseley 2015).

Finally, for models of attitudes toward the prevalence of corruption and the effectiveness of the government's anticorruption efforts, we include what we expect to be one of the more powerful control variables, corruption involvement (our dependent variable in Model 1). Being victimized by (or being involved in) a corrupt act seems almost certain to influence one's perceptions of the magnitude of the corruption problem and the effectiveness (or lack thereof) of government anticorruption efforts.[8] For our purposes, though, it is important to control for this effect in order to assess the independent impact of the local political context on citizens' evaluations of corruption and their government's efforts to fight it. To test our proposition that individuals in dominant-party contexts who report being victimized by corruption will be less inclined to see it as a problem than those corruption victims living in multiparty contexts, we include in the model an interaction term that includes a respondent's subnational regime context and whether or not she has been victimized by corruption in the previous twelve months.

Results

Table 4.1 presents the results of two logistic regression models of individuals' exposure to vote buying and corruption. In Model 1, most control variables are significant and work in the expected directions. Men are more likely to be

---

[8] Recognizing too that there will also be cases in which individuals involved in corruption may be less inclined to report it as a problem in order to justify in some way their own involvement.

Table 4.1. Experience with Corruption and Clientelism in Argentina and Mexico

VARIABLES	Victimize`d by Corruption (0 or 1)	Received Vote-Buying Offer (0 or 1)
	Model 1	Model 2
Female	−0.663***	−0.002
	(0.056)	(0.080)
Age	−0.015***	−0.005*
	(0.002)	(0.003)
Education (years)	0.019**	−0.011
	(0.008)	(0.011)
Skin Color	0.013	0.125***
	(0.019)	(0.027)
Wealth Quintile	0.089***	−0.045
	(0.022)	(0.031)
Urban	−0.162**	0.037
	(0.072)	(0.103)
Presidential Approval	−0.004***	−0.005***
	(0.001)	(0.002)
Interest in Politics	0.004***	0.006***
	(0.001)	(0.001)
Community Participation	0.009***	0.007***
	(0.001)	(0.002)
Support for Democracy		−0.002
		(0.001)
2012	0.003	0.276**
	(0.067)	(0.120)
2014	−0.304***	−0.745***
	(0.067)	(0.093)
Argentina	−0.493***	−0.212**
	(0.063)	(0.105)
DOMINANT-PARTY ENCLAVE	*0.169***	*0.228***
	(0.063)	*(0.091)*
Middle Income	−0.103	−0.085
	(0.080)	(0.115)
High Income	−0.323***	−0.538***
	(0.066)	(0.096)
Constant	0.477**	−1.492***
	(0.220)	(0.324)
Observations	7,909	6,213

Note: Standard errors in parentheses.
$*p < 0.1; **p < 0.05; ***p < 0.01$

involved in corruption than women. Similarly, higher levels of wealth, education, and civic participation all increase the likelihood an individual will have direct experience with a corrupt public official seeking illicit payment for some type of public service. All of these findings are strikingly consistent with recent research on this question (Seligson 2006).

After controlling for all of these individual-level factors, we find that simply by living in a dominant-party environment, an individual is approximately 12.5 percent more likely to report being involved in a corrupt act during the previous 12 months relative to the predicted probability of a citizen living in a multiparty context. This offers further support for the idea that corruption is more prevalent in dominant-party enclaves in Argentina and Mexico. The removal of the dominant machine from power for at least one electoral cycle seems to have helped diminish the rate of corrupt behavior among public officials. We see this stark difference in corruption victimization rates as a product of the strength and persistence of local machine politics even in the face of a national-level democratization process. However, it remains to be seen how this same political environment affects citizens' assessments of the prevalence of corruption and their government's efforts to fight corruption— our suspicion is that while individuals in dominant-party enclaves will be more likely to have firsthand experience with corruption, they will also be more accepting of such practices as "politics as usual."

The results for experience with vote-buying offers are presented in the column for Model 2, and again the effects for standard control variables are consistent with extant literature. Wealth appears to have a slight negative effect on who gets targeted for vote trafficking, but skin color, a potential heuristic for socioeconomic class, is one of the strongest predictors in the model, as dark-skinned individuals appear more likely to have experience with clientelism than their lighter skinned counterparts. Likewise, wealthy provinces appear to be less plagued by clientelism than poor provinces, which corroborates municipal-level findings in Argentina (Weitz-Shapiro 2014). Similar to corruption, individuals who are interested in politics and active in their communities also appear to be more likely targets, also echoing findings from recent studies of clientelism in Latin America (Schaffer and Baker 2015).

The key finding in Model 2 lies in the effect that living in a dominant-party enclave has on the likelihood that an individual will report receiving a vote-buying offer in the lead-up to a recent election. Consistent with our expectations, citizens living in dominant-party contexts in Argentina and Mexico are significantly more likely ($p < .01$) to have firsthand experience with clientelism than individuals in multiparty subnational regimes. This statistically significant effect translates into a *25 percent relative increase in one's probability of being targeted*—a substantive effect that outweighs even the effect of wealth. The evidence is clear: Individuals nested in dominant-party enclaves are far more likely to have first-hand experience with corruption and clientelism, just as our theory predicts and our qualitative, on-the-ground research efforts have suggested.

Turning next to the question of how life in a dominant-party system may affect one's views of the pervasiveness of corruption, Table 4.2 presents findings from our analysis of variations in respondents' views on the extent that corruption is a problem in their respective country. From the results displayed in the first two columns, we see that our expectation that citizens in dominant-party systems would be less likely to view corruption as a problem than their counterparts in a multiparty context finds some support. While there does not appear to be a difference between these two groups of respondents regarding their assessment of corruption as a problem at conventional levels of statistical significance, the sign is negative and in the "right" direction ($p < .15$). Yet this in itself is important given what we now know about the higher levels of street-level corruption in dominant-party systems, suggesting that actual experience with corruption plays less of a role in driving perceptions of corruption in these contexts. And indeed, when Model 2 includes an interaction term between corruption victimization and subnational regime context, we find significant support for this expectation ($p < .05$).

Indeed, perhaps the most compelling piece of support for our theoretical framework emerges in Model 2, in which the interaction between dominant-party enclave and corruption victimization is statistically significant at $p < .01$. For ease of interpretation, Figure 4.3 plots predicted levels of corruption perceptions associated with the four potential combinations of whether or not citizens live in a dominant-party enclave and have been victimized by corruption. What we find is that whereas being victimized by corruption has no significant impact on whether or not citizens of dominant-party systems believe corruption is high, it does have the predicted effect in multiparty contexts. In other words, even when individuals nested in dominant-party enclaves experience corruption firsthand, that experience does not translate into heightened perceptions of corruption and instead, seems to be chalked up as day-to-day politics as usual. This finding is all the more striking given

Table 4.2. Perceptions of Corruption in Argentina and Mexico

VARIABLES	DV: Perception of Corruption (0–100)		DV: Perception of Gov't Efforts to Combat Corruption (0–100)	
	Model 1	Model 2	Model 3	Model 4
Female	–0.127	–0.138	–0.136	–0.145
	(0.577)	(0.577)	(0.606)	(0.606)
Age	0.102***	0.101***	–0.011	–0.012
	(0.019)	(0.019)	(0.020)	(0.020)
Education (Years)	0.399***	0.403***	–0.588***	–0.585***
	(0.081)	(0.081)	(0.085)	(0.085)
Skin Color	0.356*	0.356*	0.326	0.328
	(0.198)	(0.198)	(0.207)	(0.207)
Wealth Quintile	0.700***	0.700***	–0.426*	–0.426*
	(0.225)	(0.225)	(0.236)	(0.236)
Urban	–0.634	–0.618	1.915**	1.923**
	(0.757)	(0.757)	(0.797)	(0.797)
Presidential Approval	–0.157***	–0.157***	0.516***	0.516***
	(0.011)	(0.011)	(0.012)	(0.012)
Interest in Politics	0.025***	0.024***	0.065***	0.065***
	(0.009)	(0.009)	(0.010)	(0.010)
Community Participation	–0.060***	–0.061***	0.015	0.015
	(0.014)	(0.014)	(0.015)	(0.015)
Corruption Victimization	0.020***	2.878***	–0.019***	–1.156
	(0.007)	(0.789)	(0.007)	(0.835)
DOMINANT-PARTY ENCLAVE	*–0.874*	*–0.048*	*3.613****	*4.239****
	(0.679)	*(0.788)*	*(0.715)*	*(0.829)*
*Victimization*Dominant-Party*		*–2.796***		*–2.125*
		(1.355)		*(1.429)*
2012	1.575**	1.587**	–1.341*	–1.332*
	(0.711)	(0.711)	(0.747)	(0.747)
2014	–2.417***	–2.444***	–0.297	–0.319
	(0.695)	(0.695)	(0.731)	(0.731)
Argentina	1.571**	1.547**	–7.577***	–7.587***
	(0.658)	(0.658)	(0.692)	(0.692)
Middle Income	–0.940	–0.837	–4.308***	–4.230***
	(0.877)	(0.878)	(0.922)	(0.923)
High Income	0.901	0.970	–2.011***	–1.960***
	(0.696)	(0.697)	(0.729)	(0.730)
Constant	74.599***	74.342***	16.409***	16.210***
	(2.326)	(2.328)	(2.450)	(2.454)
Observations	7,620	7,620	7,682	7,682

Note: Standard errors in parentheses

*p < 0.1; **p < 0.05; ***p < 0.01

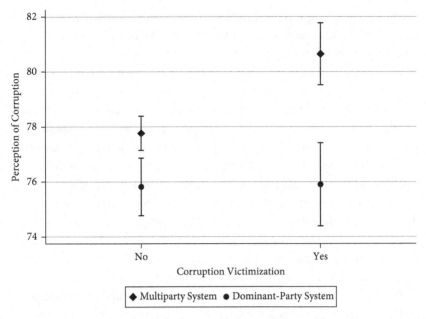

Figure 4.3. Perceptions of corruption: the interaction between victimization and subnational regime category.

that we have already established that individuals in dominant-party enclaves are significantly more likely to have firsthand experience with corruption. We now have established that despite these higher rates of corruption exposure, dominant-party citizens are less likely to view corruption as a problem.

In our third model of citizen assessments of their government's fight against corruption, we find first that our controls perform for the most part as we might expect. Education, interpersonal trust, corruption victimization, and a respondent's age all have significant and largely intuitive effects on one's views of government effectiveness in combating corruption. For example, education has a negative effect, suggesting that the more educated one is, the more critical she is of the government's anticorruption efforts. A person's ideology also has a significant impact on her perception of the government's fight against corruption—those with conservative-leaning ideologies tend to perceive the government as being more effective fighting corruption than those who self-identify on the left.

Also, as we might expect, a person victimized by corrupt behavior is significantly more likely to view her government's anticorruption efforts as ineffective. In fact, we find an almost 4-point difference in views of the government's fight against corruption between those who had and those who had not been victimized by corruption in the previous 12 months. Putting aside for a moment our focus on the role a dominant-party political context plays in shaping attitudes toward corruption, the fact that corruption victims are more likely to blame their government than nonvictims is an important, albeit largely intuitive, finding. The implication here is very clear and simple—all else equal, citizens evaluate their government and its effectiveness as much on the basis of what they experience in their daily lives as they do on what happens in the capital city or elsewhere. Bolstering confidence in government then, whether in the area of its anticorruption efforts or more general levels of system support, requires a better performing government at the local level. Though a somewhat obvious conclusion, this message seems all too often lost in the midst of national anticorruption efforts that tend to lose sight of the deleterious effects that daily, "minor" forms of corruption have on citizen assessments of their larger political system.

The strong and intuitive relationship between corruption victimization and views of government anticorruption efforts is also important for our central question concerning the impact subnational political environments have on citizens' political attitudes. In a previous model, we found that those respondents living in dominant-party systems were more likely to be involved in a corrupt act than their counterparts in multiparty contexts. This finding offers a measure of support for the idea that corruption remains a prominent feature of everyday public life in dominant-party enclaves. Knowing that respondents in these systems are more likely to be involved in a corrupt act, and that such involvement has a strong effect on one's views of government efforts to fight corruption, one might expect respondents in dominant-party systems to view their government's fight against corruption in a more negative light when compared with their counterparts in multiparty states. However, as we have argued above, if a "business as usual" attitude is more likely to prevail in dominant-party systems, then this will manifest itself in the counter-intuitive result that citizens in these systems, even those victimized by corruption, will not be nearly as critical of government "efforts" to fight corruption as those living in multiparty states where corruption is no longer viewed as business as usual.

This is precisely what we find. Specifically, respondents living in dominant-party enclaves are, on average, 3.5 points *less* critical of their government's anticorruption efforts than those individuals living in multiparty provinces and states (Table 4.2, Model 3). Why are respondents living in subnational regimes that are by all accounts more corrupt less likely to criticize their government for its anticorruption efforts? First, in two countries that have undergone democratic transitions at the national level, those individuals living in states and provinces where a single party has yet to relinquish control of the executive office will likely continue to see the overt use of and reliance on corruption and vote buying as an accepted way of playing the political game, regardless of any national-level changes in regime type. Second, with this prevalence of corruption and clientelism still exerting a powerful influence, and the limited ability of opposition forces to punish incumbents for such practices, we expect public conversations about corruption as an important issue of concern, whether in the media or political campaigns, to be minimal, thus diminishing citizen sensitivity to corruption as a problem. If corrupt behavior is viewed as simply a part of one's daily life rather than a pressing issue up for public debate, then we should expect citizens to be less critical of government's efforts to fight against it.

Do Attitudes and Experiences Change Following Transitions?

The preceding analysis has demonstrated fairly clearly that citizens of dominant-party enclaves are more likely to be targets of corruption and clientelism, but less likely to view those interactions as problematic. However, despite the heterogeneous nature of our collection of dominant-party enclaves across our two countries of interest, the possibility remains that it is not the workings of the dominant-party system that lead to higher levels of corruption and vote buying, nor the lower levels of citizen backlash against such practices. Rather, there may be a factor we have not accounted for that has driven both the persistence of dominant-party enclaves and the citizens living within them to have more distinct attitudes and experiences with corruption and clientelism than their multiparty counterparts. The results presented in this chapter to this point also fail to shed light on whether it is, in fact, a culture of corruption and clientelism that has caused dominant-party enclaves to endure. Indeed, we do see in our findings a self-reinforcing dynamic at work whereby pervasive corruption and clientelism lead to a certain level of tolerance, if not acceptance, of such practices by citizens, which, in turn, allows for their continuation. That said, in this chicken-or-egg question, we see the long-running practices of incumbent elites as the place where such citizen attitudes start. We have not come across any bit of evidence or research suggesting that the citizens of certain provinces and states in Argentina and Mexico are simply more open to corruption and vote buying than their provincial neighbors.

That said, we have a means of offering at least one test of this idea that it is not the system that produces the attitudes and experiences but, rather, the other way around or that both are the product of some missing factor for which we have not taken into account. We attempt to address those critiques here with an exploratory longitudinal analysis of how such attitudes and experiences shift following states' transitions to multiparty competition.

Whereas Argentina was added to the AmericasBarometer surveys in 2008, after which only one province transitioned from dominant-party rule, data for Mexico goes back to 2004. In 2009–2010, four Mexican states experienced alternations in the party of the governor for the first time: Oaxaca, Puebla, Sinaloa, and Sonora. We, therefore, have some ability, albeit based on a relatively small number of observations ($n = 1,528$), to examine the attitudes and experiences of citizens in these states during the dominant-party era (with data from 2004–2010) and in the years after their respective watershed elections (2012–2014) in which they ousted the PRI for the first time in more than 80 years.[9] Though this constitutes merely a preliminary glance at the attitudes and experiences under examination in this chapter, based on a limited sample, we offer this discussion as a small first step in the direction of future research on subnational dominant-party systems and what, if anything, changes once those systems are brought down.

As expected, based on the descriptive statistics presented previously, we observe a significant decline in corruption victimization in Mexican states that underwent transitions in 2009 and 2010 (Figure 4.4). This finding is consistent with our argument that once dominant parties are dislodged, the old rules of the game begin to erode. Yet we also find initial evidence that perceptions of the government's effectiveness in combating corruption declined following transitions, and that there is little change in perceptions of corruption—if anything, a slight uptick, in spite of declining victimization. Our interpretation of these results is that once transitions to multiparty competition occur, corrupt behavior on the part of government officials may, in fact, decline, making individuals less likely to have firsthand experience

---

[9] Unfortunately, the question asked regarding vote buying was not asked until 2010, preventing us from comparing rates of targeting before and after the transitions.

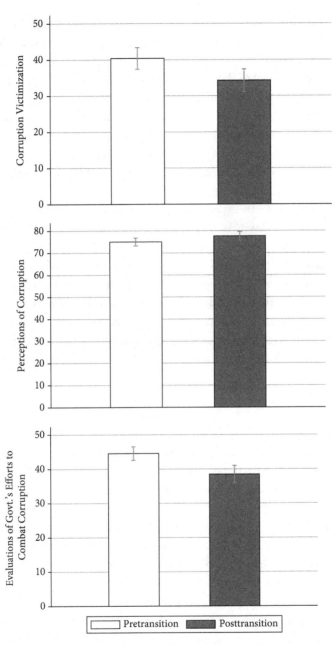

Figure 4.4. Corruption experiences and attitudes pre- and posttransition in four Mexican States.

with dirty politics. However, attention to corruption as a political issue, and, possibly, greater government oversight and transparency, may heighten the visibility of corruption in the minds of citizens, making them more aware of it and more critical of their governments' ability to rein it in. Indeed, this highlights one of the foundational problems with measuring levels of corruption through individuals' perceptions of it (e.g., Corruption Perception Index)—the very success a government may have in fighting corruption may have the unintended result of making acts of corruption more visible in the eyes of citizens and thus increase the probability that those citizens will perceive it to be a problem (Seligson 2006).

Citizen attitudes and experiences change slowly over time, but the core argument presented in this book is that living within a subnational regime characterized by a tilted electoral playing field, politicized rule of law, and the near capture of the state by the dominant party has a profound impact on how people living within those systems experience politics every day. Once dominant parties are defeated, those linkages between citizens and the systems they inhabit also begin to change. However, as long as dominant-party enclaves are in place, the attitudes and behaviors of citizens who live within them will continue to reflect the rules of the game in those systems.

Conclusion

In this examination of the role subnational political contexts play in shaping citizens' views of and experiences with clientelism and corruption, we offer strong support for the basic idea that variations in such contexts matter. When considering the bulk of research on vote buying and corruption that relies on crossnational analyses of these questions, our findings highlight the fact that important intranational differences in political environments may be muddying the waters of our understanding of how democratization affects these types of dirty politics across the developing world. Without recognizing the role that subnational political systems play in either condoning or attacking a long-standing culture of clientelism and corruption, we will miss an important part of the story behind democratic institutional change and its impact on corruption. The problem, as we argue in this chapter, is that national-level institutional change can be, and often is, trumped by subnational institutional stasis.

We now know in the cases of Argentina and Mexico that subnational regimes in which dominant-party rule has continued amid a national-level democratization process have significantly higher levels of corruption and clientelism. Though it is difficult to establish empirically without long-term panel data, there is considerable theoretical support for the proposition that these higher levels of political graft are in large part a product of the modus operandi of dominant parties. The use of corruption and clientelistic practices are, as we discussed in Chapter 2, essential characteristics of dominant-party rule and play a critical role in the electoral dominance such parties tend to exhibit. Conversely, we have good reason to posit that a principal reason corruption and vote-buying efforts are lower in multiparty contexts is that with the defeat of a dominant party comes a societal rejection of the mechanisms of governance that characterized the dominant party's time in power. Thus, the latter's defeat brings with it a heightened sense among public officials and private citizens that the old rules of the game, rules that treated the buying of votes and the use of public office for private gain as acceptable behavior, have changed. More accountable, democratic institutions, then, do seem to matter.

Having established that citizens' experiences with and attitudes toward such illegitimate practices do differ in important ways in dominant-party enclaves, we next turn to the question of how these patterns manifest themselves in citizens' views of democracy in general, the types of political behavior they engage in, and their motivations for such types of engagement. It is to these questions we now turn.

5

The View from Inside the Machine

Democratic Attitudes in Dominant-Party Enclaves

As with all of our dominant-party enclaves in Mexico, the citizens of Colima, a small state on the west coast of Mexico, had never witnessed an alternation in the party controlling the governor's office as they woke up on Election Day in June 2015. Unlike many of the dominant-party enclaves in Mexico, however, elections for the Colima governor's office had been, since 1997, relatively close affairs, with the PRI winning by an average of just under 5 percentage points. No matter how close the election, though, the PRI always emerged victorious. Even when the election was annulled in 2003 for illegal use of government programs for political purposes (making it only the second gubernatorial election to be annulled in Mexico—the first was Tabasco's 2000 election), the PRI still won the subsequent special election. And when the winning candidate in that election, Gustavo Vázquez Montes, died in a plane crash in February 2005, the PRI won the subsequent special election in April of that year, as it did the 2009 election, both times with close to a 4-point margin of victory.

But 2015 looked different. The Partido Acción Nacional (PAN) had continued to make inroads in the state, steadily increasing the number of legislative seats and mayoral offices it controlled throughout the 2000s. Further, the popularity of the PRI, both at the national and state level, had been steadily declining, and the PRI's candidate, José Ignacio Peralta Sánchez, proved to be a less-than-inspiring candidate. All of these factors provided an opening for the surprisingly populist, "man-of-the-people" PAN candidate Jorge Luis Preciado. The dynamics of this election were such that the PAN ended up winning 6 of the state's 10 mayoral elections and 10 of the state's 16 single-member legislative districts races held that year. Those bent on seeing the state's first alternation in gubernatorial power in nearly 80 years, then, surely were hopeful as they went to cast their votes on Sunday, June 7.

In the span of six months, those hopes were dashed, then revived, then dashed for good. After a lengthy delay in the reporting of results and a

Life in the Political Machine. Jonathan T. Hiskey and Mason W. Moseley, Oxford University Press (2020). © Oxford University Press.
DOI: 10.1093/oso/9780197500408.001.0001

premature declaration of victory by Mexican president Enrique Peña Nieto for Peralta on Monday, the final results were released that Wednesday, with Peralta declared the winner by a margin of 503 votes over Preciado.

The PAN immediately challenged the election on various grounds including, once again, the illegal use of government programs by the incumbent governor for partisan purposes. After the case was rejected by Colima's Electoral Tribunal, the PAN won an outright annulment of the election in a surprise ruling by Mexico's national electoral tribunal. This marked only the third such annulment of a gubernatorial election in Mexico, with Colima now holding the dubious honor of being the site for two of those three annulments.

Buoyed by the intervention of national-level institutions, hopes for opponents of Colima's political machine were revived. In the special election held on January 18, 2016, the PRI's José Ignacio Peralta defeated Jorge Luis Preciado by more than 20,000 votes and close to 4 percentage points. And the PRI's Colima machine continued running for another six years.[1]

When polled in 2010 as to whether they thought "democracy is a good or bad form of government for Mexico" 26.3 percent of Colima respondents viewed democracy as bad for Mexico, trailing only Durango (another dominant-party enclave), where an astounding 37.6 percent of respondents saw democracy as bad for Mexico, and, somewhat oddly, Tlaxcala (28.3 percent).[2] Overall, only 15.2 percent of the survey's more than 15,000 respondents across the country viewed democracy as bad for Mexico. Many in the dominant-party enclave of Colima, however, felt otherwise. With the incessant electoral malfeasance of the PRI in the state, resulting in the annulment of the 2003 and 2015 elections, along with countless other questionable incidents, particularly those involving drug cartels, occurring between those two low-water marks, it is perhaps no wonder that many citizens of Colima in 2010 viewed democracy as a system that only brought conflict and controversy to their lives.

Having established that citizens living in dominant-party enclaves confront a political system that is more likely to expose them to the seedier side of politics, whether through outright electoral fraud, vote buying, or corruption, we now explore the question of whether such relatively high levels of

---

[1] The preceding account of the 2015 Colima electoral process is based largely on Gutiérrez Rodríguez's (2015) analysis of the changing electoral landscape in Colima circa 2015.

[2] These results are drawn from the ENVUD survey data first discussed in Chapter 3.

exposure to dirty politics, whether directly or indirectly, leads to a distinct attitudinal outlook toward democracy in general among these dominant-party citizens. Our core expectation is that views from "inside the machine" when it comes to a host of key democratic norms and practices—that is, political tolerance, checks and balances, and democracy as a system of governance—are fundamentally different from those found in neighboring provinces and states where some degree of political competition has taken hold.

As we explore citizens' views toward democracy we also interrogate the utility of viewing "democratic political culture" as a national-level concept. In a developing world increasingly characterized by highly uneven democratic landscapes, scholars of political culture may be well served to dig beneath the national level when searching for the sources and consequences of a citizenry's view of their political world. With myriad examples of subnational "authoritarian enclaves" thriving amid national-level democratization processes, it seems clear that any search for evidence of linkages between regime type and the degree to which a citizenry embraces basic democratic principles may be more fruitful at the subnational level. Further, the prevalence of subnational diversity in "regime types" within a single country allows for at least some measure of analytical leverage on the question of which comes first—a democratic political culture or a democratic political system?

It is with these points in mind that we explore the democratic political cultures of dominant-party and multiparty states and provinces in Argentina and Mexico over the past decade. We find that subnational political cultures vary substantially within these two uneven democracies, and that those differences map onto the type of provincial political system under which individuals live. Though we are not able to definitively establish causality, all signs suggest that citizen attitudes toward democracy, and politics more generally, are driven as much by an instrumental, practical desire to adapt to the political cards they are dealt in their daily lives as they are driven by adherence to abstract political principles. And we contend that for many individuals, those cards can come from the local, as well as the national, political game.

We begin with a discussion of the political culture literature and then proceed to outline the reasons we see subnational divisions as an analytically useful demarcation of political culture. We then explore the attitudinal consequences of uneven democracy in emerging regimes, building on the theoretical discussion from Chapter 2 to shed light on why certain dimensions of democratic political culture appear to vary significantly across subnational regimes while others remain somewhat constant. We test this theory using data from the 2008–2014 AmericasBarometer surveys of Argentina and Mexico, and multiple subnational democracy measures culled from gubernatorial election results in each country. Based on these analyses, the uneven regime landscapes of Argentina and Mexico appear to have significant consequences for the political cultures that characterize the mass publics of these two countries. We find systematic differences in the ways that citizens of the same country view core democratic norms and processes. In conclusion, we argue that these differences may serve to further exacerbate the subnational regime divides that exist in these countries while potentially impeding progress in each country's national-level democratization project as well.

Political Culture: The Evolution of a Contentious Concept

Since the publication of Almond and Verba's seminal *The Civic Culture* (1963), a significant body of work within the comparative political behavior literature has characterized the concept of *political culture* as a national, if not regional (e.g., Wiarda 1971), description of the unique combination of political attitudes and behaviors found in a particular society (e.g., Inglehart 1988; Granato et al. 1996; Inglehart and Welzel 2005; Guiso et al. 2006; Wiarda 1971). With the aid of large-scale crossnational surveys that have emerged alongside the recent era of democratization across the developing world, the perceived importance of a society's cultural democratic credentials has informed a multitude of scholarship that explores the influence of political culture on the chances for a democratic political system to both survive and thrive (e.g., Inglehart 1988; Wiarda 1973). Proponents of this view have settled on the idea that countries contain a distinct "syndrome" of attitudes that capture a nation's fundamental political worldview that trumps whatever subnational political, socioeconomic, religious, or ethnic heterogeneity that may exist, and that this syndrome has important consequences for democratic politics within that society (Inglehart 1988).

The central argument of the "culturalist" school is that individuals' basic political norms and values shape country-level economic and political outcomes generally and have a specific impact on whether the regime in a given country is democratic or authoritarian. Echoing Almond and Verba's (1960) original articulation of the civic culture thesis, and treating years of democracy as his dependent variable, Inglehart (1990) goes so far as to claim that "over half of the variance in the persistence of democratic institutions can be attributed to political culture alone" (46). From this perspective, the causal arrow flows from mass attitudes to political institutions, and not the other way around.

Another line of research finds that elite political culture is a significant factor in whether or not a country will have a democratic regime in place. Mainwaring and Pérez-Liñán (2014), for example, home in on the degree of "normative democratic commitment on the part of powerful political players" (5) as essential in shaping the prospects of democracy within a country. Przeworski (1991), too, rests his answer to the question of why ruling elites would peacefully leave office following an electoral defeat on the idea that they have sufficient belief in their long-term prospects under democracy to accept a short-term defeat (1991). The key difference in these elite-based accounts of democratic emergence and survival from those accounts that rest on the political attitudes of the mass public is that elites often can and do play a decisive role in what specific form a nominally democratic regime takes—that is, how closely it abides by the commonly understood democratic rules of the game. In the case of our dominant-party enclaves, we would suspect, though we have no data to support this suspicion, that the incumbent elites in such systems would likely score low on most measures of a democratic political culture, supporting in a way the contention of Mainwaring and Pérez-Liñán that political elites are, indeed, decisive in determining the degree of democracy a society enjoys. This proposition, though, does not correspond with the view that the mass public's political culture is the driving force behind the degree of democracy their system exhibits.

An alternative perspective has countered the culturalist approach by arguing that a citizenry's views of and support for democratic principles are much more a byproduct of the political regime and economic conditions under which they live than they are a precursor to such country-level outcomes. In their 1996 piece, Jackman and Miller offer a systematic rebuttal of Inglehart's findings on theoretical and empirical grounds. They first argue that what Inglehart describes as a consistent "syndrome" of attitudes representing a particular culture are actually only modestly interrelated. Most importantly, when they reverse the causal arrow and examine how democracy and development influence political culture, they find more convincing evidence that institutional context structures individual-level attitudes and behaviors, rather than the other way around. They conclude that "institutional change alters the opportunities available to political actors, and, even allowing for some stickiness, thereby modifies the behavior of those actors" (Jackman and Miller 1996, 655). The argument we have developed throughout this book echoes this perspective.

While Jackman and Miller were largely concerned with rejecting the notion that political culture affects a country's "political and economic performance" (632), other scholars have sought to explicitly model the impact that political context has on attitudes toward democracy. According to this line of thought, an individual's fundamental views regarding democratic norms and processes are a byproduct of her day-to-day interactions with the political system. Muller and Seligson (1994) investigate the relationship between civic culture and democracy and find evidence that "the successful persistence of democracy over time is likely to cause an increase in levels of civic culture attitudes" (635). Similarly, Salinas and Booth (2011) find in Latin America that "acculturation to democratic attitudes occurs because of system-level rules of the political game" (53). Further, Peffley and Rohrschneider (2003) examine the relationship between political tolerance and democratization in Europe and reach a similar conclusion, arguing for the idea of "democratic learning":

> Citizens in more stable democratic nations where unpopular groups have the freedom to express their views and where the government protects those freedoms obviously have more opportunities to associate "democracy" with political tolerance and thus are more likely to learn that political tolerance is an important component of a democracy. (246)

In sum, much empirical research has investigated the relationship between characteristics of political regimes and citizen attitudes toward democracy, with a preponderance of recent work reaching the conclusion that the causal arrow largely flows from institutions to individuals.

With these general ideas in mind, we shift the conversation on regime types and political cultures to the subnational level. Specifically, we pose the following question: How might an uneven political regime landscape, characterized by dominant-party enclaves found among the subnational units *within* individual countries, influence individuals' attitudes toward core components of democracy? Our expectation is that with the highly divergent political environments found subnationally throughout the developing world in particular, national-level assessments of political culture may mask important differences in the degree to which a country's citizens support the basic norms and principles that are thought to serve as the foundation for democratic government. Specifically, we argue that in enclaves where dominant parties apply the rule of law to their own strategic ends, deploy state resources to service the machine, and engage in extensive electoral dirty tricks, citizens will adjust their understanding of democratic norms and processes in a way that will reflect these machine characteristics.

Subnational Variation in Political Culture

In this book, we offer bountiful support for the notion that individual countries differ a great deal intranationally in terms of economic and political development. Particularly in Latin America and other developing regions, some provinces and states have been slower to democratize than others (O'Donnell 1993; Snyder 2001). Across many of these countries, certain areas lag behind in terms of infrastructural development, access to technology, and levels of human capital. Illiteracy in Mexico's southeastern states (Oaxaca, Guerrero, and Chiapas) is roughly six times higher than it is in Mexico City and the country's northern states (INEGI 2017). Politically, we often find weak rule of law in such jurisdictions, higher levels of clientelism, few, if any, independent local media outlets, and limited electoral competition, even decades after national-level transitions to democracy (Fox 1994; O'Donnell 1998; Chavez 2004). But it is not only in those development laggards that we find our dominant-party enclaves. As we discussed in Chapter 3, the collection of these provincial-level political machines is quite varied and includes some of the more developed states and provinces (e.g. Edomex, Mexico, or Santa Cruz, Argentina) as well. The common trait shared by these subnational units is the entrenchment of a political group that has persisted throughout its country's political liberalization. And in some cases, these dominant-party enclaves have even served to help consolidate national democratic regimes, as ambitious provincial politicians forge mutually beneficial relationships that preserve subnational authoritarian rule (Lawson 2000; Gibson 2012).

The presence of these illiberal subnational fiefdoms has had profound effects not only on the prospects for national-level democratization, but also on citizens' form of engagement with politics and their perceptions of their country's political regime (e.g., Hiskey and Bowler 2005). Thus, where such political environments persist at the subnational level, we posit that they can also foster political cultures that bear little resemblance to what one might encounter in more democratic regions of the country.

A brief scan of the political environments and cultures found over time in the United States serves to reinforce this logic. As we have previously noted, Key's work on Southern politics in the United States (1949) highlights what many had known for years—that the South was home to a unique collection of political environments compared with the rest of the United States, marked by the single-party dominance of the Democratic Party and the disenfranchisement and pervasive violation of the civil and human rights of black Americans. Arguably it is at least in part the authoritarian nature of subnational politics in the South throughout much of the country's history that has contributed to what even today stands as a distinct political culture (see also Mickey 2015).

Operating under this notion that the regime landscapes of many emerging democracies are highly uneven, and that this unevenness should reveal itself in the political attitudes and behaviors of citizens living within those distinct systems, we then must consider how to assess a country's democratic political culture? In their oft-overlooked but illuminating article on "The Eight Spains," Linz and de Miguel (1966) put forth five decades ago an argument for the importance of studying different subnational political cultures both within *and* across nations. Utilizing data from Spain, a politically and socioeconomically heterogeneous regime at the time (and to some extent even today), Linz and de Miguel observed sharp differences in terms of religiosity, class structure, and political attitudes across the country's provinces. In reviewing their findings, they argued that students of comparative politics might benefit not only from comparing divergent political cultures within a particular country, but also from identifying a common political or socioeconomic factor present in subnational units across multiple countries and employing a comparative analysis of the political cultures of these units to support causal claims attributed to the factor those units had in common.

A cursory glance at levels of support for democracy across Latin America and *within* Argentina and Mexico in 2014 serves to illustrate Linz and de Miguel's argument from a half century ago (see Figure 5.1). We see vast differences emerge in terms of support for democracy across the Americas—from Panama, where barely half of citizens believe that democracy is the best form of government, to Uruguay, which boasts levels of support that surpass those found in Canada and the United States. Yet, a closer look at the case of Mexico illustrates how mean levels of support can mask significant subnational variation in terms of societal orientations toward democracy. Whereas certain regions in Mexico are characterized by levels of support for democracy that are on par with the United States, others possess support levels lower than those found in Honduras, a regime that many would argue has drifted toward authoritarianism over the past decade. Indeed, the numerical gap between regions *within* Mexico is on par with the gap between Canada and Haiti—two national regimes most observers would not locate in the same stratosphere in terms of democratic political cultures. We see the dominant-party enclaves we have identified across Argentina and Mexico as a critical source of this subnational cultural variation, and we explore the extent to which this common political feature of some states and provinces in these two countries produces a similar political culture that stands in contrast to those states and provinces that have some degree of multiparty competition.

The seemingly nationwide processes of economic and political development that are often seen as driving cultural change do not operate uniformly within many nations, particularly those emerging from an extended period of authoritarian rule. Thus, these "mean-spirited" analyses (Snyder 2001, 98) that form the basis for generalizations about regional and national cultures likely mask important differences in political attitudes and beliefs within these systems, rendering estimated macrorelationships between culture and economic or political outcomes misleading. In this chapter, we use survey data from Latin America to demonstrate the heterogeneous nature of national political cultures. We argue that our findings necessitate a recalibration of common conceptions of national and subnational political culture, and of causal theories that include aggregate estimates of national political culture as a key explanatory or dependent variable.

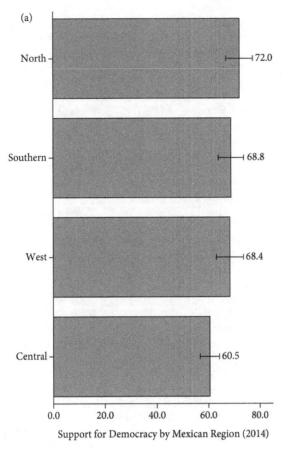

(a)

North -|—————| 72.0

Southern -|————| 68.8

West -|————| 68.4

Central -|———| 60.5

0.0   20.0   40.0   60.0   80.0

Support for Democracy by Mexican Region (2014)

Figure 5.1. Support for democracy within Mexico (Panel A) and across Latin America (Panel B).

How Dominant-Party Enclaves Shape Democratic Attitudes

We expect that subnational political context matters when it comes to citizens' support for the fundamental tenets of democracy. Given the socioeconomic, geographic, and ethnic diversity of the dominant-party states and provinces that we have identified across Argentina and Mexico, we see it as unlikely that citizens in this group of political systems would share a common political culture for reasons other than the similarities found in the

Figure 5.1. Continued

political systems they inhabit. But the question of *how* uneven democracy influences political culture remains unclear. In this section, we outline the ways in which we see subnational political context affecting the degree to which citizens express support for the fundamental principles of democracy.

Work on the concept of a democratic political culture has shifted from asking citizens about democracy directly to focusing primarily on the extent to which individuals support key components of liberal democracy, like tolerance and inclusive participation, limits on executive authority, and institutional checks and balances (Carlin 2011; Carlin and Singer 2011). Drawing from Dahl's (1971) conceptualization of "polyarchy," Carlin and Singer explore how Latin American citizens fit into different democracy support profiles, based not only on long-term explanatory factors like wealth and education, but also on short-term predictors related to economic performance and corruption victimization. Ostensibly, the prevalence of democratic values would be explained not only by individual level factors, but also the context in which citizens operate and the extent to which they are imbued with the values and norms that predominate in a particular context. At the country level, we find that many of the countries with the highest democracy scores in the region—that is, Chile, Costa Rica, and Uruguay—also boast citizenries who express support for the central tenets of liberal democracy.

As we make clear in Chapter 2, we argue that being nested within a certain type of provincial political environment should also influence how citizens view these democratic principles. If we think of one's attitudes toward politics as being shaped in part by the political game she plays or at least observes being played by political elites, then it does not require much of a leap to posit that we should see systematic differences in the degree to which citizens embrace democratic principles across distinct subnational political systems.

This proposition rests on the idea that individuals who spend their lives in less-than-democratic local political environments, in which corruption and clientelism have become business as usual, are shaped fundamentally by that experience. These individuals have little familiarity with competitive elections between ideologically distinct alternatives that take place on a level electoral playing field, they are more likely to have been targeted for vote buying and other corrupt practices, as demonstrated in Chapter 4, and they have only borne witness to dominant executives, who run roughshod over the institutions designed to check them. Moreover, these individuals live in environments in which opposing views are discouraged and, at times, even repressed. In this context, many, though not all, individuals will tend to adapt and adjust their attitudes and behaviors in ways that will improve their chances of success within this particular type of political system.

Just as Mattes and Bratton (2007) speak of "democratic learning" across African countries, where the embrace of democratic principles comes with the experiences one has with democracy, here we posit that citizens will experience the opposite—a process of "dominant-party learning"—if they live within the types of subnational systems that we have described throughout these pages. Absent much research on the ways in which subnational political contexts shape one's political attitudes, we turn to work on this question carried out at the national level. Similar to Peffley and Rohrschneider's

(2003) finding that political tolerance tends to increase in democracies over the course of time, and Rohrschneider's (1994, 1996, 1999) work on the attitudinal consequences of institutional variation between East and West Germany, we argue life in a dominant-party machine will manifest itself in the ways in which citizens engage with and view politics more generally. With this expectation, we should find that a less-than-democratic political culture prevails in these dominant-party subnational systems, producing a vicious cycle wherein individuals in these systems fail to embrace the norms of democratic politics that help nascent democracies thrive and, instead, adopt political principles, such as support for a dominant executive, that help keep the machine running.

Data and Measurement

The AmericasBarometer survey instrument once again offers us a unique opportunity to explore multiple dimensions of political culture, as it has included since its inception multiple questions intended to gauge shifting attitudes regarding key democratic norms and processes. However, democracy is a loaded concept for which definitions abound (e.g., Collier and Levitsky 1997), requiring that we ground our analysis theoretically to ensure that we fully capture the influence of subnational regime characteristics on individual-level attitudes toward democracy.

To measure democratic political culture, we draw on five different variables that approximate the extent to which individuals are committed to democratic norms and processes. The first four come from Carlin and Singer's (2011) approach to gauging "support for polyarchy"—an allusion to Dahl's (1971) seminal work on the basic rights, liberties, and practices associated with liberal democracy. In their investigation of the sources of democratic support, Carlin and Singer argue that scholars must go beyond measures that simply tap into respondents' stated preferences for democracy, given that survey questions intended to gauge support for democracy often suffer from social desirability bias or the idiosyncratic conceptions of democracy that many individuals hold (Seligson 2001; Carrión 2008). Moreover, democratic support can be a multidimensional concept containing certain dimensions to which citizens express a strong commitment, and others on which the same individuals are only partially committed, or reject entirely (Schedler and Sarsfield 2009). To ameliorate these problems, Carlin and Singer propose an approach to unearthing democratic attitudes through a focus on the constituent parts of Dahl's polyarchy: (1) support for free public contestation, (2) tolerance of inclusive participation, (3) limits on executive action, and (4) respect for institutional processes.

Particularly helpful to our study is that Carlin and Singer utilize questions included in the 2008 AmericasBarometer survey to assemble the indices that comprise support for polyarchy, and most, but not all, of these survey items have remained in the AmericasBarometer instrument through 2014. The measure for *Public Contestation* we use here gauges support for various forms of political participation, including (a) legal public demonstrations, (b) community activism, and (c) voluntarism in political campaigns. *Inclusive Participation* is an index that includes whether or not respondents believe citizens who are critical of the regime should be able to (a) vote, (b) conduct peaceful demonstrations, (c) run for office, or (d) appear on television to make speeches. It also includes support for the right of homosexuals to run for public office. Together, these two measures (rescaled 0–100) capture Dahl's first dimension focusing on the political and civil freedoms necessary for democracy to thrive.

We also run predictive models of two dependent variables that gauge how committed individuals are to democratic institutions and processes. First, we examine respondents' commitment to checks on executive power. The *Limits on Executive Action* measure is an index that includes responses to three questions: (a) whether presidents would be justified in limiting the voice of the opposition for the good of the country, (b) whether people should govern directly and not through elected representatives, and (c) whether those who oppose the majority represent a threat to the country. *Institutions and Processes* utilizes a single question that asks respondents if the executive would be justified in closing the legislature in the event of a crisis. These two indicators (0–100) provide evidence of the extent to which individuals support the institutional checks and balances Dahl argues are crucial to liberal democracy.

Finally, our fifth measure comes from the "Churchill" question, which asks citizens if, in spite of its problems, democracy is the best form of government. This variable has been used widely in research on democratic attitudes and, though not without limitations, offers a reasonably accurate measure of how individuals feel about democracy in the abstract (Kiewiet de Jonge 2016). Because Carlin and Singer find that the four polyarchy indicators tap into four separate dimensions rather than a single latent dimension, we run predictive models of each of the five variables separately, rather than group them together in one measure. We treat each variable as a continuous variable ranging 0–100 and thus employ ordinary least squares (OLS) regression for every model. Because the *Limits on Executive Action* and *Institutions and Processes* variables are coded such that higher values indicate *less* democratic attitudes, we recode each in the predictive models so that higher values in all of the dependent variables represent more support for the democratic principles being measured, meaning that we expect the coefficient for *DOMINANT-PARTY ENCLAVE* to be negative. We also include a list of control variables that the literature has demonstrated have an impact on support for democracy (e.g., age, education, economic evaluations, and religiosity) and fixed effects for the country and the year of the survey.

Results

Figures 5.2 and 5.3 provide telling initial evidence that inhabitants of dominant-party and multiparty subnational regimes differ significantly in terms of their democratic attitudes. Namely, citizens of the dominant-party provinces and states of Argentina and Mexico seem to be less tolerant of public contestation and inclusive participation on average than those citizens living in multiparty contexts and more supportive of a powerful, and potentially undemocratic, role for the executive. On the other hand, citizens of multiparty contexts are more democratic, with mean responses similar to those we observe in the United States or Canada, outpacing their counterparts in less democratic subnational contexts. These differences are all statistically significant at the $p < .05$ level and range from 4- to 8-point disparities (all variables are scaled 0–100). In particular, stark contrasts emerge between mean rates of support for executive action in dominant-party and multiparty provinces, as citizens of the former appear more likely to support a powerful leader's right to thwart minority opinions and, under certain circumstances, bypass checks and balances. It seems, then, that many citizens living within dominant-party machines, where such behavior by the executive has become routinized, grow to see this as an effective form of governance that avoids the tumult of more democratic policymaking processes.

Using the classic measure of whether or not democracy is the best system of government despite its flaws, the difference between dominant and

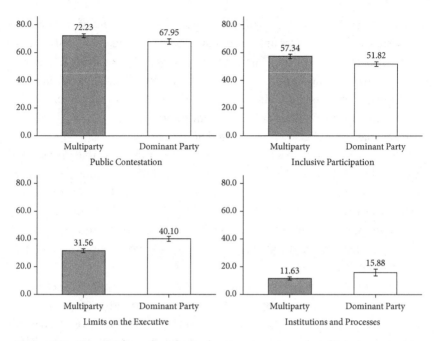

Figure 5.2. Support for polyarchy in dominant-party and multiparty contexts.

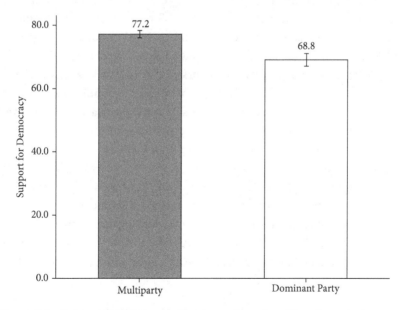

Figure 5.3. Support for democracy in one-party and multiparty contexts.

Note: It should be noted that Argentine respondents are significantly more supportive of democracy in the abstract than Mexicans—so, the mean scores for both multiparty and dominant-party systems are higher in Argentina than in Mexico. However, the differences between the two categories in each country are similar to the differences presented in Figure 5.3.

multiparty regimes is also significant. Specifically, citizens of dominant-party states and provinces are more than 8 points less likely to believe democracy is the best option. Harking back to Figure 5.1, individuals nested in multiparty regimes report average levels of democratic support that exceed those found in the United States, and the difference between dominant and multiparty regimes in Argentina and Mexico is roughly the same as that found between the United States and Mexico, or Chile and El Salvador, respectively. In sum, it appears, at least initially, that Argentina and Mexico play host to diverse subnational political cultures depending on the regime characteristics of states and provinces. However, these are only mean responses to questions regarding democratic norms and processes, and we have not begun to control for the individual- and provincial-level variables that might also influence the variation we observe across subnational contexts.

Because it remains possible that the differences we observe in terms of democratic attitudes across subnational units could be attributed to factors other than provincial regime characteristics, we next run five models of democratic support that aim to shed light on the determinants of these attitudes while controlling for other potentially important variables.[3] Table 5.1 presents findings from these OLS models, and once again we find telling evidence that the democratic political cultures of Argentina and Mexico vary significantly across subnational regime type. Even after controlling for a litany of other factors, including basic socioeconomic controls and respondents' evaluations of economic conditions that have been found to have a strong impact on support for polyarchy (Carlin and Singer 2011), subnational context appears to exert a statistically significant effect on individuals' willingness to endorse many key tenets of liberal democracy.

Focusing first on attitudes toward democratic processes (Models 3 and 4), the differences between dominant-party and multiparty contexts are stark. Individuals in the former systems are more likely to support the consolidation of power in the hands of the executive than similar citizens in multiparty subnational contexts. Moreover, from a substantive standpoint, these

---

[3] Again, all dependent variables were recoded from 0 to 100 for ease of interpretation and comparison of coefficients, and we utilize ordinary least squares regression. In the case of the *Institutions and Processes* variable, which is based on only one survey item, the dependent variable is actually dichotomous. For ease of comparison, we present the results from an estimated OLS model of this variable, given that the results from a logistic regression model are identical, substantively.

Table 5.1. Models of Democratic Support in Argentina and Mexico

	Public Contestation	Inclusive Participation	Limit Executive	Institutions and Processes	Support for Democracy
	(All Dependent Variables Coded 0–100)				
VARIABLES	Model 1	Model 2	Model 3	Model 4	Model 5
Female	−0.949*	−0.606	−0.684	2.500***	1.441**
	(0.558)	(0.554)	(0.579)	(0.895)	(0.575)
Age	0.016	−0.053***	0.097***	0.063**	0.199***
	(0.019)	(0.019)	(0.020)	(0.031)	(0.020)
Interest in Politics	0.113***	0.093***	0.041***	0.034**	0.065***
	(0.009)	(0.009)	(0.010)	(0.015)	(0.009)
Education	0.217***	0.721***	0.884***	0.694***	0.507***
	(0.079)	(0.079)	(0.082)	(0.127)	(0.082)
Wealth Quintile	0.558**	0.533**	0.865***	−0.003	0.668***
	(0.223)	(0.220)	(0.231)	(0.352)	(0.229)
Urban	−0.477	−1.279*	−1.767**	−1.165	0.922
	(0.734)	(0.738)	(0.763)	(1.207)	(0.764)
Presidential Approval	0.039***	−0.093***	−0.070***	−0.040**	0.079***
	(0.013)	(0.012)	(0.013)	(0.019)	(0.013)
National Economic Situation	−0.779*	0.013	−0.720	−0.107	2.138***
	(0.433)	(0.437)	(0.450)	(0.710)	(0.454)
Ideology	−0.343***	−0.755***	−0.782***	−0.324*	0.675***
	(0.126)	(0.121)	(0.131)	(0.193)	(0.126)
Church Attendance	−0.024***	−0.032***	−0.020***	0.002	−0.028***
	(0.007)	(0.007)	(0.007)	(0.011)	(0.007)
DOMINANT-PARTY ENCLAVE	*−0.928*	*−0.626*	*−2.428****	*−3.920****	*−2.845****
	(0.663)	*(0.660)*	*(0.688)*	*(1.071)*	*(0.685)*
Middle Income	−0.933	−2.403***	2.787***	3.254**	−1.911**
	(0.848)	(0.843)	(0.881)	(1.381)	(0.880)
High Income	5.373***	1.828***	4.294***	−1.894*	1.908***
	(0.703)	(0.693)	(0.727)	(1.106)	(0.718)
Constant	63.783***	57.183***	−45.002***	−22.798***	42.937***
	(2.188)	(2.186)	(2.274)	(3.372)	(2.271)
Observations	6,317	7,793	5,911	5,870	8,184
Fixed Effects	Yes	Yes	Yes	Yes	Yes

Note: Standard errors in parentheses.

*p < 0.1; **p < 0.05; ***p <0.01

effects are important, exceeding changes of 10 percent in terms of support for a strong executive (*Limit Executive*) and 30 percent in terms of support for key democratic institutions (*Institutions and Processes*; see Figure 5.4). While Argentines appear relatively less likely to support strong executives than Mexicans, individuals nested in similar subnational environments appear to have much in common when it comes to the effect of subnational context on democratic attitudes. Again, subnational political context appears to influence the likelihood that individuals endorse democratic norms and processes, meaning that the uneven nature of democratization in Latin America has important consequences for the attitudinal consolidation of democracy in the region.

We also see that individuals nested in dominant-party subnational systems are less supportive of democracy than their counterparts in multiparty states and provinces, controlling for a comprehensive list of individual-level variables (Model 5; Figure 5.5). This effect is substantively more important than moving from the poorest development tercile to the richest—impressive given subnational variation in terms of levels of development and the prevailing wisdom about the relationship between modernization and political culture. And as we outlined in Chapter 2, many of the dominant-party enclaves we find in Argentina and Mexico rank in the upper half of their

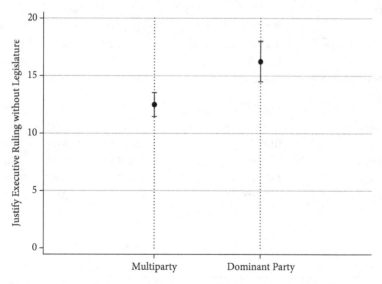

Figure 5.4. Predicted support for executive ruling without legislature.

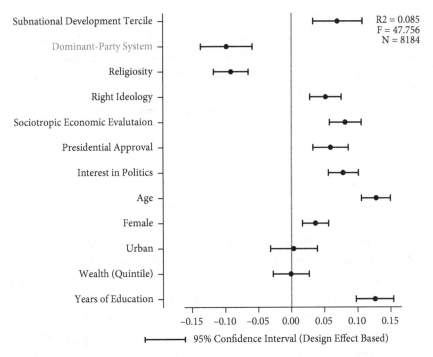

Figure 5.5. Predictors of support for democracy in Argentina and Mexico (standardized coefficients).

respective country's development levels. Despite these factors that should contribute to a stronger commitment to democratic principles, we find the opposite.

Also, as made clear in Figure 5.5, being nested in a dominant-party enclave has one of the strongest negative effects in our model on support for democracy as a system of government and overall serves as one of the strongest predictors of democratic support along with age and education. As with the case of Colima discussed in the beginning of this chapter, it seems that citizens living in dominant-party enclaves that have all the trappings of democratic systems yet fail to live up to those standards in practice are less inclined to express support for the regime at all when compared with their multiparty counterparts.

Further, the direction and near statistical significance of the coefficients for *Inclusive Participation* are suggestive of a citizenry that is less tolerant of those opposed to the government, individuals who rock the boat, than individuals living in multiparty contexts. This effect, however, is outweighed by other variables included in the model, including levels of provincial economic development. Taken together though, these results highlight the ways in which life in a dominant-party machine can manifest itself in at least three dimensions of democratic attitudes, even among individuals who are otherwise quite similar on relevant individual-level variables and nested within similar economic environments.

Causal Mechanisms: Democratic Learning and Dirty Politics

There are a few more issues to sort out with respect to the manner by which subnational regime type matters for democratic attitudes. First, do more democratic belief systems emerge immediately upon transition from dominant-party to multiparty system, or do these attitudes build slowly over time? And second, to what extent are the results we uncover here a product of the mechanisms we outlined in the previous chapter regarding corruption and vote buying?

The Evolution of Democratic Attitudes over Time

Table 5.2 presents the results from predictive models of democratic attitudes identical to those presented previously, except with the addition of an independent variable called "Years since Transition." This measure captures the length of time since multiparty regimes experienced their first alternation in the party of the governor. In the case of Argentina, the maximum value on this variable would be 27 years—the length of time between the second posttransition elections in 1987 and 2014 (e.g., Buenos Aires province, which experienced a transition from the Unión Cívico Radical (UCR) to the PJ). In Mexico, the maximum number of years since the first alternation would be 25, dating back to when the PRI first admitted electoral defeat in 1989 in the state of Baja California. In sum, the higher the number, the more experience with multiparty rule the province or state has had, and according to studies like that of Peffley and Rohrschneider (2005), the more consolidated democratic attitudes should be.

Table 5.2. Model Results with Years since Transition

VARIABLES	Public Contestation	Inclusive Participation	Limit Executive	Institutions and Processes	Support for Democracy
	Model 1	Model 2	Model 3	Model 4	Model 5
DOMINANT-PARTY ENCLAVE	−1.112 (0.868)	−0.504 (0.845)	−3.553*** (0.898)	−3.299** (1.357)	−2.823*** (0.880)
Years since Transition	−0.016	0.011	−0.098*	0.053	0.002
	(0.048)	(0.046)	(0.050)	(0.071)	(0.047)

Note: Standard errors in parentheses.
$^*p < 0.1$; $^{**}p < 0.05$; $^{***}p < 0.01$

Yet when we include years of multiparty rule in our models, holding the exact same set of control variables constant, little changes about our results. The strong effects for DOMINANT-PARTY ENCLAVE remain in the case of Limit Executive, Institutions and Processes, and Support for Democracy, and once again, the effect for Public Contestation approaches widely accepted standards for statistical significance. However, most notable is the lack of significance for our Years since Transition variable. Only on the Limit Executive dimension do we observe a statistically significant impact, and this effect pales in comparison with that of our dichotomous measure. In general, we thus find much stronger support in these models for our simple indicator for dominant-party enclaves, rather than a measure that is designed to capture the cumulative effect of experience with multiparty rule. This is not to say that experience with multiparty competition does not matter—rather, it means that when both indicators are included in predictive models of various dimensions of democratic support, the distinction between dominant-party enclaves and those that have experienced at least one alternation in the party of the governor is more pronounced.

To further probe the temporal dynamics behind the distinct political cultures we have identified across multiparty and dominant-party systems, we now return to the approach we used in the previous chapter to examine the possibility of an attitudinal shift in citizens after a transition occurs—in this case, in the same four Mexican states (Oaxaca, Puebla,

Sinaloa, and Sonora) that experienced transitions from dominant-party rule in 2009 and 2010. As we see in the graphs included in Figure 5.6, there does seem to be some indication that once the dominant party finally relinquishes power through the electoral process, a shift away from the picture of the dominant-party attitudes and behaviors we have painted in the preceding pages begins to occur. That said, we also do not expect the ouster of the dominant party to immediately transform the way citizens think about and engage with politics, as that is a process that surely will occur over an extended period of time. Nor do we expect a single election, no matter how historic it might be for a particular province or state, to magically rid the system of all traces of the "dominant-partyism" that we have catalogued previously. Indeed, if we consider the national-level transition in Mexico as an example, the PRI's ouster from the presidency in 2000 certainly did not immediately rid the nation of corruption or attempts at vote buying. However, it did heighten attention to those issues (serving as a central campaign issue of the victorious Fox campaign) and arguably posed a challenge to the "business as usual" view encouraged by the PRI's one-party system for so many years. In support of this idea, we see in Figure 5.6 that in the postdominant–party system era, support for a military coup in times of high levels of crime and corruption drops significantly, by more than 10 points for each. Conversely, a slight, albeit insignificant, drop in the overall level of support for democracy among citizens in these states suggests that in the immediate aftermath of the ouster of a dominant party, citizens seem to still reserve judgment on the merits of democracy until they see what has changed, and what has not, with the arrival of an opposition government.

If anything, this preliminary look at attitudes toward democracy in four Mexican states serves to buttress our claims regarding the primacy of institutional characteristics in shaping citizens' experiences with politics, rather than to lend support to a bottom-up explanation of subnational regime characteristics. The fact that changes in democratic attitudes like citizens' willingness to support a military coup occur *after* the local-level transition is consistent with our argument. Yet we would need to conduct a more extensive analysis of changes in attitudes and behaviors before and after transitions to make a more definitive claim on the direction of the causal arrow.

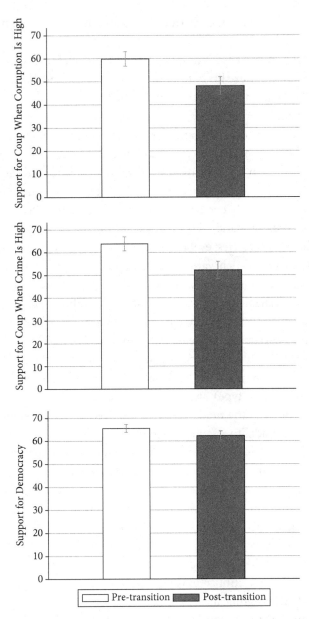

Figure 5.6. Democratic attitudes in four transition states in Mexico.

The Mediating Role of Corruption and Clientelism

In the previous chapter, we demonstrated that individuals living in dominant-party enclaves are more likely to have firsthand experience with corruption and vote buying, but less likely to view such seedy practices as problematic. Our expectation is that part of the reason why we observe a more tenuous commitment to democratic norms and processes in dominant-party contexts is because of pervasive corruption and clientelism—each of which has been found to have a corrosive effect on democratic attitudes (Seligson 2002; Cohen et al. n.d.). In other words, a heightened exposure to dirty politics in dominant-party enclaves might have a *mediating* effect on the relationship between subnational regime type and democratic attitudes.

The Sobel-Goodman test evaluates whether a mediator carries at least part of the effect of an independent variable on the dependent variable of interest (Sobel 1982), and it is often used for parsing out the effect of key causal mechanisms. Corruption and clientelism are more prevalent in dominant-party enclaves and could have a mediating role in connecting such subnational regimes to lower levels of professed support for democratic norms and processes.

A mediator (in our case, exposure to vote buying and corruption) can be said to be significant when it is positively related to the independent variable (subnational regime type) and dependent variable (democratic attitudes) and, when added to the model, reduces the effect of the independent variable on the dependent variable. While including the same control variables found in the models presented in Table 5.1, we test to determine whether part of the influence of subnational regime type on democratic attitudes flows through exposure to corruption and clientelism. Unsurprisingly, individuals in dominant-party enclaves are more likely targets for dirty politics, and experience with corruption and vote buying has a uniformly corrosive effect on democratic attitudes. In Table 5.3, we present statistics regarding the proportion of the total effect of subnational regime type that is mediated by both corruption victimization and receipt of a vote-buying offer, while reporting statistical significance for each mediating effect.

Corruption victimization is a significant mediator for each measure of support for polyarchy. In the case of *Public Contestation*, experience with corruption carries roughly 10 percent of the overall effect of living in a dominant-party enclave on support for democratic participation. Given the infinite number of factors that might mediate the relationship between subnational regime type and democratic attitudes, we view these results as

Table 5.3. Sobel Mediation Tests: Corruption Victimization and Vote Buying

	Public Contestation	Inclusive Participation	Limit Executive	Institutions and Processes	Support for Democracy
VARIABLES	Model 1	Model 2	Model 3	Model 4	Model 5
Corruption Victimization					
Sobel Test Coefficient	−0.152*** (0.051)	−0.089** 0.041	−0.120** (0.049)	−0.162** (0.067)	−0.145*** (0.046)
Percent of Total Effect Mediated	10.1%	8.2%	5.1%	5.2%	4.2%
Receipt of Vote-Buying Offer					
Sobel Test Coefficient	−0.086 (0.060)	−0.028*** (0.012)	−0.186*** (0.087)	−0.056 (0.059	−0.052 (0.048)
Percent of Total Effect Mediated	5.1%	32.3%	6.0%	2.7%	1.3%

Note: Standard errors in parentheses.
$*p < 0.1; **p < 0.05; ***p < 0.01$

important. The mediating effect of receiving a vote-buying offer is only significant for two of our key dependent variables, but in the case of *Inclusive Participation*, it appears to transmit nearly one third of the total effect of subnational regime type. These results offer compelling support for the notion that the linkages we identify in Chapter 4 as shaping citizen experiences with the provincial state play an important role in undermining democratic attitudes in dominant-party enclaves.

Overall, these results indicate that life in a dominant-party machine does manifest itself in the ways citizens think about key dimensions of democracy. Their views of the rules and processes of democracy in particular are significantly lower than those of their counterparts in multiparty regimes. While we do not claim to have conclusively nailed down the reason for this attitudinal profile of dominant-party citizens, we have offered substantial evidence that part of the answer lies in the fact that these individuals must confront on a daily basis a political machine in which corruption and vote buying are common, dominant executives run roughshod over local democratic institutions, and opponents of the machine are persecuted politically, socially, and economically.

This finding has important implications for democracy in Latin America, as living in a dominant-party province or state appears to affect individuals' commitment to democratic norms *at all levels*. These questions ask specifically about the executive branch at the national level, or democracy in the abstract, rather than merely capture individuals' affinity for their governor. Thus, not only do these cultural orientations reinforce subnational authoritarianism, but they might also provide a reservoir of support for potential undemocratic actions at the national level similar to what we have observed recently in countries like Brazil, Honduras, and Venezuela. While Latin America has certainly made great strides toward democracy over the past three decades, the fact that dominant-party enclaves can be found in many regimes across the region presents a significant obstacle to the consolidation of a democratic political culture in coming years. This marks perhaps the strongest evidence yet that dominant-party enclaves can, indeed, erode democracy from within.

Conclusion

In this chapter, we take what is an initial step toward a framework for understanding democratic political culture in uneven regimes, as clearly a great deal of work remains if we are to definitively establish the various ways in which local context shapes political attitudes and behaviors. However, these findings point us in that direction, as our analyses of Argentina and Mexico provide support for our argument that heterogeneous subnational cultures are often masked by country-level means and that subnational political contexts are a source of that political cultural heterogeneity.

This has significant consequences both for the development prospects of these subnational regimes and for democratic consolidation at the national level in a region characterized by the uneven processes of subnational democratization that serve as the focus of this book. Indeed, if local political context is decisive in shaping cultural orientations toward democracy itself, even regimes that have transitioned to democracy at the national level will have to work harder to ensure that similar processes of liberalization take place across the subnational units found within them. Individuals in uneven democracies have very different interactions with politics and the regime itself, depending on the local context in which they are embedded. This chapter argues that those divergent experiences require additional enquiry.

A clear alternative explanation to the admittedly tentative causal claim that we make regarding one's provincial political context shaping her views toward democracy is that culture comes first and, in fact, plays a role in the continuation of subnational one-party political regimes. Though this scenario is possible, it seems unlikely to us that citizens of 16 of the 54 states and provinces across two countries on two continents would share an authoritarian political culture while their compatriots living in the remaining 38 subnational units would not. If our study were confined to those U.S. states that are traditionally viewed as constituting the "Old South" with a shared history of slavery and agricultural economies, then such an alternative explanation of culture contributing to the emergence of a certain type of provincial political regime would be far more plausible. But in our study, there is sufficient heterogeneity across our 16 dominant-party provinces (circa 2014) in terms of geography, socioeconomic and human development levels, and ethnic diversity to make such a story unlikely.

In claiming that the causal arrow does not run from culture to subnational regime type, we do not mean to suggest that a society's political culture does not influence the nature of politics within that society. Indeed, as we previously discussed, the most likely scenario that we see at work in the dominant-party states and provinces of this study is one of a self-reinforcing process wherein citizens forced to play the game of machine politics (or suffer the consequences) adapt their political attitudes and behaviors accordingly, and, as a consequence, contribute to the continuation of the machine. This process, however, does not change our position that from both a theoretical and empirical perspective, the distinct attitudinal, experiential, and behavioral citizen profiles that have emerged in our dominant-party and multiparty cases are most likely a result of the distinct ways in which the game of politics is played in the two types of systems.

This story then suggests that some type of shock to this vicious cycle needs to occur in order to break out of it. Such a shock, it seems, recently (June 2016) occurred in Mexico as the PRI suffered defeat for the first time in gubernatorial elections in the dominant-party states of Durango, Tamaulipas, Veracruz, and Quintana Roo. All of these defeats were a product of internal splits within the PRI, widespread dissatisfaction with the performance of the party nationally, and the forging of opposition alliances between ideologically opposed parties in order to oust the PRI from the governor's office. This confluence of events that resulted in the watershed defeat of these dominant-party enclaves is the type of shock that appears necessary to dislodge an entrenched dominant party from power. The fact that these types of defeats have been far less common in Argentina highlights the typical absence of strong, established opposition forces in that country as well as the continued strength, until recently perhaps, of the Peronist party at all levels of government. It is with this question of how dominant-party regimes can be dislodged, and what impact that may have on the attitudes toward democracy of citizens who have lived in those regimes, that we end this chapter and move on to an exploration of how these distinct attitudinal patterns manifest themselves in the political behaviors of citizens living in dominant-party systems.

6

Severed Linkages

Distorted Accountability in Dominant-Party Enclaves[*]

If elections really boil down to "the economy, stupid," winning reelection in 2019 would have seemed to be a tall task for the incumbent governor of Santa Cruz province, Alicia Kirchner. According to a study by economic think tank Federico Muñoz y Asociados, Santa Cruz experienced the most significant economic recession of any Argentine province from 2015 to 2018—a whopping 15.7 percent decline in overall productivity (Iglesia 2019). During that time, a provincial balance-of-payments crisis resulted in diminished and delayed paychecks for thousands of public employees. On numerous occasions during Alicia's first term, many of those same public employees led work stoppages, and even violent protests in front of the provincial legislature that culminated with police repression and several serious injuries (Arias 2017). Having long been one of Argentina's wealthiest provinces, the economic maelstrom that characterized the *santacruceña* governor's entire mandate seemed too severe for even the most gifted politician to weather.

But Alicia had a few important arrows left in her quiver. The first was that her sister-in-law, ex-two-term president Cristina Fernández de Kirchner, was now on the national Peronist ticket next to presidential candidate Alberto Fernández, and the Santa Cruz governorship would be decided on the same day that *santacruceños* were also voting in the national primary elections. Due to a quirk in the Santa Cruz electoral system known as *la ley de lemas*, in which multiple candidates from the same party can run for the same office, but the votes accrued by each of those individuals are ultimately passed on to the leading party vote getter, the fact that voters were casting ballots for both their preferred presidential ticket and governor would prove important. Peronism is king in Santa Cruz, and so even citizens who might have had no

[*] Some of the results presented in this chapter originally appeared in "Severed Linkages: Distorted Accountability in Uneven Regimes" (2018), published in *Comparative Political Studies* 51(10): 1314–1350.

Life in the Political Machine. Jonathan T. Hiskey and Mason W. Moseley, Oxford University Press (2020). © Oxford University Press.
DOI: 10.1093/oso/9780197500408.001.0001

love lost for Alicia and voted for another PJ candidate eventually saw their votes count toward the final tally of the most prominent name on the ballot.

The second key factor in Alicia's favor was that Santa Cruz continued to stand as a prototype for the single-party monopolization of state resources, three decades after the inauguration of the Kirchner machine in the early 1990s. By one estimate, 45,000 of Santa Cruz's 270,000 inhabitants were public employees in 2018 (Lisoni 2018)—with roughly 50 percent of formal sector workers getting their checks from the provincial state (Sticco 2015). According to Carlos Lisoni (2018), many of the citizens who received state salaries were only temporary workers (*contratados*), rather than full-time employees (*de planta*), meaning that their economic situations were precarious—fundamentally dependent on which party holds control of the provincial government. The foundation for this capture of state resources by the Peronist Party began in earnest under Néstor Kirchner, Alicia's brother, when he was initially elected governor in 1991. He then put the finishing touches on this political machine when he succeeded in reforming the provincial constitution to allow for indefinite reelection in 1998. When Néstor departed the governorship in 2003 after winning the Argentine presidency, he left the machine running for his successor.

By this point, it should come as no surprise that Alicia won the 2019 gubernatorial election by a healthy margin, in spite of one of the most adverse economic situations of any province in the country, which was itself wracked by turmoil. In earlier chapters of this book, we visited the cases of San Luis, Argentina, and Edomex, Mexico—two dominant-party enclaves where despite wide swings in the standard metrics of an incumbent government's performance, such as economic growth and crime reduction, the ruling party has rarely (until the 2017 Edomex elections) faced a serious electoral challenge, routinely winning by double-digit margins even as their partisan counterparts at the national level suffered convincing defeats.

In this book, we have explored the ways in which such sustained dominance of a provincial political system manifests itself in terms of the political attitudes and experiences of citizens living within them. Our questions for this chapter are whether those citizens are distinct from their counterparts living in multiparty systems in terms of how they behave on Election Day, and whether their voting behavior reflects the workings of the political machine they must confront and interact with on a daily basis. Based on the evidence we offer below, it should become clear that our answer to both of these questions is a resounding "Yes."

Throughout these pages, we have discussed at length what we see as the key factors that bring about machine party dominance, focusing in particular on the strategic application of the rule of law, the equation of the local state apparatus with the party itself, and the tilting of the electoral playing field as a means of fending off challengers to the local machine. Notably absent from that discussion has been a focus on overt electoral fraud in which ballots are mismarked, miscounted, or misplaced. Though we certainly have evidence that such practices do, indeed, occur in dominant-party systems (e.g., Alvarez et al. 2008; Camp 2013; Greene 2007; Magaloni 2006), they typically are not decisive in the overwhelming electoral margins of victory that the incumbent party achieves. Rather, the bulk of these electoral landslides are made up by actual votes cast by actual citizens that are then counted in a reasonably fair fashion (Gervasoni 2018). This begs the question, then, as to whether or not citizens of dominant-party enclaves reward and punish incumbent politicians based on their perceived performance in such major issue areas as the economy, public service provision, and crime reduction. And if dominant-party citizens *do not* rely on standard performance metrics when casting their ballot, what is it that drives their continued electoral support of the machine? In this chapter, we examine this question through analysis of voting behavior in dominant-party enclaves.

While a vast literature has sought to understand how perceptions of government performance (particularly economic) factor into voters' evaluations of incumbents, much of this research has been carried out across political systems with relatively little internal variance in terms of the quality of democracy. Work on performance-based voting in uneven democratic systems, such as those found in Latin America, where such assumptions regarding the territorial dispersion of democratic norms and processes fail to hold, has been less frequent and often produced mixed results. In our view, one key to understanding these mixed findings lies at least in part in the ways that dominant-party enclaves shape the political attitudes and behaviors of those living within them.

Building on the argument and evidence presented to this point, we posit that in subnational contexts in which key elements of multiparty democracy, such as alternation in power, have taken hold, performance-based linkages between voters and their representatives should be evident. In subnational systems in which such elements *do not exist*, with a dominant party largely immune to electoral ouster through its use of a carrot-and-stick (*pan y palo*) approach to constituency relations, incumbent performance in such areas as security, public service delivery, and the economy should be less influential in the voting decisions of the electorate. Rather, as documented in Chapter 4, many individuals in these systems will base their votes on what private goods the dominant-party government provides them, rather than the incumbent's public performance. With such dynamics occurring at the subnational level across many of the region's countries, the mixed results scholars have found in crossnational analyses of economic voting, therefore, make more sense. It is not that accountability mechanisms are absent in these emerging democracies characterized by diminished or inconsistent performance voting in national elections—rather, it is that they take hold *unevenly* within national regimes characterized by disparate subnational political contexts.

By examining the electoral accountability thesis at the subnational level in two countries with highly diverse political regime landscapes, we continue our efforts to push forward our understanding of how regime unevenness manifests itself in the lives of citizens and such basic components of a democratic system as the relationship between voters and their representatives. Though we know increasingly more about when, where, and why performance-based voting is most likely to occur in democracies, we know little about what forms of electoral accountability may exist in the dominant-party enclaves that are the focus of this book. Through a comparison of the voting behavior of citizens living in these systems with their neighbors residing in multiparty systems, we gain tremendous leverage in identifying the extent to which one's local political system influences her relationship with elected officials.

In doing so, we also are able to further explore the linkage between regime unevenness at the subnational level and citizens' engagement with *national-level* political processes and actors. Building on previous research that finds that subnational system characteristics and interactions with local officials influence individuals' evaluations of national-level political processes (e.g., Cleary and Stokes 2006; Hiskey and Bowler 2005; Seligson 2002; Vetter 2002), we find support for the proposition that dominant-party systems not only affect the electoral connection between citizens and their provincial-level officials but also influence how these same citizens evaluate national-level politicians. This scaling up of the distorted electoral connections between citizens and their representatives that we find in both Argentina and Mexico has important implications for the democratization projects of these two countries, as well as the many others with similarly uneven political landscapes.

Performance and Voting in Emerging Democracies

Whether in the form of Downs's (1957) treatise on how individuals weigh economic performance when choosing candidates, Bill Clinton's 1992 U.S. presidential campaign mantra of "it's the economy, stupid" or the myriad economic explanations for Donald Trump's victory in the 2016 U.S. presidential election (Campbell et al. 2017), economic factors have long been posited to affect individuals' choices on Election Day. Indeed, the literature on economic voting is among the most well-developed lines of research in the more general topic of voting behavior. As we noted above, however, though a general consensus exists with respect to the significance of economic performance for an incumbent government's electoral prospects in established, high-quality democracies (e.g., Anderson 1995; Downs 1957; Duch 2001; Duch and Stevenson 2008; Fiorina 1981; Key 1966; Kramer 1971; Lewis-Beck 1988; Powell and Whitten 1993),[1] there is much less agreement on the role economic performance plays in the voting behavior of individuals living in emerging democracies. And with respect to voting behavior in subnational dominant-party enclaves, we know very little at all.

Initially, much of the research on this question in regions like Africa, Eastern Europe, and Latin America offered mixed results regarding the prevalence of economic voting. For example, while research across multiple African countries uncovered some evidence of economic voting, other determinants of vote choice like ethnicity have often outweighed economic variables in terms of causal importance (Arriola 2005; Posner and Simon 2002). Likewise, Stokes (1996) argues that basic economic voting models might misrepresent voters' calculus in young democracies, while Remmer and Gélineau (2003) offer evidence in Argentina for national, but not provincial, economic voting.

Recent empirical studies of emerging democracies have uncovered a more robust relationship between economic considerations and support for the incumbent but find that this relationship is contingent on regime characteristics (Gélineau and Singer 2015; see also Singer 2011). For example, research on countries emerging from the breakup of the Soviet Union suggests that economic voting depends, in part, on the nature of the incumbent party's

---

[1] It should be noted that the relative impact of performance evaluations has been liked to contextual factors and characteristics of individuals (e.g., Anderson 2000; Carlin and Singh 2015; Gomez and Wilson 2001; Powell and Whitten 1993).

relationship to the democratic transition itself, as the decision confronting voters in transitional elections is distinct from the "referendum model" of economic voting derived from established democracies (Tucker 2006). Benton (2005) finds that Latin American voters can hold *multiple* parties accountable for poor performance in contexts characterized by frequent economic crisis, when more than one party is associated with past economic downturns. Singer and Carlin (2013) offer a useful summary of this extensive literature, highlighting the role that "political, economic, and institutional contexts of elections" (740) play in the extent to which individuals base their votes on the state of the economy in emerging democratic systems.

"Clarity of responsibility" has emerged as the mechanism most often used to explain crossnational variation in performance-based voting, with some institutional frameworks better enabling voters to apportion blame for economic struggles than others (e.g., Powell and Whitten 1993; Anderson 2000; Duch and Stevenson 2008; Carlin and Singh 2015). Parliamentary democracies with cabinets composed solely of members from the prime minister's party offer an example of a high level of clarity of responsibility, whereby virtually any government misstep is more easily attributed by voters to the party in power (Anderson 2000; Duch and Stevenson 2008; Powell 2000; Powell and Whitten 1993; Whitten and Palmer 1999). Conversely, in the case of coalition governments, systems with multiple veto points (e.g., the president, legislature, and central bank), or nonconcurrent elections, attributing culpability is a much more difficult task and is thus associated with lower levels of economic voting (Anderson 1995; Samuels 2004). Duch and Stevenson (2008; see also Carlin and Singh 2015) find that where there is a high degree of state control over economic policy, voters are more likely to punish incumbents for perceived mismanagement. Federal systems also have been found to muddy the waters, making blame attribution more difficult for voters as they must balance the relative culpability of provincial and national-level politicians for an economic downturn (Atkeson and Partin 1995). The clarity of responsibility logic also applies to polarized contexts, which offer distinct ideological alternatives, and presidential systems in which the president's party also possesses a majority in the legislature (Gélineau and Singer 2015). As Carlin et al. (2015a) note in their summary of performance-based voting research in Latin America, "heterogeneity in performance voting not only reflects voters' distinct agendas but also voters' ability to assign responsibility for policy outcomes" (279).

These works underscore the important role that institutions can play in moderating the electoral connection between voters and their representatives by either highlighting or diminishing the salience of recent performance in voters' evaluations of their elected officials. Missing from this research, however, is a focus on the impact that such practices as clientelism and corruption, which we have identified as essential parts of dominant-party machines, might have on voters' decision calculus. We, therefore, take as our point of departure this focus on the ways in which formal political institutions influence how people vote and proceed to look at the determinants of voting behavior in a set of subnational political contexts in which informal institutions such as vote buying are commonplace. As we have outlined in previous chapters and discuss in more detail in this chapter, our expectation is that voters in dominant-party enclaves will behave in ways that do not comport with the economic voting perspective. Rather, the driving forces behind voting behavior in local contexts characterized by dominant-party machines will be less about the incumbent government's overall performance in such areas as the economy and public service provision, and more about the specific private relationships the system has developed with citizens.

Accountability in Dominant-Party Systems

Taking as a given the regime unevenness we find in emerging democracies across the world, our core expectation in this book is that the political attitudes and behaviors of citizens living in uneven regimes will differ, in part, as a function of the distinct subnational political contexts in which they find themselves. With respect to electoral accountability, in subnational contexts in which at least minimally competitive elections have taken hold and citizens have evidence that alternation in the party of the governor can happen, we should find that voters behave in ways consistent with the expectations of the performance-based voting literature that rests on the core assumption that voters are willing and able to hold their elected officials accountable for their performance in office, economic and otherwise.

On the other hand, when no concrete evidence exists that those in power will ever relinquish that power, this core assumption of the performance-based voting literature will *not necessarily hold*. As elaborated in Chapters 2 and 3, several features of such dominant-party enclaves suggest that rather than rely on standard performance-based metrics on which to base their evaluations of incumbent governments, citizens will, instead, be driven by the clientelistic linkages that tend to prevail in such contexts (see Chapter 4) and the risk-aversive behavior that those same officials hope will be a consequence of citizens' equation of the dominant party with the state (Morganstern and Zechmeister 2001).

If an individual sees no chance of "throwing the bums out" with her vote, one alternative becomes toleration of, if not participation in, the game of dominant-party politics in which selling one's vote, pursuing economic gains through the state, and "going along to get along" becomes a strategy of survival, if not prosperity. Simply put, our expectation is that when an individual's provincial political system does not provide or allow for democratic linkages between citizen and state, the mechanisms driving the performance-based voting thesis will falter, leaving one's vote choice, if, indeed, she chooses to vote, influenced by other factors such as the incumbent's ability to selectively provide what should be public goods as a way to reward and punish voting behavior.

Moving to how these subnational dynamics might affect individuals' engagement with their national political system, we recall Tip O'Neill's well-worn aphorism, "all politics is local" (1993). Much of what citizens know and believe about politics likely comes from their experiences in their own communities. When individuals are embedded in distributive networks, in which the dominant machine touts itself as the sole purveyor of economic advancement, and citizens learn that politics is a fundamentally clientelistic, rather than programmatic, game at the provincial level, we argue that these norms and behaviors can seep into the ways in which they engage with and evaluate even their *national*-level politicians. Whereas potential heuristics regarding the current state of the economy, the quality of public services, or levels of insecurity weigh heavily on the minds of individuals who see the connection between party platforms and policy outcomes on a day-to-day basis, such cues might evade the voting calculus of citizens situated in less democratic contexts. As Greene (2007) notes in his "resource theory" of single-party dominance (6), a key tool for incumbents in dominant-party systems is the use of "dramatic resource advantages . . . to supplement policy appeals with patronage goods that bias voters in their favor" (5). If accountability mechanisms between constituents and politicians are distorted in dominant-party enclaves, these distortions may then also affect how citizens evaluate national-level institutions and actors (Cleary and Stokes 2006; Vetter 2002).

At first glance, our expectations regarding the relative absence of performance-based voting connections in dominant-party enclaves may seem to challenge extant work that finds support for such connections. On the contrary, we view it as simply another way to evaluate the idea that voters *in a functioning democratic system* will rely on their views of the economy and other metrics of incumbent performance as reasonably effective heuristics to guide their voting behavior. The absence of evidence for performance-based voting in dominant-party enclaves, in our minds, suggests not that the underlying theoretical insights for such types of voting behavior are wrong, but, rather, that the political system in question has severed that particular form of electoral connection between citizens and representatives. As such, we expect to find support for this basic proposition through *the absence* of performance-based voting in dominant-party enclaves.

We should also point out that if voters in dominant-party enclaves do rely on incumbent performance as a basis for their vote, then a system in which the ruling party has never ceded power should offer an ideal "most likely" test for the "clarity of responsibility" proposition that the more unambiguous the chain of command is within a political system, the more voters will reward or punish that party based on its performance in such areas as the economy (e.g., Powell and Whitten 1993). Indeed, it is difficult to imagine a system with more clarity than one dominated by a single party and/ or individuals for decades. There is, then, a possibility, that we, in fact, find stronger evidence for performance voting in dominant-party enclaves than we will in multiparty systems. Given all that we have said about the workings of dominant-party enclaves in the preceding pages, however, our expectations lie on the side of finding limited evidence for such performance-based voting in dominant-party contexts.

A third scenario, of course, is that the standard performance metrics, such as the economy, healthcare, and security, simply do not affect the voting behavior of any citizens at the provincial level, regardless of the type of subnational political system they live in. Rather, public healthcare, levels of security, and economic conditions of a province may be viewed as beyond the control of its governor and, instead, as the responsibility of the national government, or the complex web of responsibility at the national level might make even performance-based voting for the president less likely. In this case, we should find limited evidence of performance voting regardless of whether the provincial political system is dominated by a single party or has transitioned to a multiparty environment.

In order to fully test these possibilities, we explore the role that three distinct performance metrics play in the electoral calculus of voters in dominant-party and multiparty systems. Recognizing that the standard pocketbook and sociotropic (or national) economic evaluations may, in the minds of voters, be outside the domain of their subnational elected officials, we explore the connection between citizens' evaluations of and experiences with not only the economy but also two other areas of government performance that are arguably more directly related to provincial-level governing responsibilities and highly relevant to the daily lives of most citizens: security and healthcare.

Data and Measurement

To test our argument, we once again turn to the AmericasBarometer data from the 2008, 2010, and 2012 national surveys of Argentina and Mexico along with our simple, but to this point effective, indicator of one's subnational political context—whether or not alternation in control of the gubernatorial office has occurred within the previous 25 years.[2] Since 2004, the AmericasBarometer has measured performance evaluations and vote intentions using national probability samples of voting-age adults in dozens of countries throughout the Western hemisphere. These surveys, carried out every two years, include close to 4,500 respondents in both Argentina and Mexico when we pool the national samples from 2008, 2010, and 2012.

Dependent Variables: Prospective Vote for Governor and President

Because we cannot measure respondents' evaluations of key issue areas immediately prior to the latest election, we rely on items that ask for the respondent's "prospective vote choice" for president and governor as our dependent variables in the models in this chapter.[3] The wording of the items

---

[2] We lack data on gubernatorial vote choice and sociotropic economic evaluations for Mexico in 2014, requiring that we confine our analysis to the period from 2008 to 2012.

[3] Given problems related to vote recall, even in important elections like those for president and governor, we believe prospective vote choice is a preferable measure notwithstanding potential issues of endogeneity that we address in this chapter.

is as follows: "If the next presidential/gubernatorial elections were being held this week, what would you do?" The options include (1) "Wouldn't vote," (2) "Would vote for the incumbent candidate or party," (3) "Would vote for a candidate or party different from the current administration," and (4) "Would go to vote but would leave the ballot blank or would purposely cancel my vote." Because our only clear expectations concern whether or not an individual will support the incumbent party, we recode the variable 0 = vote for an opposition party or candidate and 1 = vote for the incumbent. We also, however, pursue an alternative approach that makes full use of the survey response options provided to respondents in our two prospective vote items.[4]

The presidential election item was included in each survey year (2008, 2010, 2012) for both countries, allowing for a total of 6,993 respondents, while the gubernatorial election item only appears in the 2010 Mexico survey and the 2010 and 2012 Argentine surveys, resulting in an N of 3,425. Given the dichotomous nature of the dependent variable(s), all of the results presented in this chapter come from logistic regression models of prospective vote choice. Following Linz and de Miguel's (1966) advice regarding comparative studies of subnational units in multiple countries, and the approach utilized in previous chapters, we model prospective choice on pooled data from both countries, while also including fixed effects for country and year.[5]

---

[4] Following the example of Duch and Stevenson (2008), multinomial logit models are probably the best choice for modeling performance voting using individual-level data, particularly when there are multiple options for opposition parties. However, given that the AmericasBarometer only offers respondents the options of (1) the incumbent, (2) *any* opposition party, (3) abstention, and (4) casting an invalid ballot, we would only be comparing two outcomes—that is, voting for the incumbent candidate or party vis-à-vis an opposition candidate or party—as our theoretical approach does not produce any clear observable implications regarding abstention or invalid voting. We, therefore, present results of logistic regression models in this chapter, comparing only prospective votes for the incumbent and opposition, while reporting results from full multinomial logit models in the Appendix Tables A.4–A.11. From a statistical standpoint, these approaches are almost exactly the same and produce nearly identical results.

[5] To account for the possibility that the two countries are simply too different to pool together in models of vote choice, we run separate country-specific models and report results in the Appendix (Tables A.12–A.13). The results are largely consistent with findings from the pooled sample.

Gauging Performance Evaluations: Beyond the Economic Vote

To measure individuals' performance evaluations, we utilize questions from the AmericasBarometer surveys that ask respondents about their personal and national economic circumstances, as well as their evaluations of the government's performance in terms of security and public health services. The first of the economic questions measures "pocketbook" evaluations, or an individual's assessment of her personal economic situation (see Appendix for question wording). This item has been found by some to have an important impact on vote choice in democratic contexts (e.g., Markus 1998). The second question measures an individual's "sociotropic" evaluation of the economy—that is, how she views the larger national economic picture, independent of her own personal situation (Kiewiet 1983; Kinder and Kiewiet 1981). Each question has been recoded 0 (negative)—100 (positive) for ease of interpretation.

As we noted previously, respondents may reasonably view the economy as a national issue, outside the domain of their provincial governor. As such, we also explore citizens' evaluations of other relevant areas of government performance. The first concerns citizens' evaluations of their local public health services. Here we employ a measure that explicitly asks respondents to assess the adequacy of their local health system, asking the following: "And thinking about this city/area where you live, are you very satisfied, satisfied, dissatisfied, or very dissatisfied with the condition of public health services?"[6] Given that in both Argentina and Mexico, decentralization reforms over the past 30 years have transferred much of the responsibility for the provision of such public services as education and healthcare to the provincial and local levels (e.g., Falleti 2010), we should expect individuals' responses to this item to help explain their expected vote for the governor.[7]

Our final performance metric focuses on the issue of crime. Here we employ an item that asks respondents the following: "To what extent would you say the current administration improves citizen security?"[8] Admittedly, this item contains considerable ambiguity in terms of which level of "incumbent government" it is referring to, provincial or national. However, we argue that

---

[6] For all question wording and descriptive statistics, see the Appendix Table A.1.
[7] This question was only included in the 2012 AmericasBarometer surveys, resulting in a smaller N in all models that include this variable.
[8] 100-point scale; 0 = "Not at all"; 100 = "A lot."

evaluations of the government's handling of issues related to security should matter for both local- *and* national-level vote intentions, given the primacy of the issue in both Argentina and Mexico, and the extent to which levels of government cooperate in combatting crime.[9]

For each policy area, we have some reason to believe that these performance-based considerations will weigh particularly heavily on the minds of voters in Argentina and Mexico. Given the territorial unevenness in terms of violent crime rates in Mexico (see Molzahn et al. 2013), as well as the country's multiple layers of law enforcement, we expect citizens to hold both state- and national-level officials responsible for perceived levels of insecurity. Moreover, despite the fact that Argentina has relatively low violent crime rates by regional standards, Argentines ranked second in Latin America in terms of their *perceptions* of insecurity during the years under study (LAPOP 2012). And as Pérez (2015; see also Cruz 2008) finds in his assessment of crime and voting in Latin America, it is perceptions of insecurity, rather than actual crime victimization, that most often drives voter evaluations of incumbents (342). This policy area, then, should be one that is particularly salient in subnational contexts in which performance-based voting occurs. With respect to healthcare, most citizens have direct experience with their country's health system, ranging from those that have received high-quality care to those unable to access any type of care. Though government responsibility for healthcare varies and is often complex, given this issue area's prominence in the lives of most individuals, attribution of blame and credit may be directed toward both national and subnational officials, particularly given the fact that the survey item explicitly asks respondents about the quality of healthcare in their community.

To assure that we are making valid inferences about the association between performance evaluations and prospective vote choice across subnational contexts, we include a number of control variables in each of the vote choice models presented in this chapter. First, in each model, we control for several factors that are thought to affect individual voting patterns, including sex, age, wealth quintile, level of education, whether the individual lives in an urban or rural area, and her relative interest and involvement in politics. We also include an indicator for whether or not the person is a member of the same party as either the incumbent governor and/or president (depending

---

[9] We also used another security-related variable, which simply measures perceived levels of insecurity with no mention of the current government, and the results were similar.

on the model), as well as a three-category variable that provides a measure of provincial level of development. We account for country- or time-specific effects by including dummy variables for the country (base category = Mexico) and year of the survey (base category = 2008). The models also include all other performance evaluations, and an indicator for citizen preferences regarding the state's role in generating employment, which is discussed in the following section.[10]

Further, to ameliorate the potential problem that certain variables may drive vote choice more in one country than the other, we include controls for several factors that have been highlighted as important in the literature on voting patterns in Argentina and/or Mexico. In Mexico, voting is essentially voluntary, whereas Argentina maintains a compulsory voting system, albeit with weak penalties. However, we include a control for past turnout to attempt to capture habitual voters. In both regimes, we expect that vote trafficking might influence vote choice (e.g., Fox 1994; Stokes 2005); therefore, we include a variable for whether or not respondents have received an offer of some kind of material reward in exchange for their vote in past elections. Given Mexico's relatively higher levels of religiosity (LAPOP 2012), we include a control variable for the importance of religion to respondents. Last, to account for the potential that ethnicity might be an important driver of vote choice in Mexico, but not Argentina, we include a dummy variable for indigenous self-identification. Because several of these questions were only asked in 2010 and 2012, we also run reduced models of presidential vote choice on larger samples, which allows us to draw from the 2008 national surveys of Argentina and Mexico as well.

Given the parsimonious nature of our measure for dominant-party enclaves, and that this simple dichotomous variable undoubtedly overlooks gradations of electoral competition within the dominant-party category, we also include a more nuanced measure of subnational democracy to serve as a control for variations in competitiveness. In his work on fiscal federalism and subnational democracy in Argentina, Gervasoni (2010b, 2018) uses provincial electoral data and factor analysis to produce subnational democracy scores that tap two key dimensions of democracy: contestation and constraints on power (see Dahl 1971). We employ a modified version of his measure for use across both Argentine provinces and Mexican states, taking

---

[10] We include all performance variables with the exception of health service evaluations, which come from a question that was only asked in 2012 and, thus, would greatly reduce the number of observations.

into account the relevant differences in the subnational electoral laws of the two countries. For a detailed explanation of the construction of these subnational democracy scores, see the Appendix.

Results

Before fully analyzing the extent to which voters in dominant-party enclaves based their electoral decisions at least in part on the incumbent's performance, we explore the mechanisms we posit are at work that make dominant-party citizens less likely to use government performance as a guide to their vote—widespread support of an extensive role for the state in economic affairs and common experiences with vote buying. First, we find that citizens living in dominant-party enclaves tend to report higher levels of support for the state as a primary provider of employment. We view this as an indication of the extent to which dominant-party citizens equate the local political machine with the state. In addition to their higher odds of encountering clientelism and corruption (Chapter 4), then, we contend that this preference for an active state will correlate with support for the machine and will lessen the importance of perceived incumbent performance in the voting calculus of dominant–party system citizens.

We then proceed to analyze performance voting for the governor across distinct subnational political contexts. Here we find strong evidence for performance-based electoral evaluations among citizens living in multiparty systems. In other words, in multiparty contexts, citizens appear to behave exactly as we would expect—the more they approve of the incumbent's performance in a certain issue area, whether it is the economy, crime, or healthcare, the more likely they will be to express their electoral support for the incumbent. Conversely, we find a much weaker relationship—and on certain performance metrics, no relationship at all—in dominant-party enclaves. Across all three of the issue areas we examine, respondents' views of incumbent performance in dominant-party systems makes little difference in whether or not they will support the incumbent governor or party on the ballot.

We conclude our analysis with an assessment of the extent to which these differences in respondents' reliance on performance as a tool to evaluate incumbents at the provincial level also emerge in their electoral evaluations of national-level incumbents. Our findings suggest that it is, indeed, the case that an individual's subnational political context shapes not only her electoral decision at the provincial level, but also when evaluating national-level officials.

Causal Mechanisms: State Dependence in Dominant-Party Enclaves

One key component of our argument regarding dominant parties' ability to remain in power rests on the efforts by incumbent officials to cultivate the perception that the machine is tantamount to the state in order to secure political support. In such a system, we then should find a citizenry that tends to be more in favor of state involvement in the economy, for example, than those citizens living in systems in which the economic power of the state is not deployed in the name of the dominant party (e.g., Gervasoni 2010b; Greene 2007; McMann 2005). As Magaloni (2006) and others (McMann 2005) have argued, one consequence of state penetration in economic affairs will be that voters will likely be more risk averse in casting their ballots, as they fear that ousting the hegemonic party might result in them losing their economic lifeline developed under the dominant-party system (see, e.g., Morgenstern and Zechmeister 2001). As we have noted before, we fully recognize that within our category of dominant-party enclaves, there likely exists substantial variation with respect to such factors as the degree of economic dependence among citizens (see Giraudy 2015), but as a general distinguishing characteristic of dominant-party enclaves, we view the conflation of the party with the state apparatus as vital to understanding the political attitudes and behaviors of citizens nested in such systems.

The AmericasBarometer includes a battery of questions in each round that gauge citizen preferences regarding the proper role of the state in managing the economy. One of these items measures support for the notion that the state should be the primary source of employment, asking, "The [country] government, more than the private sector, should be primarily responsible for creating jobs. To what extent to do you agree or disagree with this statement?" If we are correct in our claim that officials in dominant-party regimes intentionally seek to conflate the party with the state, we expect that connections between an active state and one's economic livelihood should be stronger in dominant-party enclaves than in multiparty contexts. As a consequence, we should observe in dominant-party systems that one's preference for an active state role in generating employment is associated with her level of support for the incumbent, while in multiparty states, there should be no such connection between one's views on the proper role of the state in the economy and her degree of support for the incumbent.

When we subject this interaction to multivariate regression, controlling for demographic variables, partisanship, ideology, and other performance evaluations (see Appendix for full model results), we find that views regarding the state's responsibility to provide employment seem to be associated with supporting the incumbent in dominant-party enclaves, but not in multiparty regimes (Figure 6.1). These analyses are only preliminary, as Argentine provinces and Mexican states differ a great deal in terms of rates of public employment, and the degree to which dominant-party systems endeavor to cultivate dependence on the provincial state (Giraudy 2015). However, we argue that they are illustrative of the mechanisms that we see working to diminish the role of incumbent performance for voters in dominant-party enclaves.

We utilized a similar approach to assess the influence of vote buying on vote choice in dominant-party enclaves, but results were inconclusive. While we know from Chapter 4 that clientelism is more widespread in dominant-party systems, we find little evidence that it is actually *more effective* in such contexts—in other words, targets and nontargets of clientelistic exchange appear similarly likely to support the incumbent machine in dominant-party

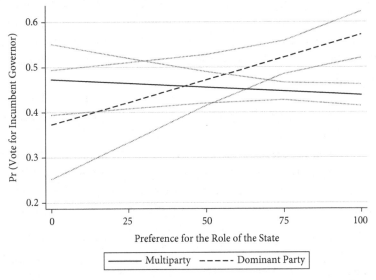

Figure 6.1. Preference for active state role in providing employment and gubernatorial vote choice. Pr = probability.

enclaves. One potential reason for this null result is that vote buying might actually be more strategically useful when elections are competitive. Weitz-Shapiro (2014) finds that in municipalities where elections are tight and a large share of the voting population is poor, clientelism is more prevalent, given that parties view it as particularly effective under such conditions. Another reason could be that citizens in dominant-party states and provinces receive their "reward" for loyalty to the machine via other forms of exchange—namely, public employment or more regularly disbursed social programs.

Performance-Based Voting in Gubernatorial Elections in Argentina and Mexico

Having established that voters in dominant-party systems are more likely to be exposed to vote-buying offers and street-level forms of corruption, and that higher levels of support for state involvement in the economy are associated with support for the incumbent in such contexts, we now look at whether or not these dominant-party enclave characteristics translate into distinct patterns of voting behavior among citizens living in such systems.

In Table 6.1, we report results from four predictive models of gubernatorial vote choice in Argentina and Mexico.[11] Our theoretical perspective entails an interactive relationship between subnational regime type and performance evaluations, wherein such considerations will be more strongly correlated with prospective vote choice in multiparty contexts than in dominant-party states or provinces. Because our dichotomous measure for whether or not a province/state has undergone a transition is comparable across the two national contexts, we pool the data from Argentina and Mexico while including a country dummy and a comprehensive set of control variables.[12]

Focusing on the coefficients for the interaction terms, we find that three of the four coefficients are negative and significant at conservative levels ($p < .05$). In the case of sociotropic economic evaluations, having a positive view of the overall economic situation of the country is strongly associated with supporting

---

[11] If we run models of gubernatorial vote choice that do not include an indicator for subnational regime type at all, on the whole performance evaluations do tend to correlate with vote choice in Argentina and Mexico. In other words, if we ignored subnational context, we might come to very different conclusions regarding the presence of performance voting in each of these regimes.

[12] Again, see Appendix for country-specific models run on split samples.

Table 6.1. Performance Evaluations and Gubernatorial Vote Choice by Subnational Regime Type (2010–2012)

VARIABLES	Prospective Vote for Governor (1 = Vote for Governor's Party; 0 = Vote for Opposition Party)			
	Model 1	Model 2	Model 3	Model 4
Female	0.293***	0.297***	0.101	0.305***
	(0.100)	(0.100)	(0.175)	(0.100)
Age	–0.002	–0.002	–0.006	–0.002
	(0.004)	(0.004)	(0.006)	(0.004)
Wealth (quintile)	0.036	0.036	0.042	0.037
	(0.039)	(0.039)	(0.070)	(0.039)
Interest in Politics	–0.003*	–0.003	–0.001	–0.003
	(0.002)	(0.002)	(0.003)	(0.002)
Education (level)	–0.310***	–0.309***	–0.543***	–0.314***
	(0.078)	(0.078)	(0.138)	(0.078)
Urban	–0.085	–0.073	0.087	–0.081
	(0.134)	(0.134)	(0.278)	(0.134)
President Copartisan	–0.003	–0.015	0.331	–0.041
	(0.173)	(0.174)	(0.336)	(0.174)
Governor Copartisan	1.339***	1.353***	1.158***	1.354***
	(0.154)	(0.154)	(0.333)	(0.154)
Voted in Last Election	–0.001	–0.001	–0.001	–0.001
	(0.001)	(0.001)	(0.004)	(0.001)
Indigenous	–0.267	–0.296	0.372	–0.286
	(0.318)	(0.318)	(0.765)	(0.317)
Importance of Religion	0.006***	0.006***	0.003	0.006***
	(0.002)	(0.002)	(0.003)	(0.002)
Received Vote-Buying Offer	–0.251*	–0.265*	–0.411	–0.261*
	(0.138)	(0.138)	(0.257)	(0.138)
Government Should Provide Jobs	0.001	0.001	–0.001	0.001
	(0.002)	(0.002)	(0.004)	(0.002)
Middle Income	0.054	0.091	0.892*	0.060
	(0.166)	(0.166)	(0.491)	(0.165)
High Income	–0.481***	–0.457***	–0.762***	–0.454***
	(0.127)	(0.127)	(0.252)	(0.127)
Subnational Democracy Score	–0.528***	–0.545***	–0.513***	–0.551***

Continued

Table 6.1. *Continued*

VARIABLES	Prospective Vote for Governor (1 = Vote for Governor's Party; 0 = Vote for Opposition Party)			
	Model 1	Model 2	Model 3	Model 4
	(0.083)	(0.083)	(0.150)	(0.084)
Argentina	0.026	0.026		0.047
	(0.158)	(0.158)		(0.158)
2012	0.867***	0.856***		0.853***
	(0.145)	(0.144)		(0.145)
Government Security Evaluation	0.010***	0.010***	0.011***	0.012***
	(0.002)	(0.002)	(0.003)	(0.002)
Pocketbook Economic Evaluation	0.000	−0.000	−0.008	0.000
	(0.003)	(0.003)	(0.005)	(0.003)
Sociotropic Economic Evaluation	0.013***	0.010***	0.020***	0.010***
	(0.003)	(0.002)	(0.005)	(0.002)
Health Services Evaluation			0.009**	
			(0.004)	
Dominant-Party Enclave	0.384	−0.128	1.543*	0.379
	(0.243)	(0.327)	(0.838)	(0.245)
Dominant–Party*Sociotropic	*−0.011***			
	(0.005)			
Dominant-Party*Pocketbook		*0.001*		
		(0.006)		
Dominant-Party*Health Services			*−0.032***	
			(0.013)	
Dominant-Party*Security				*−0.009***
				(0.004)
Constant	−0.862**	−0.785*	0.609	−0.884**
	(0.413)	(0.416)	(0.817)	(0.414)
Observations	2,130	2,130	793	2,130

Note: Standard errors in parentheses.

*p < 0.1; **p < 0.05; ***p < 0.01

the incumbent governor or her party in multiparty regimes but appears virtually unrelated to voting for the incumbent in dominant-party enclaves (Model 1). A similar story emerges in the case of citizens' evaluations of local public health services (Model 3). With respect to respondents' views of the

government's performance on issues relating to security, we find that in multiparty states those individuals with positive views of the government's handling of crime and security are significantly more likely to vote for the incumbent
governor than their counterparts with negative assessments of the government's
anticrime efforts (Model 4). For respondents in dominant-party enclaves, on
the other hand, evaluations of security provision have no significant association
with evaluations of the incumbent governor. In these provinces and states, the
chances of casting a vote for the incumbent are essentially the same regardless
of one's views on the government's performance in the area of security. The only
such pattern of findings that do not emerge as significant are those related to
pocketbook voting, for which there appears to be no difference in dominant-
party and multiparty systems (Model 2). This is not particularly surprising,
given the more oblique connection between personal economic circumstances
and government responsibility (e.g., Lewis-Beck 1988).

Figure 6.2 illustrates the divergent role that evaluations of government
efforts to improve security seem to play among individuals living in multiparty regimes and those living in dominant-party enclaves. In the former
group, a minimum to maximum change in one's perception of government
efforts to improve security nearly doubles the probability of supporting the
incumbent governor. In dominant-party enclaves, however, respondents'
evaluations of their government's anticrime efforts are weakly related to support for the incumbent (Figure 6.2). Thus, across evaluations of the overall
economic situation, citizen security, and the quality of health services—all
of which are at least partly provided for by local political actors in Argentina
and Mexico—we see the same pattern. In multiparty states, respondents'
prospective vote choice seems to be correlated with evaluations of government performance, while in dominant-party enclaves, performance, at least
in these issue areas, does not seem to matter nearly as much.[13]

---

[13] Regarding the issue of causality, one could argue that partisan attachments are driving performance evaluations, which is why they are correlated with vote choice—indeed, Pickup and Evans
(2013; Evans and Pickup 2010) present compelling evidence to that effect. This perspective contends
that respondents might say the incumbent has done a good job combatting insecurity because they
already support that party, which, in turn, biases their evaluations. Throughout the chapter, we imply
that performance evaluations motivate vote choice, albeit without making overly strong claims regarding causality, knowing that with a cross-sectional analysis, there is real potential for reverse
causality. However, we do not think that this potential criticism undermines our results for one key
reason: Even if one's prospective vote is driving performance evaluations, that would still constitute
evidence that *some* connection between vote choice and performance exists in certain provinces, but
not others. Further, and perhaps most importantly, we can think of no reason why the potential for
reverse causality would exist in multiparty but not dominant-party states.

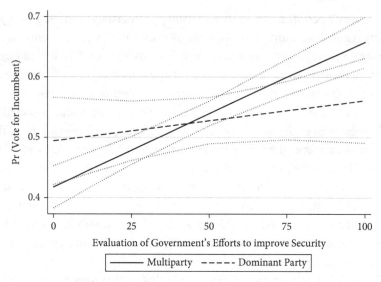

Figure 6.2. Evaluations of government's efforts to improve security and gubernatorial vote choice. Pr = probability.

Before moving to an analysis of how subnational political contexts influence national-level vote considerations, it is worth noting the largely consistent and intuitive performance of our extensive battery of control variables. As should be expected, when a respondent identifies with the party of the governor, she is more likely to offer support for the incumbent. Conversely, the more educated a respondent is the less likely she is to support the incumbent, speaking perhaps to the anti–status quo bias of more educated respondents.

Finally, and most significantly for this analysis, we find that the more electorally democratic a state or province is, based on our subnational democracy index, the less likely a respondent will be to support the incumbent. That this control appears to adequately capture the competitiveness of a state and produces a strongly significant, intuitive, and consistent result across the four models suggests that our dichotomous categorization of multiparty and dominant-party systems is, indeed, tapping a concept that, while certainly related to a system's electoral context, is in important ways independent from the competitiveness of gubernatorial elections. While competitive elections have often been viewed as a characteristic of high-quality democracies, and consistently uncompetitive elections as a sign of a less democratic regime, we have several examples from our two countries in which the authoritarian elements of dominant-party enclaves become most evident when the dominant party faces a credible electoral challenge. As noted in previous chapters, the 2017 gubernatorial election in the dominant-party state of Edomex serves as the most recent example of this. Faced with the prospect of losing power for the first time, the PRI's state political machine became highly visible and active (Semple 2017). This same tendency for a political machine to roar even louder when confronted with a viable electoral challenge can also be seen in the senatorial elections in San Luis, as described in Chapter 1.

Does Dominant-Party Context Matter for National Elections?

Having established that there is a stronger connection between performance evaluations and gubernatorial vote choice in multiparty provinces than in dominant-party systems, and that, instead, considerations related to the economic role of the provincial state and prevailing patron–client relationships seem to characterize relations between voters and their elected officials in dominant-party settings, we ask another vital question: Do these distinct subnational electoral environments influence how individuals weigh performance in *national* elections?

We might expect to find less evidence of this divergent pattern of performance-based voting in prospective presidential elections, given the potential disconnect between provincial and national politics. However, as we discussed previously, we view the severed electoral connections we have found at the subnational level to likely shape the ways in which individuals determine their vote choice for national-level offices as well. An individual conditioned to evaluate politicians based on whether an offer has been made for their vote, or whether their job with the state will remain intact, will likely apply these same decision-making criteria during a presidential election. Just as one's attitudes toward democracy and the national political system appear to be influenced by the characteristics and modus operandi of her provincial political system, so, too, might her thought process when it comes to casting a vote for the president.

As we present in Table 6.2 (and Figures 6.3 and 6.4), we do, in fact, find suggestive evidence that electoral connections between the president and voters differ substantially across dominant-party and multiparty regimes. The model results displayed in Table 6.2 assess the relative weight that

Table 6.2. Performance Evaluations and Presidential Vote Choice by Subnational Regime Type (2008–2012)

VARIABLES	*Prospective Vote for President* (1 = Vote for President's Party; 0 = Vote for Opposition Party)			
	Model 1	Model 2	Model 3	Model 4
Female	0.063	0.044	0.055	0.061
	(0.072)	(0.071)	(0.106)	(0.106)
Age	−0.008***	−0.008***	−0.006	−0.005
	(0.002)	(0.002)	(0.004)	(0.004)
Wealth (Quintile)	−0.090***	−0.081***	−0.145***	−0.143***
	(0.028)	(0.028)	(0.041)	(0.041)
Interest in Politics	−0.003**	−0.002	0.003	0.003*
	(0.001)	(0.001)	(0.002)	(0.002)
Education (Level)	−0.208***	−0.178***	−0.309***	−0.312***
	(0.056)	(0.056)	(0.082)	(0.082)
Urban	−0.040	−0.031	−0.100	−0.103
	(0.094)	(0.093)	(0.146)	(0.146)
President Copartisan	3.275***	3.314***	2.816***	2.778***
	(0.154)	(0.153)	(0.239)	(0.239)
Voted in Last Election			−0.000	0.000
			(0.002)	(0.002)
Indigenous			−0.420	−0.434
			(0.356)	(0.356)
Importance of Religion			0.001	0.001
			(0.002)	(0.002)
Received Vote-Buying Offer			−0.041	−0.057
			(0.145)	(0.145)
Middle Income	−0.356***	−0.353***	−0.135	−0.115
	(0.112)	(0.111)	(0.183)	(0.182)
High Income	−0.033	0.008	−0.067	−0.038
	(0.089)	(0.088)	(0.137)	(0.137)
Subnational Democracy Score	−0.284***	−0.282***	−0.145*	−0.167*
	(0.057)	(0.056)	(0.086)	(0.086)
Argentina	0.594***	0.762***	0.061	0.067
	(0.089)	(0.087)	(0.170)	(0.169)
2010	−0.518***	−0.581***		
	(0.092)	(0.091)		
2012	−0.033	−0.007	1.152***	1.137***

Table 6.2. *Continued*

| VARIABLES | Prospective Vote for President (1 = Vote for President's Party; 0 = Vote for Opposition Party) | | | |
	Model 1	Model 2	Model 3	Model 4
	(0.086)	(0.085)	(0.151)	(0.150)
Government Security Evaluation	0.018***	0.022***	0.021***	0.023***
	(0.001)	(0.002)	(0.002)	(0.002)
Sociotropic Economic Evaluation	0.016***		0.018***	0.016***
	(0.002)		(0.003)	(0.003)
Dominant-Party Enclave	0.210	0.161	0.121	0.187
	(0.174)	(0.170)	(0.274)	(0.278)
*Dominant-Party*Sociotropic*	*−0.008**		*−0.010*	
	(0.004)		*(0.006)*	
*Dominant-Party*Security*		*−0.005*		*−0.009**
		(0.003)		*(0.004)*
Constant	−1.039***	−0.746***	−1.439***	−1.460***
	(0.255)	(0.250)	(0.398)	(0.399)
Observations	4,648	4,672	2,236	2,236

Note: Standard errors in parentheses.
*$p < 0.1$; **$p < 0.05$; ***$p < 0.01$

sociotropic and security evaluations play in respondents' prospective vote choice. These are two areas where presidents typically bear some responsibility for performance in the eyes of voters. We find that for respondents in multiparty systems, sociotropic evaluations are more powerfully associated with presidential vote choice than they are in dominant-party enclaves (Models 1 and 3). Likewise, citizens' perceptions of the government's efforts to combat insecurity also seem to more strongly correlate with presidential vote choice in multiparty provinces than in dominant-party systems (Models 2 and 4).

Figure 6.3 displays the predicted probability that a respondent would report intentions to cast a vote for the incumbent president as a function of her views of the economy, after controlling for the other factors we have included in the model. We then run a similar model with an interaction term for security evaluations and dominant-party systems (Figure 6.4). In both cases, we find that such evaluations appear to matter more in the presidential vote

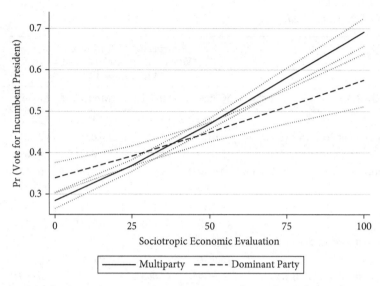

Figure 6.3. Sociotropic economic evaluations and presidential vote choice. Pr = probability.

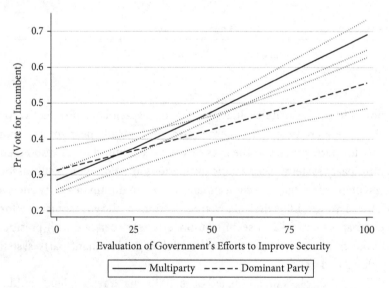

Figure 6.4. Evaluations of government's efforts to improve security and presidential vote choice. Pr = probability.

considerations of respondents living in multiparty systems than they do in dominant-party enclaves.

The coefficients for these interactions are statistically significant at $p < .05$ and $p < .10$ levels, respectively. However, it seems clear from the findings that the dynamic we identified at the subnational level is not quite as stark when applied to the national level. Performance evaluations of the president do seem to matter in dominant-party enclaves, just not as much as they do in multiparty systems. For example, whereas in multiparty provinces an increase from the least favorable to the most favorable evaluation of the national economic situation produces a near 40-point increase in the likelihood that a particular individual will support the incumbent president vis-à-vis a candidate from another party, a similar change produces only a 20-point increase in dominant-party systems (Figure 6.3). We observe a similar dynamic when it comes to evaluations of government efforts to improve security and presidential vote choice (Figure 6.4). Performance evaluations of presidents, thus, seem to matter in dominant-party enclaves, but significantly less so than they do in multiparty contexts.

In sum, these findings offer some support for the notion that in subnational systems in which viable political competition has taken root, performance-based evaluations serve as valuable heuristics on which citizens can lean when deciding how to cast their ballot. Indeed, our respondents in competitive local political environments appear capable of making somewhat sophisticated attributions of blame depending on the policy area. On the other hand, dominant-party enclaves distort performance-based voting, as individuals nested within political machines vote based on other considerations and are less likely to behave in the way so often described by political behavior scholars focused on advanced democracies. These findings also hold, to a lesser extent, for national elections, as local political environments seem to influence the extent to which performance evaluations correlate with *presidential* vote choice.

Conclusion

With the decline of Mexico's oil industry in the past 20 years, the state of Campeche, almost completely reliant on petroleum, has suffered more than a decade of economic recession. Its average gross state product "growth" rate between 2005 and 2011 was *negative 4.4 percent* (Rodríguez 2012, 254). The state's economic woes have continued in recent years, with its economy registering a fourth consecutive year of negative growth in 2017, shrinking an astounding 10.4 percent (INEGI 2019). Despite these nearly 15 years of economic malaise, widespread reports of high-profile incidents of corruption, and stagnant, if not declining, human development indicators (e.g., the state registered the highest maternal mortality rate in the country in 2013 [OECD 2015, 7]), as of 2019 the PRI had continued its nearly 90-year hold on the state's executive branch, winning the election in 2009 by 8 percentage points and increasing that margin of victory to 9 points in 2015. In this chapter, we have taken a further step toward a better understanding of how such clear signs of poor governance go unpunished by voters.

At their core, arguments for performance-based voting depend on the assumption that at least a minimal degree of democratic accountability exists within a political system between voters and elected officials, and that economic and other policy performance indicators will provide voters with a useful and easy-to-access metric with which they can enforce such accountability on Election Day. What we have examined in the preceding pages is the idea that this assumption does not hold for all democratic political systems today, particularly across the developing world.

As we have emphasized throughout this book, a defining characteristic of emerging democracies, from the former Soviet Bloc countries to Latin America, is a high degree of *intranational regime unevenness*. This internal heterogeneity has always existed—for evidence of that one need only look at the U.S. South throughout much of the 20th century. What is distinct about the recent global democratic landscape is how pervasive this unevenness has become (Gervasoni 2018). While established democracies such as the United States and European countries have arguably become more homogenous in terms of their internal democratic quality, the world is now dominated by relatively young, imperfect, and highly uneven democratic systems, many of which are beginning to reveal more and more authoritarian tendencies (e.g., Freedom House 2018). This global unevenness makes any crossnational study of performance voting problematic because a national label of "democracy" may, in fact, tell very little of the story going on within a particular country.

In this chapter, we look at the consequences of this unevenness for how citizens engage with and hold accountable their elected officials across distinct subnational electoral environments. Our findings suggest that we have identified yet another important, underexplored analytical path for scholars of political behavior that should help us better understand both the democratic institutional requirements for accountability mechanisms to operate and the implications of a highly uneven democratic landscape for voting behavior. In both Mexico and Argentina, voters in states and provinces living in dominant-party enclaves such as Santa Cruz and Campeche rely less on performance-based evaluations as a guide for how to vote, in gubernatorial elections *and* presidential elections, than do their counterparts in multiparty systems. Though much work remains to be done to fully understand the connections between dominant-party citizens and their elected officials, we have taken a first step in establishing that our conventional understanding of those connections as they exist in more democratic systems is mistaken.

In addition to highlighting the powerful role that subnational political institutions can play in shaping the political attitudes and behaviors of individuals, we also add an important caveat to the "clarity of responsibility" thesis that has received much attention and support in recent research (e.g., Carlin and Singh 2015; Duch and Stevenson 2008). In our cases of dominant-party enclaves, we have perhaps the clearest line of responsibility possible—the same party dominating politics for more than two decades. With this clarity, then, we might expect to find strong evidence of performance-based voting on the part of citizens who know exactly which party is responsible for governing outcomes in their state or province. Instead, due to the mechanisms we have identified that undercut, or sever, the lines of traditional electoral accountability between voter and elected officials, we find virtually no evidence of performance-based accountability at the ballot box. Thus, this chapter provides another strong example of the ways in which local political context influences individuals' political behavior, in this case how they evaluate their provincial *and* national elected officials. In the following chapter, we proceed to analyze one more potential consequence of dominant-party enclaves—*who* participates in politics, and *how*?

7

Stacking the Deck

Political Participation in Dominant-Party Enclaves

On June 16, 2019, Gildo Insfrán was elected governor of Formosa province for the seventh consecutive time. The election was not much different from previous ones—despite being one of Argentina's poorest, most unequal provinces, an overwhelming 71 percent of *formoseños* chose to renew their provincial executive for another term. When the governor took to Twitter on Election Night to congratulate the voters of Formosa on a great "celebration of democracy," he joyfully proclaimed that "together, we are invincible"—a statement that, after four decades of uninterrupted dominant-party rule, few in Formosa could reasonably dispute.

Over the course of his 24 years in power, Insfrán has built one of the most powerful provincial machines in Argentina. It was Insfrán himself who succeeded in reforming the provincial constitution to allow for indefinite reelection in 2003 (La Nación 2003), and he has since consolidated his hold on power through positioning himself as the embodiment of the provincial state, which in a far-flung, impoverished province like Formosa is the primary source of economic opportunity. Hugo Beck notes in his 2012 article on the Insfrán machine in Formosa, "the footprint of formoseño Peronism on political life since 1983, and especially since 1995, makes it difficult to differentiate the state from the governing party" (26). According to Beck, roughly 60 percent of *formoseños* depend on the provincial state for employment or social assistance, representing one of the highest rates in Argentina.

At the core of Insfrán's political dominance is a sophisticated clientelistic operation that endeavors to reward loyalists and punish opponents, not only on Election Day but throughout the interelectoral period as well. Never has that been more apparent than in the 2019 election. In the days preceding the vote, Insfrán ordered an advance on bonuses owed to state employees and pensioners that were supposed to be distributed at the end of June. He also delayed the arrival of utility bills that are normally mailed the first week of every month (Boerr 2019). These measures are consistent with a system

Life in the Political Machine. Jonathan T. Hiskey and Mason W. Moseley, Oxford University Press (2020). © Oxford University Press.
DOI: 10.1093/oso/9780197500408.001.0001

through which, "based on the needs of the most precarious sectors of society, the party uses public employment, housing, public works, targeted social assistance plans, and help with daily subsistence as elements of exchange" for political support, which includes voting and attendance of official party events (Beck 2012, 9).

But the means of control utilized by the Insfrán machine go beyond mere co-optation. The Formosa machine routinely threatens citizens with losing their jobs, with being denied access to public housing, or by preventing them from accessing social programs, if they are caught rocking the boat. Insfrán's machine has targeted civil society organizations for persecution, on occasion deploying provincial police to break up marches by autonomous indigenous groups in the eastern part of the province and has even invented grounds for detaining judges who issue unfavorable decisions (Roberts 2017). In an interview in which an opposition politician complained about issues related to extreme poverty and a lack of basic public services in rural parts of the province, the member of the Socialist Party eventually backtracked, saying, "Please, don't put any of this [in your article] . . . don't put my name. The last time they beat me up. They almost killed me" (Roberts 2017, "Dos advertencias"). The Formosa priest and former candidate for governor Francisco Nazar summed up the overwhelming obstacles to resisting dominant-party hegemony in Formosa:

> Fear and a lack of judicial recourse are the cause of a deterioration of the rule of law that all of us live here in Formosa. It manifests in the lack of an independent judiciary, the absence of criminal investigation, and total impunity in cases of human rights violations, abuses of power, and limits placed on freedom of expression . . . there is the feeling that we are all spied upon, and that those in positions of political power are protected by complete impunity. . . [the result is that] there aren't real channels for effective political participation, and it's a virtual impossibility to seek justice via formal juridical avenues (Nazar 2004, "Algunas cosas de nuestra realidad").

The case of Formosa draws our attention to a critical question regarding the impact of dominant-party enclaves on the citizens nested within them: How do the carrots and sticks deployed by machine parties affect how citizens participate in politics? In subnational contexts in which citizens are forced to either "go along to get along" or live in a persistent state of fear and persecution, what factors determine which citizens choose to leave the sidelines and enter the fray that is dominant-party political life? Undoubtedly, the determinants of political participation in dominant-party enclaves are quite different from what we would observe in fully democratic countries, and even in neighboring provinces and states where some degree of multiparty competition has taken hold. In this chapter, we tackle the question of the impact dominant-party enclaves have on *who* participates in politics, and *how*.

When considering the question of how a subnational political system shapes citizens' frequency and mode of participation in politics, we can draw quite a bit from crossnational research on the topic. An abundance of evidence, for example, suggests that participation tends to be higher in "consensus" systems of democracy when compared with their majoritarian counterparts (Karp and Banducci 2008; Lijphart 1999; Norris 1997; Anderson and Guillory 1997). We can also safely surmise that the 99.97 percent (give or take) of eligible voters who reportedly turned out to vote in North Korea's 2015 local elections did so in large part due to the characteristics and mobilizing tactics of that country's political regime (CNN 2017). Moving to a somewhat less extreme example, we have a rich and methodologically diverse body of research that highlights the various tools employed in such one-party regimes as pre-2000 Mexico to mobilize citizens politically, both on Election Day and for progovernment rallies when necessary (e.g., Camp 2013; Greene 2007; Magaloni 2006). Similarly, a growing body of research has highlighted political systems that intentionally inculcate economic dependence on the state to influence the scope and form of a citizenry's political engagement (e.g., McMann 2006).

With a few notable exceptions, however, we know very little about how subnational political systems shape individuals' participation in politics, and in what ways. Certainly Key (1949) and Mickey (2015) have shed much light on how the U.S. South's particular subnational one-party systems of the early-to-mid-20th century influenced the nature of participation in those contexts (see also Black and Black 1989). The clearest, and most obvious example, of the impact these subnational systems had on participation is found in the abysmally low voter turnout rates for blacks living in those states during that era (Key 1949). But in the current era of highly uneven emerging democracies, we lack systematic work on the ways in which distinct subnational systems of government that often exist alongside one another *within the same country* shape the patterns of citizen participation in politics that emerge within these subnational units.

We begin this chapter by reviewing extant research on political participation in less-than-democratic regimes, most of which has focused on crossnational variation in political behavior, rather than on within-nation differences in how citizens engage with politics. As we have noted in previous chapters, we see participation in dominant-party systems driven in large part by those key regime characteristics that allow such systems to persist—electoral malfeasance, the political application of the rule of law, and the deployment of the provincial state in the name of the dominant party machine. Here we focus primarily on voter turnout, participation in protests, and civic activism and explore how the distinct characteristics of dominant-party enclaves we have outlined to this point shape who participates in politics, and how.

Our expectations are threefold. First, we expect that common demographic predictors of participation in liberal democracies do not necessarily have the same impact on participation in dominant-party enclaves. We focus in particular on education, which we argue has a different effect on participation in contexts where the most politically aware citizens are those most likely to know the game is rigged. Second, we expect that partisanship exerts an important effect on the likelihood that an individual participates in a dominant-party system, whereas it is likely to have a lesser effect on participation patterns in multiparty regimes. Finally, we conclude by examining how efficacy is associated with participation in dominant-party enclaves. Instead of exhibiting drastically lower rates of internal and external efficacy, citizens of dominant-party enclaves seem to be characterized by *efficacy gaps* between individuals who count themselves among the politically favored class and those who do not.

In analyses of AmericasBarometer survey data from Argentina and Mexico (2008–2014), we find once again a striking role for one's subnational political system in the ways in which she engages with politics. These findings further support our contention that any effort to empirically evaluate, and understand, patterns of political attitudes and behavior in uneven democracies needs to account for the distinct subnational political environments found *within* those nationally democratic regimes.

Political Participation in Less-than-Democratic Regimes

Though we do not have much in the way of research on participation across distinct subnational political systems as a guide to our analysis of differential patterns of political behavior across the 23 provinces of Argentina and the 31 states of Mexico,[1] we can learn quite a bit from existing research on this question at the national level. From research on participation in democracies, for example, we know that such individual-level characteristics as education, age, gender, income, and, attitudinally, one's assessment of the economy (e.g., Dahlum 2018; Smets and van Ham 2013; Verba and Nie 1972) and political efficacy (Niemi et al. 1991) are important predictors of the degree to which she participates in politics. From this research we also find that in established democracies there tend to be lower levels of the more overt forms of clientelism-induced participation in which citizens exchange their political voice for either monetary or nonmonetary rewards (Stokes et al. 2013).

Yet crossnational research from advanced democracies tells us little about how citizens engage politically with more authoritarian political regimes—a research question that poses significant obstacles for empirical inquiry and requires a different set of assumptions regarding the motivations of participants in politics. One key takeaway from the limited work there is on participation in nondemocratic regimes is that the *amount* of participation often obscures the *motivations and quality* of that participation. Indeed, even when participation is widespread, elections in authoritarian regimes often serve a number of purposes for dictators intent on remaining in power, instead of communicating citizens' true preferences (Gandhi 2008; Geddes 1999). Various empirical studies have documented how authoritarian leaders utilize regular elections to demonstrate the futility of government opposition (Simpser 2005), to co-opt that opposition (Lust-Okar 2005), or to gain information about where they need to shore up weaknesses (Brownlee 2007).[2] In virtually all of these cases, the incumbent machine utilizes aggressive clientelism (Lust-Okar 2006) and intimidation (Schedler 2006) to ensure that their supporters are overrepresented at the polls, and that the outcome of the election is never in doubt. Even protest is not as autonomous at it might seem in nondemocratic regimes, as revealed in Robertson's (2007) study of labor strikes in Russia, where work stoppages are wielded as a bargaining chip between regional and national political elites rather than serving to communicate the grievances of workers. In sum, efforts to delve deeper into

[1] As noted earlier, we treat Mexico's Federal District as distinct from the country's remaining 31 states, while recognizing that it has often been considered the 32nd state and, indeed, achieved full statehood in 2018.
[2] See Gandhi and Lust-Okar (2009) for their thorough review of the literature on elections in nondemocratic countries.

the mechanics of political participation in nondemocratic regimes have shed light on the systematic efforts of government officials to manipulate *who* participates in politics and *how* they engage the political system.

An important implication of these studies is that the individual-level determinants of political participation tend to be quite different in nondemocratic regimes than they are in consolidated democracies. As noted in previous chapters, McMann's (2006) work on the authoritarian enclaves of the former Soviet Union highlights the ways in which "economic autonomy," or the lack thereof, can fundamentally shape how citizens decide to participate in politics. Croke et al. (2015) go one step further and offer support for what they describe as "deliberate disengagement"—a dynamic in which the well-established positive relationship between education levels and participation found in established democratic systems is, in fact, reversed in electoral authoritarian regimes. In less overtly authoritarian, but still not fully democratic, regimes we also have a number of works that highlight the connection between regime characteristics and citizens' participation in politics. In Argentina, for example, Auyero et al. (2009), focuses on the relationship between patronage politics and mass mobilizations of citizens in certain instances. Similarly, Magaloni's work (2006) is representative of an abundance of research on the mobilizing techniques of the PRI in Mexico during its 80-year run as that country's ruling party (e.g., Camp 2013).

Among the most detailed documentation of political behavior in an authoritarian regime is Shi's *Political Participation in Beijing* (1997), based on surveys carried out surrounding the 1984 and 1988 elections in China. Similar to other studies of nondemocratic regimes, Shi finds that being educated actually makes individuals *less* likely to participate in politics, given that the dominant Chinese Communist Party (CCP) historically "considered the educated the prime target of departicipation, deliberately discriminating against them and imposing much harsher punishment on them than on others for their intransigent behavior" (148). Shi notes that while "all the explanations suggest that the educated should vote more than other groups . . . the data analysis show exactly the opposite," which he attributes to "a subculture among the educated that makes them extremely sensitive to the risks associated with their political behavior" (148). He also finds that members of the CCP are overrepresented in nearly all forms of political participation, outnumbering unaffiliated voters by 15 percent in the 1988 elections (166). In spite of this relatively bleak picture, Shi does find evidence that political outsiders express some degree of political efficacy operating at the local level through community- and work-related organizations, suggesting that nonmembers of the politically favored class look outside of formal modes of political participation in an authoritarian system in order to articulate their interests.

In sum, crossnational work on political participation in nondemocratic regimes not only offers a multitude of reasons to support our contention that we should find systematic subnational differences in participation patterns within uneven democracies but also provides a theoretical and empirical guide for how to find them. In the following section, we draw from the lessons offered by this extensive body of research at the national level to explore participation dynamics within dominant-party enclaves.

Political Participation in Dominant-Party Enclaves

In exploring the behavioral consequences of uneven democracy, we focus on three key repertoires of political participation: voting, protest, and civic activism. The key distinction between multiparty and dominant party regimes that we see concerning citizens' engagement with politics is not the *amount* of their participation but, rather, the *mode* and *apparent motivation* of that participation. Existing within nationally democratic regimes, dominant-party enclaves are constrained in some ways by the need to at least appear somewhat democratic, and as such they do not seek to thwart participation entirely, as outright repression of such activities as voting and civic activism would raise flags at the national level (see Gibson 2012). Rather, incumbents in these systems selectively cultivate participation in order to enhance their claim on power (Greene 2007; Magaloni 2006). As such, dominant parties rely heavily on the persistence of clientelistic relationships between citizens and the state that are designed to ensure that loyal partisans are disproportionately represented at the ballot box, in the streets, and in community life.

We argue that these distinct subnational political contexts influence the political behaviors of citizens through multiple pathways. In particular, we focus again on the mechanisms that we have highlighted throughout this book that provide the backdrop for the less-than-democratic political profiles of citizenries living in dominant-party political contexts. The first such mechanism lies in the prevalence of clientelistic relationships between citizens and elected officials in dominant-party systems. Though we certainly make no claim that such relationships are absent in multiparty systems, there is clear and robust evidence that in both Mexico and Argentina, an individual living in a dominant-party context is significantly more likely to be familiar with, if not actively participate in, a relationship with elected officials that rests on the "sale" of her political voice in exchange for private goods of some sort (see Chapter 4).

As these types of relationships persist, largely unchallenged by a viable political opposition, citizens increasingly view these interactions as the only way through which they can extract goods, and representation, from the state, and, as such, these exchanges also become the basis on which individuals evaluate the performance of their elected officials (see Chapter 6). Nichter and Peress refer to this dynamic as "demand fulfilling," highlighting "the important role of citizen demands in clientelism" (2017, 1111). These variations in the degree to which clientelistic exchanges characterize relationships between citizens and their provincial government officials provide one source for the behavioral differences that we posit exist between citizens of dominant-party and multiparty regimes. As Gandhi and Lust-Okar (2009) point out in their overview of research on participation in authoritarian regimes, "patronage distribution and control over resources" (408) are essential tools for incumbents in such systems to generate electoral support (see also Greene 2007).

This mechanism also manifests itself through the efforts of dominant parties to capture, and utilize for electoral purposes, the resources of the state. Gervasoni (2010b) presents compelling evidence that citizens of less democratic Argentine provinces are more likely to depend on the state for their economic livelihood when compared with their counterparts living in competitive systems. This low level of economic autonomy in dominant-party contexts, where one's "ability to earn a living independent of the state" (McMann 2006, 28) is limited, reflects the degree to which dominant parties seek to become tantamount to the state itself and, as a consequence, also can be expected to influence the ways in which citizens engage with their political system. Citizenries of dominant-party states may be less inclined to involve themselves in politically risky behavior that would challenge the status quo and threaten their relationship with the incumbent government (McMann 2006). As Greene (2007) notes, opposition in dominant-party systems raises "the opportunity cost of foregoing the material advantages that they would have received by joining the dominant party, such as a stipend, kickbacks, or access to an old boys' network of business contacts and favors" (5). If participation, as many have argued (e.g., Verba and Nie 1972), is driven at least in part by one's resources, then for both clientelism and dominant-party capture of the state, what we might call one's heightened vulnerability to losing access to job opportunities or social programs becomes important as well in explaining the decision to participate and the nature of that participation.

A related mechanism harks back to this chapter's opening anecdote regarding Formosa province. In systems in which citizens fear legal retribution from the provincial machine for speaking out against it, they might alter how, and how much, they participate in politics. As we have documented throughout this book, dominant parties often seek to deploy the rule of law for political purposes, and this extends to how they respond to protests critical of their performance, or municipalities that fail to demonstrate the requisite devotion to the party on Election Day. In fieldwork in San Luis, Argentina, we heard multiple accounts of police repression during the *multisectorial* protests of 2004. One social movement leader was knocked unconscious by a police officer brandishing a nightstick and woke up in jail. Whereas in full democracies, participating in a street demonstration or joining a civil society organization in pursuit of social change would hardly constitute risky behaviors, dominant-party citizens might hesitate to mobilize against the regime not merely for fear of economic retribution, but also out of a desire to avoid legal persecution.

The final mechanism we posit as driving differences in the behavioral patterns of individuals living in multiparty and dominant-party contexts involves the continued efforts of dominant-party elites to slant the electoral playing field in their favor and the resultant differing levels of electoral competition we typically find in the two systems because of those efforts. We view this rigged electoral game as manifesting itself most clearly in the degree to which citizens feel politically efficacious within their subnational political system. In systems in which the ruling party has never lost, and in elections that by all accounts should be tightly contested but instead turn out to be comfortable victories, political efficacy, or the feeling that one can effect change in politics, will tend to be low among opponents of the machine. Conversely, within that same dominant-party system, those individuals who have cast their lot with the machine will likely feel highly efficacious, albeit in an instrumental sort of way, as they reap the material benefits of their political affiliations. This political efficacy gap, in turn, should translate into distinct patterns of political participation in dominant-party contexts, depending on whether individuals count themselves as supporters of the ruling machine or regime opponents.

Though participation rates may be similar in dominant-party and multi-party contexts, we contend that the motivations behind such participation will tend to be different. In dominant-party enclaves, we expect participation to be motivated by incumbent officials and the carrots and sticks they use to "(dis)incentivize" citizens. As such, participation will likely be disproportionately populated by government supporters, with "protests" often taking the form of progovernment rallies, and voter turnout driven by a desire for private goods rather than by accountability concerns. Another quote from an interview in San Luis regarding the *multisectorial* protests speaks to the power that dominant parties can wield over supporters who depend on them for their livelihood:

> After the [2001] crisis that devastated the entire country, San Luis province experienced several important social mobilizations that sought a response from public officials to the poverty and economic precariousness generated among a large portion of society . . . Massive social protests uniting multiple sectors marched through the main streets in the capital making their claims. Thousands participated, and the provincial police forces responded with violence. *What's worse, many of the beneficiaries of social plans were called by the governor—in this case, Alberto Rodríguez-Saá—to lead a counter demonstration.*[3]

Conversely, opponents of the regime in such systems, and those who simply refuse to play the dominant-party's political game, will be more likely to disengage from politics altogether, along the lines of Croke et al.'s "deliberate disengagement" (2015). In multiparty contexts, conversely, we expect to find no such relationship between partisan sympathies and patterns of political engagement. Further, we expect to find evidence that education predicts political participation in ways similar to those in advanced democracies.

Combined, these three mechanisms should result in government sympathizers being the more likely participants in politics, engaging in a variety of behaviors designed to serve the incumbent machine. For example, in great contrast to multiparty systems in which demonstrators tend to be critics of the incumbent government (see Silva 2009; Boulding 2014; Moseley 2018), we expect many "protesters" in dominant-party systems to

---

[3] Author's translation; interview with movement organizer, as it appears in Moseley (2018, 146). Italics added for emphasis.

express support for their elected officials, with their street-level participation simply one manifestation of that support, driven by expected rewards from the government.[4] Overall, while voters, protesters, and community activists in multiparty states should match standard profiles of political participants found in many democratic countries around the world, those most likely to protest and vote in dominant-party enclaves tend to directly challenge that conventional wisdom regarding the determinants of political participation.

Similarly, we expect the distinctive characteristics of dominant-party systems to also influence which citizens engage in politics directly through contacting political officials in order to solve a problem. This form of participation in many ways captures a defining element of a system based on clientelistic relationships. Just as citizens in such a system are available to "take to the streets" when called upon by political elites, so, too, do those political elites make themselves available to citizen/clients in order to solve specific problems and "fulfill requests" (Nichter and Peress 2017, 1087). Emblematic of this personalist approach to politics that characterizes dominant-party systems was Venezuelan president Hugo Chávez's radio call-in show "*Alo Presidente*" in which Chávez would respond directly to citizen grievances, simultaneously inculcating tremendous loyalty among his core constituency and demonizing his opponents. In such a political context, it is no surprise that those citizens most likely to engage in these types of personal contacts with elected officials will be government supporters. Conversely, in less personalist, more established democratic systems, one's views toward the incumbent should be far less decisive in identifying who seeks out help from political officials. Once again, this expectation is grounded in a fundamental quality of dominant-party systems—citizen-incumbent relations built on the private provision of rewards for loyal supporters and punishment for opponents. We now turn our attention to the task of marshaling empirical support for these expectations.

---

[4] We suspect, but do not test here, that system opponents in dominant-party enclaves may be more likely to turn to violent protest tactics, given their inability to influence politicians through less costly formal and informal vehicles for representation (Moseley 2018). However, we lack a measure for aggressive protests in Argentina and Mexico, so we focus here on reported participation in elections, civic activism, and street demonstrations.

Data and Measurement

To test our argument, we once again turn to data from the 2008–2014 AmericasBarometer national surveys of Argentina and Mexico and subnational democracy measures constructed from gubernatorial elections. As discussed previously, our concern here is with understanding differences in *who* participates in politics across multiparty and dominant-party subnational political systems, in an effort to shed light on the underlying motivations of that participation. In order to capture a full range of *how* citizens participate, we focus our analytical lens on (1) voting, the most basic form of participation in a democracy; (2) street demonstrations, an informal repertoire of participation and one that, due to its very public nature, can potentially increase the chances that a citizen will receive either punishment or rewards from the incumbent government; and (3) civic activism, a bedrock mode of participation in any ostensibly democratic context (Putnam 1993). Civic activism can be overtly political (e.g., petitioning a local authority for help or participating in party activities) or nonpolitical (e.g., neighborhood associations, parent organizations, or simply working to solve local community problems). We initially focus on explicitly political community-level activities in this chapter but return to potential variation in nonpolitical forms of community participation in the discussion of efficacy.

For voting, we use a simple measure for past turnout in the most recent presidential election, drawn from a question asked in each iteration of the AmericasBarometer surveys. To measure protest, we utilize a question that gauges whether or not individuals report having engaged in at least one peaceful protest during the previous 12 months. This provides a straightforward measure to investigate the possibility that characteristics of protestors vary across subnational regime contexts. Finally, we utilize a variety of survey items created by LAPOP that measure nonpolitical activism through respondents' participation in parent–teacher associations, labor organizations, and any effort to "help solve a community problem." We also model two more explicitly political measures of civic engagement, including participation in political party meetings and contacting local officials. As noted above, this latter form of participation should be most distinct across dominant-party and multiparty contexts, with incumbent supporters in dominant-party systems significantly more likely to engage in such contacts than opponents, while in multiparty systems, incumbent support or opposition should be far less determinative of who contacts political officials.

As with much survey-based work on political participation, the fundamental weakness of all the measures used here is that they rely on respondents' self-reports about past behavior. Such self-reports tend to be "noisy," and can overestimate the frequency of actual acts of participation by respondents.[5] Recognizing this issue, we see no systematic reason why respondents in either multiparty contexts or dominant-party enclaves would be more (or less) inclined to misrepresent their past political behaviors. Unable to resolve these measurement problems, we rest our analysis on the assumption that misreporting of past political behaviors will occur with similar frequencies across the distinct political contexts and categories of respondents we explore in this chapter, thus minimizing the chances that our findings will be systematically skewed in one direction across all of our analyses and distinct dependent variables. Through analysis of these three distinct forms of participation, we hope to offer robust support for the notion that subnational political context does, indeed, have a wide-ranging impact on the ways in which citizens engage with their provincial political system.

Aside from the primary independent variable of subnational regime type, there are several other important factors we include in the analyses in this chapter that are essential to our theory, as well as those variables that will help us root out spurious relationships. One key prediction of our theory is that education will have a more subdued impact on participation in dominant-party enclaves than in multiparty systems, as more politically aware individuals might opt out of participating in machine politics. This prediction finds initial support in a simple correlation analysis in which we estimate predicted turnout rates by educational attainment (Figure 7.1). Without controlling for other factors, it seems that education is, indeed, negatively related to participation in elections in dominant-party enclaves, whereas it is positively correlated with turnout in multiparty regimes, similar to what we would expect from the literature on voting in established democracies.

Our second key expectation is that participation will generally be biased toward government supporters in dominant party regimes, whereas incumbent support will be less vital in predicting participation in multiparty contexts. To measure government support, we rely on two items. The first measures whether or not individuals would vote for the incumbent if a hypothetical gubernatorial election were to take place that week. This provides

---

[5] Among the many works on this question, for overreporting of voting, see, for example, Ansolabehere and Hersh (2012), Berent, Krosnick, and Lupia (2016), and Silver et al. (1986).

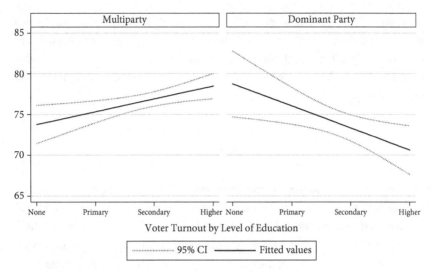

Figure 7.1. Education and voter turnout by subnational regime category.

us with a general measure for a seemingly large number of provincial inhabitants who are at least marginally attached to the incumbent machine. The second measure seeks to identify core party identifiers of the incumbent dominant party—in most cases the PRI and PJ, the two parties at the helm of most of our dominant-party political machines in Mexico and Argentina, respectively. This party identification measure will capture those individuals who are closer to party networks and more active in party organizations than individuals who simply report their intention to vote for the incumbent governor. Our expectation is that by using these two measures, we will observe distinct patterns of participation among supporters of the incumbent governor and core party members in dominant-party enclaves, compared with multiparty contexts.

Finally, we also include a number of controls found in standard vote intention and other participation models in an effort to account for the other most significant factors associated with political participation. These include standard demographic and socioeconomic characteristics such as gender, age, income, and whether the respondent lives in an urban or rural setting. In addition, we use a presidential approval measure and an interest in politics item to capture the potential impact these factors may have on an individual's participation levels. We also use the same measure of the level of development of each province in order to account for the possibility that overall economic development levels have some influence on participation rates within a province. For this measure, we continue to categorize our provinces and states into either "high income," "middle income," or "low income" categories based on the relative rank of the gross state product per capita within each country.

Results

The results in this section come from estimated logistic regression models (for dichotomous dependent variables) of citizen participation in politics. All models include fixed effects for country and year. As we seek to determine how subnational political context affects patterns of political participation among supporters and opponents of the incumbent government across Argentine provinces and Mexican states, the most important coefficient in most models will be the interaction between the variables that measure partisan affiliation and subnational regime type, each of which is dichotomous. We also include interactions between years of education and subnational regime category, to capture the expectation that education exerts a different effect on political participation in dominant-party systems than that typically found in democratic systems.

Our principal expectation is that for all three forms of political participation, activism will be most likely among loyal regime supporters in dominant-party enclaves, while in multiparty contexts no such partisan dynamic will exist with respect to who participates. In other words, whereas in dominant-party enclaves, incumbent governments stack the deck in terms of incentivizing their constituents to engage with politics via traditional modes of political participation, in multiparty contexts we expect not to observe such a strong correlation between party sympathies and rates of participation but, rather, find patterns that are similar to those found in more established democracies. We also expect that, in keeping with the logic of "deliberate disengagement" (Croke et al. 2016), and based on the correlation analysis presented in Figure 7.1, education will have a stronger positive impact on the likelihood that individuals in multiparty contexts will participate than on those living in dominant-party enclaves, where many individuals who understand the nature of the system are likely to opt out of actively participating in the machine's political game.

Table 7.1 presents results from our first three estimated models of participation—reported turnout in the most recent presidential election.

Table 7.1. Models of Past Turnout in Argentina and Mexico

VARIABLES	DV: Turnout in Last Presidential Election (0 or 1)		
	Model 1	Model 2	Model 3
Education	0.057***	0.040***	0.064***
	(0.007)	(0.014)	(0.008)
Wealth	0.029	0.082**	0.027
	(0.019)	(0.038)	(0.019)
Urban	0.153**	−0.113	0.151**
	(0.064)	(0.135)	(0.063)
Female	0.193***	0.138	0.187***
	(0.049)	(0.096)	(0.049)
Age	0.048***	0.046***	0.048***
	(0.002)	(0.004)	(0.002)
Presidential Approval	0.002**	−0.004**	0.003***
	(0.001)	(0.002)	(0.001)
Interest in Politics	0.007***	0.003*	0.008***
	(0.001)	(0.002)	(0.001)
2010	−0.131*		−0.132*
	(0.069)		(0.069)
2012	0.057	0.440***	0.063
	(0.071)	(0.162)	(0.070)
2014	−0.020	0.579***	−0.094
	(0.071)	(0.128)	(0.070)
Argentina	0.514***	0.349**	0.498***
	(0.055)	(0.136)	(0.055)
Middle Income	−0.036	−0.131	−0.022
	(0.073)	(0.167)	(0.073)
High Income	−0.028	0.069	−0.009
	(0.060)	(0.117)	(0.060)
Incumbent Party Member	0.749***		
	(0.128)		
Incumbent Party Supporter		0.880***	
		(0.112)	
DOMINANT-PARTY ENCLAVE	0.002	−0.192	0.305**
	(0.060)	(0.160)	(0.135)
*Party Member*Dominant-Party Enclave*	*0.441**		
	(0.242)		

Continued

Table 7.1. *Continued*

VARIABLES	DV: Turnout in Last Presidential Election (0 or 1)		
	Model 1	Model 2	Model 3
Supporter*Dominant-Party Enclave		*0.701****	
		(0.247)	
Education*Dominant-Party Enclave			*–0.030***
			(0.013)
Constant	–2.316***	–2.091***	–2.404***
	(0.190)	(0.357)	(0.192)
Observations	10,425	2,830	10,425

Note: Standard errors in parentheses.
*p < 0.1; **p < 0.05; ***p < 0.01

The key finding in Model 1 is the significant sign for the interaction between dominant-party regime and party membership, which is positive and significant at $p < .10$. This interaction term indicates that, ceteris paribus, being a member of the incumbent governor's party has a stronger positive effect on voter turnout in dominant-party enclaves than in multiparty contexts. Model 2 produces similar results for the interaction between support for the incumbent governor and subnational regime category. Figure 7.2 illustrates the fact that incumbent supporters are significantly more likely to turn out to vote than nonsupporters in dominant-party systems, with an increase from .57 to .86 in the probability of having voted in the most recent presidential election. In multiparty systems, conversely, support for the incumbent governor was only associated with a .15 increase in the probability of turning out. Simply put, and as we expected, supporters of the dominant machine are better represented in elections than nonmembers. Another finding of note here is that nonsupporters in multiparty systems appear more likely to vote than nonsupporters in dominant-party systems. This finding speaks to the idea that opposition supporters in multiparty contexts are less inclined to see the electoral game as rigged and thus more likely to engage with the system on election day than are opponents of a dominant-party machine, in which turning out to vote for any election may be viewed as not worth the effort and/or tacit support for the machine itself. It should also be noted that our turnout item for these models is for *presidential* elections—further

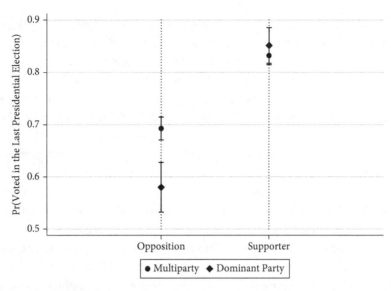

Figure 7.2. Voter turnout by incumbent support and subnational regime category. Pr = probability.

underlining our argument that the subnational dominant-party contexts that are the focus of this study have important consequences for national political processes as well.

Other variables that seem to exert a positive effect on the likelihood that individuals report voting in the last presidential election include education, gender, age, and interest in politics, consistent with much of the extant literature on the topic. Yet, once again we find support for our expectations in Model 3, when we see that one's education level is a far stronger predictor of turnout in multiparty systems than it is in dominant-party enclaves—compelling evidence for the notion that citizens who understand the nature of a dominant-party machine might opt out of participating altogether—regardless of the election. The positive effect for education on turnout in multiparty regimes is roughly double that of the effect found in dominant-party enclaves. In other words, while education has a slight positive effect on electoral participation in dominant-party contexts controlling for other factors, that effect pales in comparison with the effect it would have in full democratic settings. This result echoes findings from competitive authoritarian countries (Croke et al. 2016) and lends further credence to the argument that political participation differs fundamentally *within* uneven democracies by subnational regime context.

These findings, then, offer the first bit of support that political participation in dominant-party systems reflects the incentive structure created by incumbent officials to reward loyal supporters for their political support and, perhaps, punish those who oppose the system. Supporters of the incumbent government are likely to participate in important national elections at higher rates, while nonsupporters might sit out the electoral process altogether. When considered in the context of an emerging democracy in which citizen engagement in politics is an important component in the development of a democratic political culture, these findings suggest that a systematic disengagement of one subset of the country's citizenry occurs with each subnational dominant-party machine that continues to persist well into the country's democratic maturation process. Meanwhile, those most likely to participate in these dominant-party enclaves are those individuals who support the continuation of the machine that serves them at the subnational level. Though we have limited empirical evidence, a plausible consequence of this heightened level of participation by subnational machine supporters in national-level elections is greater support for the same machine-driven politics at the national level that these individuals profess support for in their home province. We will return to the troubling implications of these findings in our concluding chapter, but at this point we turn next to an exploration of other forms of political participation in dominant-party systems.

Having established that voter turnout seems to differ based on partisanship and local political context, and that education exerts a diminished effect on electoral participation in dominant-party systems, we proceed to analyze how patterns of protest participation vary at the subnational level in Argentina and Mexico. Table 7.2 presents results from logistic regression models of reported protest participation from 2008 to 2014—one of the most important noninstitutional forms of political voice in Latin America today (Moseley 2018). In Model 1, we find that the interaction term between party member and dominant-party enclave is not significant. However, in Model 2, we find that the coefficient for *Supporter*Dominant-Party Enclave* is positive and statistically significant at the $p < .05$ level, suggesting that those individuals who express support for the governor in a dominant-party system are, indeed, more likely to turn out for a progovernment rally compared to government supporters in multiparty contexts.

Figure 7.3 clarifies our interpretation of this finding, as it appears that being a government supporter decreases the probability of participating

Table 7.2. Models of Protest Participation in Argentina and Mexico

VARIABLES	DV: Protested in Past 12 Months (0 or 1)		
	Model 1	Model 2	Model 3
Education	0.032***	0.018	0.031**
	(0.012)	(0.018)	(0.014)
Wealth	0.068*	0.089*	0.069**
	(0.035)	(0.050)	(0.035)
Urban	−0.425***	−0.809***	−0.428***
	(0.138)	(0.232)	(0.138)
Female	−0.093	−0.005	−0.095
	(0.088)	(0.125)	(0.088)
Age	−0.005*	−0.012***	−0.005
	(0.003)	(0.004)	(0.003)
Presidential Approval	−0.004**	0.002	−0.003*
	(0.002)	(0.002)	(0.002)
Interest in Politics	0.017***	0.019***	0.017***
	(0.001)	(0.002)	(0.001)
2012	−0.500***	−0.300	−0.488***
	(0.110)	(0.187)	(0.110)
2014	−0.435***	−0.538***	−0.465***
	(0.108)	(0.159)	(0.106)
Argentina	0.623***	0.843***	0.616***
	(0.100)	(0.200)	(0.100)
Middle Income	−0.156	0.070	−0.155
	(0.157)	(0.249)	(0.157)
High Income	0.067	0.068	0.070
	(0.109)	(0.162)	(0.109)
DOMINANT-PARTY ENCLAVE	−0.015	−0.448*	−0.041
	(0.123)	(0.271)	(0.294)
Dominant Party Member	0.241		
	(0.166)		
Dominant Party Supporter		−0.217	
		(0.144)	
*Party Member*Dominant-Party Enclave*	*−0.025*		
	(0.310)		
*Supporter*Dominant-Party Enclave*		*0.737**	
		(0.340)	
*Education*Dominant-Party Enclave*			*0.003*
			(0.026)
Constant	−2.891***	−2.548***	−2.890***
	(0.327)	(0.491)	(0.331)
Observations	7,898	2,809	7,898

Note: Standard errors in parentheses.

*p < 0.1; **p < 0.05; ***p < 0.01

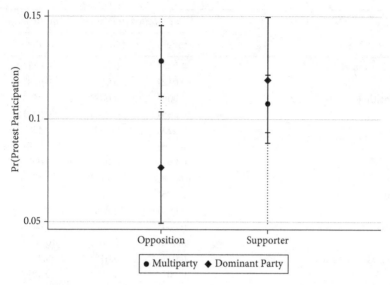

Figure 7.3. Protest participation by incumbent support and subnational regime category. Pr = probability.

in a street march or demonstration in multiparty contexts by about .02 but *increases* the likelihood of protesting in dominant-party systems by about .08. In multiparty systems, that is, we find what we would expect to see in any democratic system: Opponents of the incumbent governor are more likely to take their dissatisfaction to the streets. The opposition in dominant-party systems, however, behaves differently. Most important, we see strikingly low rates of protest participation among opponents of the incumbent governor in dominant-party enclaves, perhaps reflecting either the fear of retribution and/or the resigned acceptance of the status quo that individuals who do not support the dominant-party machine likely experience. Supporters of the machine, conversely, are slightly *more* likely to participate in "protests" than their opposition counterparts, a finding that corroborates qualitative accounts from provinces like San Luis where loyalists are often incentivized to take to the streets in support of their political patron. Finally, unlike the finding for education and voting across subnational political contexts, the interaction between education and subnational regime category seems to be insignificant, perhaps because protest as a form of political participation, when not incentivized by the incumbent machine, may provide an outlet for the political voice of educated individuals that does not imply support for the machine itself.

To this point, these findings offer further support for our contention that the participation patterns of citizens living in dominant-party systems will reflect, in part, the governing characteristics of the system in which they live. When considered at the crossnational level, such a proposition and set of findings are rather common. For example, we have a fairly well-established understanding of the ways in which such features as majoritarian electoral systems or parliamentary forms of government affect citizens' level of participation in politics (see, e.g., Norris 1997; Anderson and Guillory 1997). Similarly, scholars of subnational politics in the United States have leveraged cross-state variations in direct democracy policymaking procedures to highlight the participatory benefits of these forms of state-level politics (e.g., Tolbert et al. 2003). Yet, we know of very few, if any, works that systematically explore the pernicious ways in which a subnational dominant-party machine shapes the behavioral patterns of both supporters and opponents across a range of modes of participation. Here we have carried out just such an analysis on voting and protest and find evidence consistent with our theory across both. We now turn to a third form of participation, local civic activism, a type of behavior for which we expect the machine will once again leave a heavy imprint on who participates and why.

Table 7.3 reports findings from six separate models of two forms of political activism, seeking help from a local official and attending a party meeting, which constitutes the third repertoire of participation we consider in this chapter. Here again, we find persuasive evidence that the individuals most likely to participate in this form of politics differ fundamentally across multiparty and dominant-party contexts, as local machines in the latter have constructed a system of rewards and punishments that make it more likely to find supporters of the system actively engaged in local politics than opponents. In four of the estimated models of participation we observe significant effects for the key interaction under examination, and in all six models the interaction has the predicted sign.

In theory, having direct contact with one's local representative is one of the most important manifestations of the representational connection between citizens and their elected governments. In dominant-party enclaves, supporters of the incumbent are more likely to enjoy the benefits of this direct linkage than opponents of the dominant machine (Models 1–3). Figure 7.4 illustrates that being a supporter of the incumbent governor increases one's probability of having solicited a local authority for assistance by .08—a nearly 50 percent relative increase in probability compared with government

Table 7.3. Models of Political Activism in Argentina and Mexico

VARIABLES	DV: Solicited Help from Local Official (0 or 1)			DV: Participated in a Party Meeting (0 or 1)		
	Model 1	Model 2	Model 3	Model 4	Model 5	Model 6
Education	−0.029*	−0.010	−0.009	0.024	−0.000	0.009
	(0.016)	(0.008)	(0.009)	(0.017)	(0.009)	(0.010)
Wealth	−0.103**	−0.134***	−0.135***	−0.098*	−0.063**	−0.062**
	(0.045)	(0.023)	(0.023)	(0.050)	(0.025)	(0.025)
Urban	0.321**	0.510***	0.510***	0.326**	0.361***	0.354***
	(0.147)	(0.069)	(0.069)	(0.164)	(0.076)	(0.076)
Female	0.396***	0.249***	0.248***	−0.150	−0.177***	−0.177***
	(0.113)	(0.058)	(0.058)	(0.125)	(0.063)	(0.063)
Age	0.003	0.005***	0.006***	−0.003	−0.001	0.000
	(0.004)	(0.002)	(0.002)	(0.004)	(0.002)	(0.002)
Presidential Approval	0.002	0.001	0.001	0.006**	0.002	0.003*
	(0.002)	(0.001)	(0.001)	(0.002)	(0.001)	(0.001)
Interest in Politics	0.011***	0.011***	0.011***	0.024***	0.021***	0.022***
	(0.002)	(0.001)	(0.001)	(0.002)	(0.001)	(0.001)
Middle Income	−0.429**	−0.131	−0.122	−0.332	−0.408***	−0.395***
	(0.207)	(0.084)	(0.084)	(0.211)	(0.093)	(0.092)
High Income	−0.409***	−0.354***	−0.346***	−0.794***	−0.538***	−0.529***
	(0.133)	(0.069)	(0.069)	(0.149)	(0.075)	(0.075)
2010		0.000	0.001		0.023	0.034
		(0.084)	(0.084)		(0.085)	(0.084)
2012	0.453**	0.017	0.024	−0.217	−0.358***	−0.336***
	(0.191)	(0.083)	(0.083)	(0.208)	(0.090)	(0.089)
2014	0.475***	0.373***	0.331***	−0.339**	−0.158*	−0.233***
	(0.160)	(0.082)	(0.081)	(0.170)	(0.091)	(0.090)
Argentina	−0.333*	0.002	−0.002	0.157	−0.061	−0.075
	(0.177)	(0.064)	(0.064)	(0.180)	(0.070)	(0.070)
DOMINANT-PARTY ENCLAVE	−0.103	0.256***	0.320**	−0.096	0.294***	0.661***
	(0.210)	(0.070)	(0.138)	(0.234)	(0.077)	(0.154)
Incumbent Supporter	−0.211			−0.232		
	(0.133)			(0.151)		
Incumbent Party Member		0.266**			0.325***	
		(0.112)			(0.115)	
Supporter*Dominant-Party	0.681**			0.789***		
	(0.268)			(0.291)		

Table 7.3. *Continued*

VARIABLES	DV: Solicited Help from Local Official (0 or 1)			DV: Participated in a Party Meeting (0 or 1)		
	Model 1	Model 2	Model 3	Model 4	Model 5	Model 6
*Party Member*Dominant-Party*		*0.078*			*0.445****	
		(0.178)			*(0.178)*	
*Education*Dominant-Party*			*–0.006*			*–0.032****
			(0.014)			*(0.015)*
Constant	– 2.538***	–3.079***	–3.109***	– 2.929***	–2.690***	– 2.820***
	(0.408)	(0.220)	(0.222)	(0.451)	(0.236)	(0.238)
Observations	2,826	10,440	10,440	2,824	10,433	10,433

Note: Standard errors in parentheses.

$*p < 0.1; **p < 0.05; ***p < 0.01$

opponents. Notably, incumbent governor supporters in dominant-party systems have the highest rates of reported contact with local officials, likely illustrating a tendency for some citizens to expect a payoff from local officials for "going along to get along" in a political game that is rigged.

Models 4–6 demonstrate that local political context has a similar influence on one's likelihood of participating in party meetings—another important representational connection in any political system. The gap here is even more pronounced, with dominant-party supporters reporting rates of participation in political organization meetings of almost twice those of government opponents (Figure 7.5). In multiparty regimes, a more subtle partisan difference in terms of patterns of political activism emerges, offering further evidence from yet another arena of political engagement that dominant-party regimes can, and do, systematically manipulate political participation to their benefit.

We recognize that such a finding is by no means a revelation for the many scholars and observers of such regimes, either at the national or subnational level, over the years. Indeed, even for just Argentina and Mexico, we have countless reports of political elites extralegally influencing which citizens gain privileged access to the state and how citizens behave politically. What

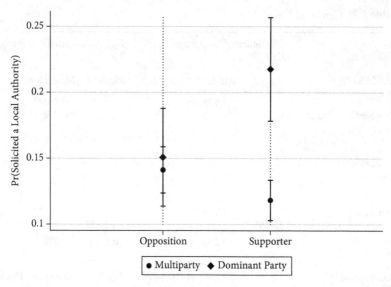

Figure 7.4. Solicitation of local official by incumbent support and subnational regime category. Pr = probability.

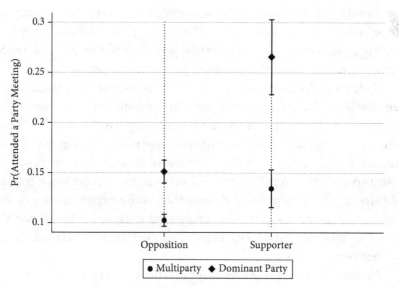

Figure 7.5. Participation in party meetings by incumbent support and subnational regime category. Pr = probability.

we offer here, however, is an empirical evaluation of the consequences of these dominant-party tools from the perspectives and behaviors of the citizens themselves, as revealed through analysis of survey data. In other words, we know a lot about what dominant-party political elites do to distort and undermine democratic institutions and norms in order to stay in power, but here we offer one of the first systematic accounts of how these efforts influence those who find themselves stuck in these machines.

In Model 6, the interaction between dominant-party enclave and education is also significant at $p < .05$, suggesting again that education exerts a different effect on participation in political organizations in dominant-party systems than in multiparty contexts. Figure 7.6 plots predicted probabilities associated with varying levels of education and participation in political meetings across dominant-party enclaves and multiparty regimes. The results are striking. Whereas education has the predicted (albeit slight) positive effect on political activism in multiparty regimes, where we argue political life is more reminiscent of established liberal democracies, education exerts an important *negative* effect on political organization attendance in dominant-party enclaves. We interpret this finding as another piece of evidence that in provinces and states where the game is rigged, and where politics is characterized by the three central characteristics driving political attitudes and participation in dominant-party enclaves, more educated members of society will choose to opt out of the political process. This finding echoes results from nondemocratic regimes in Africa (Croke et al. 2015) and research from China (Shi 1997), and it highlights the extent to which very different political regimes can be nested within the same national context and produce distinct patterns of participation as a consequence.

Though each of the above analyses of the relationship between one's subnational political context, her partisan sympathies, and her proclivity to participate in politics carries with it the usual caveats and cautions relating to causality and measurement issues, when taken together the picture we are left with is one that is consistent with the general narrative developed throughout this book—subnational dominant-party enclaves produce decidedly different patterns of political attitudes and behaviors that run counter to our general understanding of the ways in which democratic citizenries typically behave. By ignoring this subnational dynamic, we risk losing sight

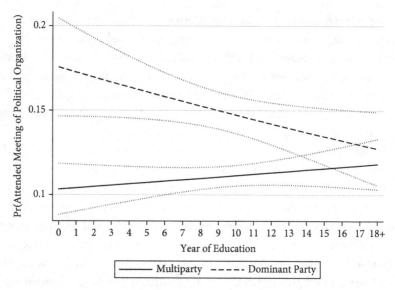

Figure 7.6. Participation in party meetings by education and subnational regime category. Pr = probability.

of a critical impediment to the development of active and engaged publics across the world's many cases of uneven democracies.

Efficacy and Participation in Dominant-Party Enclaves

Underlying much of the preceding discussion is the idea that in dominant-party enclaves, both opponents of the local machine and educated members of society are left out of the political arena, implying reduced levels of political efficacy among a large swathe of citizens within those locales. Yet, when we examine average levels of internal and external efficacy across dominant-party enclaves and multiparty systems, we find similar rates of individuals who view themselves as capable of understanding important political issues (internal efficacy) and believe that politicians are willing to listen to "people like them" (external efficacy). This might reflect the fact that one or both of these two forms of political efficacy are independent of subnational regime dynamics and, instead, are largely driven by national regime characteristics.

We suspect, though, a different explanation that once again involves the differential impact a dominant-party context will have on supporters and opponents of the machine. Though we should expect in any type of political system to find lower levels of external efficacy among opponents of the incumbent government, we expect this efficacy gap between opponents and supporters to be larger in dominant-party systems, due to supporters' privileged access to representatives of the system and the obstacles opponents face to such access. Given the importance of efficacy in understanding who participates in politics (Finkel 1985), if we were to uncover differences in efficacy between government supporters and opponents in dominant-party enclaves that might also shed some light on the mechanisms underlying patterns of political participation in contexts of machine rule.

Focusing on mean levels of internal and external efficacy, or the degree to which individuals believe they understand the most important political issues in their country and are heard by politicians, respectively, a snapshot glance at the disparity between incumbent supporters and opponents across multiparty and dominant-party systems reveals an important consequence of uneven democracy. The individuals who have most "bought in" to the type of dominant-party politics we document throughout this book exhibit some of the highest rates of internal and external efficacy, and substantially higher mean levels than nonmembers of the incumbent party (Figure 7.6). As others have noted, dominant-party enclaves are sustained not only by clientelism and intimidation, but also by generating buy-in among loyal supporters of the machine (Magaloni 2006). These graphs offer some initial individual-level support for the existence of such buy-in, as loyal partisans of incumbent machines exhibit high levels of confidence that they understand the true nature of politics, and that politicians care about what people like them think.

Regarding internal efficacy, the most important takeaway from Figure 7.7 is that government supporters report significantly more confidence in their understanding of the political system than opponents in dominant-party enclaves, while there is only a slight discrepancy between supporters and opponents emerges in multiparty contexts. Our interpretation is that this efficacy gap results from differential access to state resources based on partisanship in dominant-party machines. In our view, within dominant-party enclaves certain individuals obtain high levels of government responsiveness based on their status as loyal supporters of the incumbent machine and their ability to have direct contact with public officials and the local party apparatus, while citizens who refuse to "buy in" are left out in the cold. In high-functioning democracies, partisanship should have little effect on one's ability to understand politics—but within dominant-party machines, where

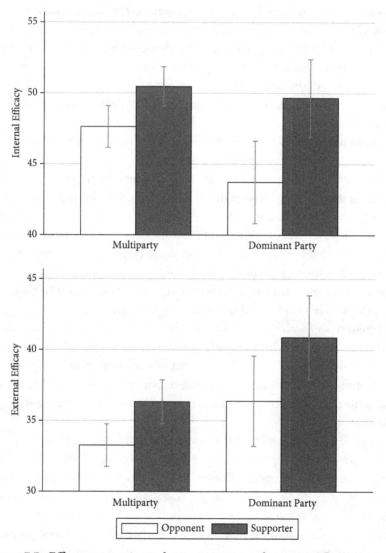

Figure 7.7. Efficacy among incumbent supporters and opponents by subnational regime type.

one stands with respect to the incumbent party appears to be vital in shaping internal efficacy.

On external efficacy, the notable result is that dominant-party supporters report higher levels of confidence that politicians care about what people like them think than all other groups, among which we fail to uncover statistically significant differences. We admit to being somewhat perplexed by the higher mean level of external efficacy among dominant-party opponents than their counterparts in multiparty states and provinces. More than anything, this highlights the need to further pursue this line of inquiry in the future in an effort to understand the political psyche of individuals living in a machine.

When assessing the findings as a whole, though, we find that while overall levels of external and internal efficacy appear somewhat similar in dominant-party and multiparty subnational regimes, a deeper investigation reveals important internal dynamics in terms of which citizens feel more efficacious. A sizeable efficacy gap between government supporters and opponents in dominant-party enclaves, particularly in terms of the degree to which citizens feel they understand politics, probably plays an important role in shaping who participates in politics in those states and provinces—indeed, in multiparty states and provinces, only a minimal partisan gap emerges.

Before moving on, one other reason why we might observe similar overall levels of efficacy across dominant and multiparty systems comes from Shi's (1997) work on political participation in Beijing. He finds that, despite their relative marginalization in official politics, political outsiders in China often seek out other avenues for advancing their interests locally, whereby they obtain some degree of efficacy that is generally not available to them through elections or party activities. Following this logic, those individuals who are most aware of the way the game of politics is played in their dominant-party system, and thus most aware of their inability to influence that machine in any meaningful way, will seek out other forms of voice, in this case at the neighborhood level. We do find some evidence that dominant-party opponents are more active in religious organizations, parent–teacher associations, and neighborhood improvement committees than their multiparty comments, but fully understanding how dominant-party citizens substitute political participation with local activism would require a deeper investigation.

Do Dominant-Party Opponents Fear Retribution?

Throughout this chapter, we have argued that dominant-party machines utilize a combination of carrots and sticks to incentivize their supporters to participate in politics, while discouraging their detractors from rocking the boat. Our thinking on the matter has been shaped by conversations we have had with citizens in dominant-party enclaves, combined with news reports regarding the strategic politicization of the rule of law in Argentine provinces like Formosa and San Luis, and Mexican states like Edomex and Colima. But obtaining quantitative data that sheds light on the thought processes of political activists in dominant-party enclaves is difficult, if not impossible—if citizens nested in political machines really are fearful to speak out against their provincial government, it would seem that they, much like the opposition party politician in Formosa mentioned in the introduction to this chapter, would be reluctant to admit so in an interview with a stranger.

We know that rates of protest are lower in dominant-party enclaves than in multiparty states and provinces (Figure 7.8)—these data corroborate findings from Moseley (2018), in which he uncovers a curvilinear relationship between the quality of subnational democracy and rates of peaceful protest wherein the *least* democratic Argentine provinces play host to the lowest

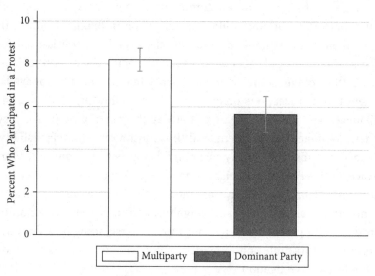

Figure 7.8. Reported protest participation by subnational regime type.

levels of street mobilization. Moseley reasons that protest is less common in the most closed political systems because machine parties more actively repress social movements that are critical of the governing party. When contention does arise, he finds that it more frequently results in violent conflict between protestors and state actors, similar to the episodes described by activists in Formosa and San Luis.

We lack high-quality measures for police repression at the individual level across Argentina and Mexico, but there was a special battery of protest-related items included in the 2010–2014 AmericasBarometer national surveys of Argentina, which was inspired by the high incidence of protest in that particular national case. One survey item asks respondents who report having participated in a peaceful street march or demonstration if that mobilization resulted in a clash between police and activists—a useful proxy for measuring experience with repression, given the peaceful nature of the protests reported by survey respondents. Of the 4,412 individuals who were interviewed in Argentina from 2010 to 2014, 660 (15 percent) claimed to have protested. Of those, 16 percent of the respondents ($n = 75$) replied "yes" to the question about having experienced a clash with police. A much smaller number of those individuals lived in dominant-party enclaves ($n = 37$), but nearly one third of those individuals claimed to have been confronted by police during demonstrations, compared with only 18 percent of those interviewed in multiparty contexts (Figure 7.9).

Given the small sample size from only one of the countries included in our study, it would seem imprudent to make sweeping generalizations about police repression in dominant-party enclaves based on the data summarized in Figure 7.9. But these results are consistent with anecdotal evidence like that presented at the beginning of this chapter and results from Moseley's (2018) analysis of protest across Argentine provinces—a higher percentage of dominant-party citizens, in spite of potential issues related to social desirability, claim to have been involved in clashes with police when they mustered up the courage to take to the streets. In sum, these data suggest that dominant-party machines shape political participation not only through incentivizing supporters to show up on Election Day, but also through intimidating opponents into quiescence. As the opposition gubernatorial candidate and activist in Formosa, Francisco Nazar, said, the *formoseños* "live in in a regime that behind the disguise of democracy hides a true dictatorship . . . there are not public freedoms, they persecute you, they threaten you" (La Nación 2017b, as quoted in Gervasoni 2018, 65). In dominant-party

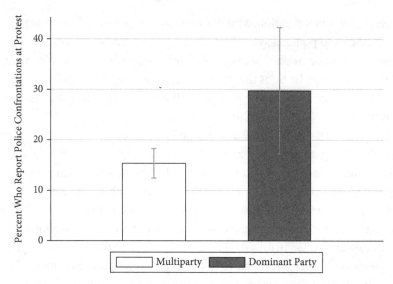

Figure 7.9. Percent of protest participants who reported police confrontation at protests by subnational regime category (Argentina 2010–2014).

enclaves, the choice to participate in political life is a more complicated one, in which citizens must weigh a set of carrots and sticks that are far less prevalent in multiparty regimes.

Conclusion

From one perspective, the findings we present in this chapter should not come as a surprise. Indeed, the fact that patterns of political participation in dominant-party systems differ from those patterns we would expect to find in multiparty contexts has an abundance of empirical and theoretical support from scholars working across a diverse set of cases, ranging from the one-party South in the United States to the hegemonic party rule of the PRI in Mexico throughout much of the 20th century. In contrast, from another perspective, our findings here and elsewhere challenge in a fundamental way the "whole-nation bias" (Linz and de Miguel 1966) that has characterized much of the political behavior work in emerging democracies over the past 30 years. Though an increasing number of scholars have recognized the highly uneven nature of these democratization processes around the world, few have taken the next step to explore the attitudinal and behavioral consequences of such unevenness.

In the preceding pages, we have taken that step and find significant divides running through both Argentina and Mexico that manifest themselves in the ways citizens within these countries engage with their political system. Whether in terms of the simple act of voting, the decision to take to the streets in support of or in opposition to a particular cause, or contacting a political official to ask for help, we find strong differences across subnational political contexts in both countries in terms of which citizens are most likely to engage in these behaviors. What these findings offer then is compelling evidence for contextual influences on an individual's political behavior patterns and, more generally, a democracy gap within two countries widely considered, at the national level, to be relatively democratic.

Dominant party machines "stack the deck" to ensure that loyal supporters have an outsized influence in elections and in their communities, which undoubtedly results in unequal political influence across partisan lines. They incentivize their supporters with carrots—whether it be a cushy government job, a much-desired social assistance plan, or food and medicine—in the days leading up to the election. They intimidate their opponents with sticks—threatening to fire them for insubordination or repress them if they dare to take to the streets and criticize the incumbent machine. The result is that participants in dominant-party politics do not constitute a representative cross-section of society—rather, they are less educated citizens who are largely government supporters and have made the decision (conscious or not) to go along to get along. And thus, the machine keeps chugging along.

What the results presented in this chapter suggest is that citizens within the same country, just as opposition party members living in the U.S. South throughout much of that country's history, have fundamentally different relationships with and access to their political representatives. Further, studies of political behavior and democratization that do not take into account the subnational divides that characterize many emerging democracies will not capture these distinct relationships that citizens have with their political system. If one of the core questions guiding the study of politics around the world remains "who gets what, when, and how?" (Lasswell 1936), then knowing the role that subnational regime characteristics play in answering it seems a vital step for comparative scholars of emerging (and established) democracies the world over. Our findings from two of those countries, Argentina and Mexico, offer all the more reason to begin taking that step.

8

Conclusion

On its face, the *merendero* program in San Luis seems like good social policy. Established during an economic downturn in Argentina characterized by spiking poverty levels and high inflation, the provincial government stepped up to the plate, offering the neediest children in the province a safe neighborhood space where they would have access to basic foodstuffs that many of their parents were probably struggling to provide. *Merenderos* have also been used to distribute tablet computers and other school materials, conduct free doctor's visits and administer vaccines, and supply sports equipment and provide playing fields. Similar social welfare programs have had enormous success in reducing poverty and increasing educational attainment in Argentina and across Latin America over the past two decades, and the *merenderos* in San Luis would seem to be a quintessential example of this trend.

Yet a more careful examination of the program's origins reveals less benign motivations on the part of the provincial government. The Rodríguez-Saá machine established the *merenderos* on August 22, 2017, on the heels of a resounding defeat for Adolfo's senatorial campaign in the primary elections on August 13. The initial plan would establish 400 sites throughout the province, each run by a party operative (Mayor 2017). Other journalistic accounts put the number of *merenderos* at closer to 5,000, with reports that parents were required to accompany their children to the sites, at which point they would engage in conversations with loyal party operatives and be encouraged to participate in party events (Perfil 2019). In a leaked WhatsApp audio attributed to a party staffer who had attended a meeting with the governor, the individual said, "For each child, there needs to be an adult . . . what he (Alberto) needs is votes . . . we need to convince 150,000 to vote (for Adolfo) in October" (El Puntano 2017). In another leaked audio, Alberto told a party leader that heads of *merenderos* who attended opposition rallies should be fired (Perfil 2019).

When digging into the *merenderos'* day-to-day operations, the partisan chicanery becomes even more apparent. The profile photo for the

Life in the Political Machine. Jonathan T. HiskeyJonathan T. Hiskey and Mason W. Moseley, Oxford University Press (2020). © Oxford University Press.
DOI: 10.1093/oso/9780197500408.001.0001

"Merenderos San Luis" Facebook page features a professionally designed logo that says "22AG," which has the dual meaning of commemorating the date that the program was established and promoting Alberto's 2019 campaign for governor (*Alberto Gobernador*). The Facebook group contains dozens of photographs of Alberto visiting children at the *merenderos*, many of whom are wearing shirts with the 22AG logo. In other photos, children pose in front of propaganda posters lining the walls of the facility, flashing the peace sign universally associated with Peronism in Argentina. On one particular post from October 16, 2018, which contains a flyer for the celebration of the annual Peronist "Day of Loyalty" the following afternoon, one woman replies with a question: "Good evening. I'm part of a merendero. Is tomorrow's rally obligatory as well?"

The case of the *merendero* program in San Luis highlights the degree to which dominant party machines can sink their talons into the citizens they represent. The individuals accessing the goods and services provided by *merenderos* undoubtedly *need* them—these are effectively "problem-solving web[s]" (Auyero 2000, 110) that help poor and working-class people make ends meet when times get tough. But the *merenderos* double as an important arm of the dominant-party machine that mobilizes supporters, threatens dissenters, and inculcates children with positive orientations toward the machine. When contemplating the future of dominant-party enclaves and the citizens they produce, as we will do in this chapter, this last point stands out. When children as young as five or six years old begin to view the PJ operative at their neighborhood *merendero* as a source of snacks and soccer balls, and the man on the posters plastered on the walls, who stops by every now and then to give hugs and hand out gifts, as some kind of benevolent paternal figure, political socialization and machine indoctrination become one and the same.

In this book, we make the case that the persistence of dominant-party enclaves in national-level democracies erodes democratic attitudes and behaviors from within. Clientelism and corruption are pervasive in dominant-party systems, and citizens' exposure to the dirty politics of their provincial regime incentivizes many to "go along to get along." At a moment in which the attitudinal consolidation of democracy in Latin America appears increasingly in doubt (Cohen et al. 2017), the persistence of less-than-democratic subnational regimes—and their effects on citizens who happen to live within them—becomes an even more important topic for study.

This closing chapter first serves to summarize our central argument and the evidence we bring forth to support it. Through our investigation of multiple dimensions of democratic public opinion and political behavior, we believe this book paints a compelling portrait of how subnational politics facilitates or hinders the development of an active and vibrant democratic citizenry. Second, we explore several key implications of our findings for research on political behavior in Latin America and beyond, including lessons regarding the limitations of crossnational studies, the extent to which we can generalize our findings to other democracies globally, and how to situate our analysis within the context of global democratic erosion.

We continue on a more optimistic note, by briefly exploring potential ways in which dominant-party systems can be defeated, giving way to multiparty competition that serves to reinforce, rather than undermine, democratic politics at the national level. We again draw on the cases of Argentina and Mexico, which we argue produce starkly different prognoses in terms of the future life span of dominant-party enclaves. Whereas in Argentina, there appears to be no real threat to dominant-party survival in many of the country's provinces, recent elections in Mexico have resulted in the PRI's defeat in traditional strongholds like Quintana Roo, Tabasco, and Tamaulipas. Even in Edomex, it appears the decades-long run of the PRI may be coming to a close, with its recent (2018) watershed loss in the mayoral election in Atlacomulco, a muncipality long considered the "cradle" of the once-dominant political party (Montes and de Córdoba 2017). From these cases, and the growing research on the demise of such regimes (e.g., Petersen 2018), we see that dominant-party enclaves are not invincible, and we offer a roadmap for how democratizing forces can prevail in such contexts.

In our discussion of the ways in which subnational dominant-party rule can be ended, we also return to a question to which we allude throughout the book: Do changes in citizen attitudes and behaviors provoke regime change, or do individuals merely respond to what are fundamentally elite-level dynamics? As we state in the initial presentation of our theory, we tend to favor the latter dynamic, without entirely ruling out the potential for a recursive relationship between institutions and behavior. Whereas we observe little evidence for an impending democratic sea change in the years leading up to the dominant-party's defeat, there are indications that democratic attitudes and behaviors have begun to consolidate in the near-decade following those transitions.

Finally, we bring the reader's attention to several avenues for future research that this book begins to explore or makes reference to but, due primarily to limitations of our data, has yet to systematically investigate. In our view, the findings presented in these pages are only the tip of the iceberg—moving forward, political behavior research must continue to investigate how local regimes shape individuals' ideas and opinions regarding politics, and whether or not (and how) they choose to enter the political arena themselves.

What Have We Learned?

Despite the pervasiveness of regime unevenness across the world's emerging democracies, and an abundance of research on the persistence of subnational authoritarianism in recently democratized countries (e.g., Gervasoni 2018; Gibson 2005, 2013; Giraudy 2015), we know little about the significance of these subnational divides for important economic, political, and social outcomes. Here we address the ramifications of dominant-party enclaves for national-level democracies by examining how living within a political machine influences citizens' political attitudes and behaviors. This book represents, to our knowledge, the first systematic effort to address the *consequences* of uneven democratization processes in emerging regimes.

In Chapter 2, we outline our theory of divided regimes. We argue that three key characteristics of dominant-party enclaves—(1) strategic application of the rule of law, (2) the conflation of state and dominant party, and (3) the systematic slanting of the electoral playing field—have important consequences for how individuals nested within such regimes think about and engage with politics. By strategic application of the rule of law, we mean the dominant party machine's ability to alter or circumvent established standards for legality to tilt the political playing field in their favor. This could mean sanctioning sophisticated vote-buying schemes, awarding construction bids to political allies, or utilizing law enforcement to disproportionately target and punish the opposition—practices that skirt legality and often become the domain of party machines in provinces devoid of institutionalized uncertainty (Chavez 2006).

Corruption is likely the most visible manifestation of this first trait of machine politics. In dominant-party systems, powerful machines can exploit a lack of institutional checks on power to misuse public funds and positions of

influence for political and economic gain. Thus, we argue that we should observe higher levels of corruption victimization in dominant-party enclaves
compared with multiparty environs. Our case studies of Edomex and San
Luis highlight the degree to which corruption becomes the name of the game
in dominant-party systems, as the political machines in both subnational
regimes capitalized on their position of strength to pack the local bureaucracy with loyalists, intimidate the opposition, and accumulate vast sums of
personal wealth.

We see the conflation of party and state, where the former monopolizes
and strategically deploys resources from the latter, as a second critical characteristic of dominant-party enclaves that influences the ways in which
citizens think about and engage with politics. One tried-and-true tool of governance for dominant-party incumbents is the selective use of state resources
in ways that reward and punish supporters and opponents, respectively. By
expanding the size of the public sector or rewarding loyal voters with cash
or food at election time, dominant parties can make citizens vulnerable
to the withdrawal of those benefits, and thus more risk averse in contemplating their political allegiances. We, therefore, find that in such contexts,
traditional performance metrics used by voters in established democracies,
like the state of the economy or one's assessment of the government's performance in such areas as fighting crime and providing adequate healthcare, are
less consequential, as individuals grow accustomed to a sort of "perverse accountability" (Stokes 2005) that reinforces hierarchical clientelistic linkages
and thus reduces the likelihood that dominant parties will be voted out of
office.

Finally, we argue that the relatively low level of electoral uncertainty characteristic of most dominant-party systems has important consequences for
how individuals think about and engage with politics. The resulting low
levels of political efficacy among opponents of the incumbent machine,
which come with the near certainty that the dominant party will prevail on
Election Day, reduce the odds that these individuals will participate in politics, thus ceding the political arena to machine loyalists. Rather than view
elections as an opportunity to replace the incumbent with a party more responsive to their policy demands, individuals in dominant-party systems
tend to view the electoral process as an opportunity to extract short-term
benefits in the absence of real competition. We also expect contentious participation to be less frequent in dominant-party systems, particularly among
government opponents, given that when it emerges it tends to result in

police repression by machine parties, as in the case of San Luis during the *multisectorial* protests of 2004–2005.

We present evidence to support our theory beginning in Chapter 4, where we demonstrate that citizens of dominant-party systems are more likely to be victimized by corruption and approached for clientelistic vote buying than their counterparts in multiparty contexts. These differences are statistically significant ($p < .01$) and substantively match or supersede the contributions of many other factors commonly linked to the chances that an individual will be exposed to these forms of dirty politics. This increased probability of first-hand experience with such under-the-table tactics is a key mechanism of our theory, given its potential downstream effects on democratic attitudes, vote choice, and various forms of political participation.

Perhaps more surprising than the higher prevalence of dirty politics in dominant-party systems is the evidence we offer for the prevalence of a "business as usual" attitude among dominant-party citizens, whereby individuals tend not to view corruption as a problem, instead viewing such tactics as an everyday feature of the political game they must play. To this point, we find that those *victimized* by corruption in dominant-party systems are no more likely than nonvictims to view corruption as a problem whereas in multiparty contexts, corruption victimization, as might be expected, is a strong predictor of the probability that an individual believes corruption is a problem. We are left, then, with citizens in dominant-party systems who are more likely to be victims of and exposed to the seedier side of politics but, perhaps in part due to this heightened exposure, are less likely to view these behaviors as problematic. Rather, being forced to pay off a cop to avoid harassment or being propositioned by an incumbent politician to sell one's vote in exchange for any number of forms of payment becomes, simply, a part of one's daily life in the machine.

Chapter 5 represents our initial foray into exploring how this dominant-party game of politics influences the ways in which individuals view democracy and the critical norms and processes that underlie such a system of government. Drawing on Carlin and Singer's (2011) approach to measuring support for polyarchy (Dahl 1971), we evaluate how living within a dominant-party system affects several dimensions of democratic attitudes, including support for inclusive participation and public contestation, a willingness to limit the power of the executive, respect for core institutions and processes, and a preference for democracy over any other system of government. We find that, on four of the five dimensions, individuals nested in dominant-party enclaves are significantly less democratic than their multi-party counterparts.

Most notable from these results is the fact that many of the questions used to construct the "support for polyarchy" index specifically reference national-level institutions, offering strong support for our contention that the deleterious effects of local-level dominant-party machines extend to attitudes and behaviors relevant to the national-level consolidation of democracy. In terms of support for democracy as the best system of government, living in a dominant-party system has among the strongest *negative* effects in our model, which includes a complete set of controls identified in the literature as key drivers of views toward democracy. With these findings, then, we move from identifying dominant-party citizens as likely victims of, and perhaps active participants in, dirty politics to finding that their general attitudes toward democracy, both in the abstract and with specific regard to the national-level institutions and norms that underlie their own democratic systems, are serving as a drag on the development of a democratic culture.

We next shift our lens to electoral accountability in Chapter 6 and find yet again a dominant-party citizenry that seems to reflect many of the undemocratic tendencies of the system in which they live. Here, we argue, and find evidence for, the idea that that dominant-party enclaves will thwart the performance-based representational linkages that are so central to the foundations of democracies. Rather than determine whether or not they will support the incumbent based on traditional performance metrics like sociotropic or pocketbook economic evaluations, security efforts, or public service quality, many individuals in dominant-party systems appear to be driven more out of concern for maintaining their favored status vis-à-vis the local machine, or, conversely, simply view the act of voting as a ritual with little connection to the behavior of government officials. Thus, many seemingly universal lessons from extant research on economic voting appear not to apply to dominant-party enclaves. More surprising perhaps is that these results hold, though not as powerfully, for national elections as well, offering another piece of evidence that much of, if not all, politics is, in fact, local. We also add to our picture of a dominant-party citizenry that appears to be moving farther away from the democratic norms and behaviors that we expect those living in a democratizing national system to exhibit.

Our final empirical chapter explores patterns of political participation in uneven regimes, including voter turnout, civic activism, and protest. Our expectation is that, in an effort to stack the deck in their favor come election time, dominant parties motivate participation by loyalists at least partially through selective incentives, while discouraging potential opponents much in the ways we explored in San Luis, Argentina, and Edomex, Mexico, through overt or implied threats. Our models of turnout and civic participation reveal that, as predicted by our theory, government supporters are more likely to participate in a diverse array of political activities than opponents in dominant-party systems, but not in multiparty contexts. In other words, the proincumbent slant to political participation is only present in dominant-party enclaves. We also find that whereas opponents are more likely to take to the streets in multiparty regimes than government supporters, as one would expect from the protest literature (e.g., Moseley 2018), supporters of the incumbent party are actually just as likely to participate in protests as opponents in dominant-party systems. Thus, even this traditional domain of conscientious objectors seems to have been hijacked by the local machine in dominant-party enclaves. Finally, we find that protestors in dominant-party enclaves are more likely to encounter police repression when they take to the streets, as predicted by extant literature (e.g., Moseley 2018) and anecdotal evidence from the case study of San Luis offered in Chapter 3. What this finding suggests is that demonstrating against the incumbent machine carries with it significant costs for government opponents and might contribute to their decision to remain on the sidelines of political life.

Implications for Studies of Political Behavior

The findings presented to this point have a number of important implications for studies of political behavior in general, and particularly those that endeavor to examine patterns of political participation and attitudes at the local level. Here, we address several in turn.

Limitations of Crossnational Studies

As should be evident from the preceding pages, we view the systematic comparison of subnational political systems and, in our case, their effect on the political attitudes and behaviors of citizens living within them, as critical in developing a fuller understand of the drivers of the ways people think about and engage with politics. We are certainly not the first to call attention to the importance of the many subnational divides that run through countries, but relatively few have pursued in a systematic fashion the impact of these divides on citizens' political attitudes and behavior. As we have referenced multiple times throughout the preceding pages, V. O. Key (1949) stands as perhaps the founding father of subnational comparative political analysis with his extensive study of the one-party states of the U.S. South. Interestingly, though, Key's work focused more on uncovering the similarities and differences that existed *within the one-party South* rather than exploring the implications of the political divide that separated those states from the rest of the United States.

Where Key's analysis does step beyond the borders of the South, and in many ways anticipates the work of Gibson (2013) and others 40 years later, is in the role he identifies for the one-party South in supporting national political agendas—a role that helped explain why such a repressive, undemocratic set of subnational political systems could coexist with a national system that many viewed as the shining example of democratic rule. A key (no pun intended) lesson from this analysis that we have applied in the preceding pages is the critical, and often forgotten, influence that subnational systems have on the quality of a country's democratic system as a whole. Mickey's 2015 work on the various paths toward democracy that the one-party systems of the U.S. South followed, and the political, social, and economic implications of those paths, offers a recent example from the American politics subfield of the type of work that awaits for scholars of the many emerging, and uneven, democracies around the world. Though more and more work has emerged over the past 20 years to help us understand the roots of subnational authoritarian enclaves (e.g., Fox 1994; Snyder 2001; Gibson 2005, 2013; Gervasoni 2010b, 2018; Giraudy 2013, 2015), relatively few have examined the impact of such divides on the lives of individuals who reside within them. It is this gap that we have tried to address in this study.

While work on the implications of such divides has been rare in work on political behavior, this is not the case in the area of development studies, both within academia and work coming from the international development community. Echeverri-Gent's subnational analysis (1992) of poverty alleviation programs in India highlighted the importance of state-level electoral competitiveness in explaining variations in the development outcomes of such programs. More squarely in the development community, the United Nations Development Programme in recent years has devoted considerable resources to identifying and exploring the implications for human development of various subnational divides, noting that "[t]he HDI [Human Development Index] provides a snapshot of average national performance in human development. However, averages can obscure large disparities within countries" (Watkins, 2006, 269). The UNDP report goes on to disaggregate the HDI along regional, gender, and ethnic lines, revealing, for example, that within China, "urban Shanghai would rank 24 in the global HDI league, just above Greece, while rural Guizhou Province would rank alongside Botswana" (271). In a similar vein, we find in Chapter 5 that support for democracy among citizens living in the dominant-party systems of Argentina and Mexico is on par with the levels of support found in El Salvador, while those Argentines and Mexicans living in multiparty subnational systems report levels of support for democracy that exceed those found in the United States. In short, just as the UNDP looks at the "same country [and finds] different worlds" (270), we, too, find fundamentally distinct patterns of political attitudes and behaviors developing within single countries. And in a world now characterized by highly uneven political regimes that populate the gray area between outright authoritarian systems and fully democratic ones, attention to the subnational contours of these uneven landscapes is all the more important in efforts to understand how and why individuals engage with politics in distinct ways.

How Far Does the Theory Travel?

As in any comparative study of two countries, albeit a study with over 50 subnational units serving as the focal point of the analysis, one question certain to arise among readers is how far our findings from the provinces and states of Argentina and Mexico might travel. Our answer, simply, is "Quite far." Though certainly a speculative answer, as we have done limited work outside of the countries of this study, we view the idea that one's subnational political system will influence the ways in which she thinks about and engages with politics as one that should be applicable across a wide range of countries and cultures.

Digging into the well-worn notion that "all politics is local" we have a long history of political theorists who have attached great importance to that government which is closest to the people in terms of shaping their more general views toward and engagement with democratic politics. As Gannett noted, Tocqueville's writings on America viewed, "political life in the local town

[as] the indispensable catalyst for both creating and sustaining a successful democracy" (2005, 721). This role for subnational government in the deepening of a country's democracy has been made all the more critical in an era of decentralization, whereby efforts to bring government closer to the people have resulted in the empowerment of subnational political officials the world over (see Eaton 2004; Falleti 2010).

A fundamental premise underlying hopes that decentralization will bring increased citizen participation in politics and strengthened ties of accountability between citizens and their elected officials is that the institutions of democratic accountability created at the subnational level, whether in the form of elections or citizen oversight boards, will function as designed. And if they do, the potential for contributing to the growth of a democratic citizenry is substantial, with such positive effects extending beyond the borders of the subnational unit in question. As Stoyan and Niedzwiecki (2018) find, "increased regional authority through self-rule [i.e., decentralization] positively affects voting participation . . . [with] individuals living in countries with higher levels of authority, . . . in their own territory are more likely to turnout to vote" (34). In other words, as we have claimed throughout this work, subnational democratic institutions have great potential to contribute to the formation of democratic citizens.

What is at times forgotten in discussions of the potential benefits of decentralization, however, are the consequences for citizen's political attitudes and behaviors when the institutions of decentralization do not work as designed but, rather, are captured by elites to serve their own narrow interests. As Hiskey and Seligson (2003) find in their study of the impact of Bolivia's decentralization program on citizens' attitudes toward democracy, "decentralization can bolster citizen levels of system support at the national level . . . [but] the renewed emphasis on local government can have the opposite effect of producing *more negative* views of the political system when the performance of local institutions falters" (64). These findings echo those of many others from across the developing world, and what they tell us is simply that no matter the country or culture, subnational political systems can have powerful *positive* or *negative* effects on the ways citizens view and engage with their political world more generally. It is this idea that we see as applicable across time and space. Our work on the subnational landscapes of Argentina and Mexico, then, serves merely as a first step in understanding how subnational political dynamics shape the contours of a country's national political regime.

Uneven Regimes and the Global Erosion of Democracy

Reports from around the world seem to increasingly point to the deterioration of democratic norms and procedures—whether in the case of the rise of populist leaders in established democracies or the continued instances of electoral violence in emerging democracies (Diamond 2015). Michael Abramowitz, president of the Freedom House organization, writes in the opening to the 2018 *Freedom in the World* report that "democracy is in crisis. The values it embodies—particularly the right to choose leaders in free and fair elections, freedom of the press, and the rule of law—are under assault and in retreat globally" (Freedom House 2018, 1). While such trends have many contributing factors, we offer the persistence of subnational dominant-party systems, and the impact they have on citizens living within them, as one such obstacle to the deepening of national-level democracies. With dominant-party elites actively working to undermine and distort the accountability mechanisms of democracy, and many dominant-party citizens tolerant of, if not complicit in, the operation of the system's machine, a country's national-level democratization project will almost invariably be slowed.

On what basis do we make this claim that dominant-party systems at the subnational level undermine democratic projects at the national level? As we have tried to catalogue throughout the preceding pages, the most pernicious feature of the dominant-party systems we have described is the efforts by dominant-party elites to co-opt, and make complicit, significant segments of the mass public. The fact that dominant-party citizens are less inclined to view corruption as a problem, despite (or perhaps because of) being more likely to have experience with it, is but one indication of how a dominant-party system can undermine the development of a democratic citizenry that is willing and able to play its oversight role in the operation of a high-functioning democracy. More generally, the influence dominant-party systems appear to have on the general orientation toward democracy held by citizens living within them is equally problematic for the deepening of democracy. At a minimum, societal support for the basic idea of democracy is essential for it to flourish as a system of government, and in today's world, as Abramowitz notes, there are relatively fewer people with concrete memories of the vicissitudes of authoritarian rule:

> Perhaps worst of all, and most worrisome for the future, young people, who have little memory of the long struggles against fascism and communism, may be losing faith and interest in the democratic project. The very idea of democracy and its promotion has been tarnished among many, contributing to a dangerous apathy. (Freedom House 2018, 1)

We view the deleterious effects of life in a dominant-party system, whether as a tacit supporter or vocal opponent, as central to understanding the decay from within that appears to be eroding many of the world's emerging and, in some cases, established democracies. The fact that the current global democratic landscape is pockmarked with so many subnational dominant-party systems then does not bode well for democracy moving forward. That said, one other lesson we can draw from Mexico, if not Argentina, is that such subnational obstacles to democracy are not impervious to change, for no matter how hard dominant-party elites may try to insulate themselves from such change, they can, and often do, fail.

Pathways out of Uneven Democracy

While they are often exceedingly difficult to dislodge given the structural advantages we outline throughout this book, dominant parties do lose elections. Here we outline some of the factors that can contribute to transitions from single-party dominance to multiparty competition, drawing from our critical cases of Argentina and Mexico. The two most important factors, in our view, are (1) opposition parties' ability to construct short-term alliances with so-called "strange bedfellows" and (2) the extent to which dominant parties' control over economic opportunity within their borders can be challenged. In the case of Argentina, there is little evidence to suggest uneven democracy is on the way out, due to the absence of a consistent national-level alternative to the Peronist Party (at least until 2015) and the continued economic power granted to governors of less populous provinces through the federal coparticipation scheme. In Mexico, on the other hand, recent PRI losses in states like Tabasco, Tamaulipas, and Quintana Roo provide some grounds for optimism regarding the trajectory of the country's uneven regime. We address each case in turn.

Entrenched Dominant-Party Enclaves in Argentina

There is little evidence to suggest dominant-party enclaves are under threat in Argentina. Of the 16 multiparty provinces in our analysis, 12 had transitioned by 2000, offering some indication that if dominant-party systems were to be dislodged, it was likely to occur in the first three or four posttransition elections. As of 2014, the end of our empirical analysis, Río Negro was the last Argentine province to transition from dominant-party rule, doing so in 2011 in an unusual case due both to the fact that the UCR had been the dominant party since 1983, and that the first non-UCR governor, Peronist Carlos Soria, was murdered early in his first term in office by his wife. One province—Jujuy in 2015—has transitioned from dominant-party rule to multiparty competition since the end of the period under study, highlighting the difficult obstacles faced by machine opponents in Argentina. We return to the case of Jujuy at the conclusion of this discussion.

A peculiar wrinkle with respect to Argentina's uneven regime is the extent to which governors of dominant-party systems have achieved national prominence in Buenos Aires. Carlos Menem—who served as president of Argentina from 1989 to 1999 and whose tactics inspired scholarship on "delegative democracy" (O'Donnell 1993), "neoliberalism by surprise" (Stokes 2001), and "institutional weakness" (Levitsky and Murillo 2005; Spiller and Tommasi 2009)—famously hailed from the dominant-party enclave of La Rioja, where in the decade prior to his election as president he constructed his own political fiefdom.[1] Néstor and Cristina Fernández de Kirchner controlled the executive branch from 2003 to 2015 and, like Menem, began their political careers in one of Argentina's least democratic provinces: Santa Cruz (Gervasoni 2018). Even Adolfo Rodríguez-Saá held the presidency for a brief moment in 2001, having established himself as one of the preeminent PJ power players throughout his many years as governor and senator from San Luis.

---

[1] Menem was actually the governor of La Rioja for the first time before the military coup in 1976, after which he was removed from office by the military junta.

Gibson's (2012) treatise on "boundary control" sheds light on the symbiotic relationship that can emerge between provincial machines and democratically elected presidents. In Argentina, the strength of dominant-party governors is heightened by one of the world's most malapportioned legislatures, which grants executives from small provinces, in particular, significant bargaining power in both houses of congress (Diamond and Plattner 2006; Samuels and Snyder 2001). Given their disproportionate influence and the small populations of their home provinces, legislators hailing from more far-flung areas of the country are much less expensive targets for dealmaking than those from populous areas like Buenos Aires and Córdoba (Scartascini and Tommasi 2012; Spiller and Tommasi 2009). Given that none of the dominant-party enclaves in Argentina are among the five largest in terms of population (Buenos Aires, Buenos Aires capital, Córdoba, Mendoza, and Santa Fé), governors of such less-than-democratic provinces thus wield significant bargaining power in the capital. In sum, it appears that rather than being bit players nationally or even shunned, governors from dominant-party systems are often central to national politics in Argentina.

Among the likely culprits for the perpetuation of dominant-party rule in Argentina is the coparticipation scheme elaborated on in Chapter 3, which many have argued results from the country's extremely malapportioned legislative chambers, and the weakness (at least until recently) of national-level alternatives to the Peronist Party. As Gervasoni (2010b, 2018) demonstrates convincingly, the more "rentier" the provincial regime, the more likely governors are to consolidate power and drift away from liberal democracy. Argentina's coparticipation system disproportionately favors peripheral provinces with small populations and has inadvertently vested massive political power in the governors of such provinces. Using federal transfers, which are decoupled from local taxes, governors can build bloated public sectors populated primarily by loyalists and punish potential opponents who choose not to go along to get along. This disproportionate economic influence undoubtedly reinforces dominant-party rule in provinces like La Rioja, Santa Cruz, and San Luis.

The other factor working in favor of dominant-party systems in Argentina is the absence (at least until recently) of a national political party to rival the Peronists. Historically, the UCR has been strong in Argentine cities, universities, and in the *campo* (the country's agricultural sector) but lacked territorial penetration in less developed parts of the country. Though the UCR has held the presidency on two occasions—with Raúl Alfonsín in the 1980s and Fernando de la Rúa from 1999 to 2001—no non-Peronist government had been able to finish its term in office since Argentina returned to democracy in 1983, largely due to the muscle of the Peronist Party throughout the country and in the Buenos Aires *conurbano* (greater urban area).[2] But in 2015, the mayor of Buenos Aires capital and founder of the Propuesta Republicana (PRO, which would become central to the Cambiemos coalition), Mauricio Macri, won the presidency. Cambiemos's successful presidential election was accompanied by a gubernatorial victory in Jujuy in 2015 and impressive gains in the 2017 midterm elections in Buenos Aires province, each of which were territories long dominated by the PJ. However, Macri would go on to lose his bid for reelection in October 2019 amid a crippling inflation rate and stunted economic growth, although he was able to buck the trend and finish his term.

On this note, we return to the case of Jujuy, Argentina's northernmost province, which in 2015 witnessed the end of the PJ's three-decade domination of provincial politics. In the lead-up to the 2015 gubernatorial election, Gerardo Morales, a national senator and member of the UCR, became part of the Cambiemos coalition in Jujuy, led by then-presidential candidate Macri's party (PRO), the UCR, and a collection of smaller parties. In October, he ousted incumbent governor Eduardo Fellner by more than 20 points—the first time the PJ had suffered defeat in a gubernatorial election since Argentina's return to democracy in 1983.

Morales' decision, along with his coalition partners, to band together in an effort to defeat the PJ was clearly decisive in paving the way for his victory. In the press conference announcing the creation of Frente Cambia Jujuy, Morales proclaimed:

> We have a great task of reparation before us. It doesn't matter how many insults, threats, or defamations we have received. In response to the violent, the decadent, and the demonstrated failures, we answer with our convictions, with peace and tolerance; with a real plan and with dreams (for Jujuy). We are the strength and the change: a new government.[3]

Morales went out of his way to thank the various presidential candidates aligned with the parties making up the coalition, claiming, "they have

---

[2] See Auyero's (2007) excellent account of the 2001 lootings in the *conurbano* outside Buenos Aires, which he argues persuasively were organized by Peronist operatives.

[3] Authors' translation. "Se lanzó el Frente Cambia Jujuy. 'Aquí está el nuevo gobierno.'" http://www.cambiajujuy.com.ar/info.php?id=2

understood our reality (in Jujuy) and the challenges we face as a country and in Jujuy, where change will require an even greater effort" (2). It seems unlikely that such a sweeping victory would have been possible without this support from politicians in Buenos Aires, and the collaboration between multiple parties in Jujuy. The principal challenge confronting such coalitions is that when they actually win, they have trouble governing given the diversity of viewpoints demanding a seat at the table. And it is difficult to know if such coalitions can survive over the long haul—only that they are necessary to precipitate the defeat of the dominant party. Yet in Jujuy, it appears the PJ's 2015 defeat was only a harbinger of things to come, as the once-dominant party was handily defeated again by Cambiemos in 2017 and nearly surpassed by the Frente de Izquierda y de los Trabajadores (FIT) from the left. In sum, while the deck has long been stacked against opposition parties in Argentine dominant-party enclaves, given the economic strength of the provincial state and territorial weakness of minority political parties nationally, the rise of Cambiemos and potential for electoral coalitions between a multifarious band of democratizers did the trick in Jujuy and might elsewhere in the years to come.

Dominant-Party Decline in Mexico

Since 2010, we have seen the overturn of nine dominant-party systems in Mexico, leaving, in 2020, only five states where the PRI has never lost control of the executive branch (Campeche, Coahuila, Colima, Hidalgo, and Edomex). What have been the ingredients of this subnational sea change taking place within Mexico over the past several years? In many respects, the factors that seem most important in explaining the recent ousters of dominant-party systems at the subnational level are the same ones that help explain the demise of the PRI's national dominant-party system in 2000.

With virtually every one of the recent defeats of the PRI and its first-time ouster from the governor's office, several features were in place. As Petersen (2018) convincingly demonstrates, "elite fracture, defection of groups from the authoritarian elite to the opposition, and opposition unification" (36) have been essential components to these ousters. With some exceptions, these factors are similar to those that ultimately contributed to the downfall of the PRI at the national level in 2000.

The victory of PAN candidate Vicente Fox in the 2000 presidential election is widely seen as the final step in Mexico's move away from a one-party authoritarian system to a multiparty democracy. Preceding that victory was the fracture of the PRI in the late 1980s, with the formation of the Partido Revolucionario Democrático (PRD) by disaffected *PRIistas*, a highly contentious battle among several PRI candidates for the party's nomination for the 2000 presidential race, and the general coalescence of the opposition, albeit without a formal coalition, around Fox as the candidate of change.

A second key factor in that watershed election was voter turnout, or lack thereof. As Klesner explains, "The PRI had built its hegemony on its capacity to turn out voters in rural Mexico. In July 2000 it failed at this essential task" (2001, 110). We can see, then, that both at the national and subnational levels, the defeat of a dominant-party system depends on the formation of opposition alliances and the awakening of the citizenry to the possibility that the dominant-party can, in fact, lose an election. It was for this reason that Fox's campaign slogan in 2000 was, simply, "*Ya!*," roughly translated as "It's time!" His campaign was able to convince enough voters to break out of the chains of the PRI's one-party machine and, as a result, bring an end to a 70-year-old dominant-party system. The basic lessons of this regime change can be, and have been, applied to efforts to rid the country of state-level dominant party systems. Though such efforts did not prevail in the 2017 elections in Edomex, it seems only a matter of time before that particular dominant-party system also crumbles under the weight of a determined opposition, a fractured dominant-party elite, and continued struggles for these latter officials to maintain the tenuous bargain they have struck with the general public in order to sustain a dominant-party subnational system in the midst of a maturing national-level democracy.

Next Steps

What next? The first, and most important, answer to this question concerns a matter of data collection. To our knowledge, there are few examples of surveys in emerging democracies that are representative at the state or provincial level. While we believe that the evidence we bring to bear from the AmericasBarometer surveys of Argentina and Mexico is convincing, given the nationally representative nature of those surveys and the extensive battery of relevant items they entail, our analytical leverage and findings would no doubt be strengthened by surveys that were fully representative of populations residing in dominant-party enclaves. Political behavior scholars would do well to zero in on local regimes for future crosslevel studies of how context and subnational institutions influence attitudes and behaviors, perhaps leading to the construction of a database of provincial-level survey projects.

Another topic left unexplored in this book, given our emphasis on those political systems that have never experienced an alternation in the party of the governor, is the possibility that dominant-party systems can resurface after the initial transition has occurred. This echoes Huntington's (1991) emphasis on the "two turnover test," which he argued was critical to identifying the establishment of democracy. At first glance, there are a number of provincial and state regimes in Argentina and Mexico in which initial transitions took place, only to be replaced with new machine-like systems. In Misiones, Argentina, for example, the UCR yielded the governorship to the PJ in 1987, which then morphed into the Frente Renovador de la Concordia in 2003, an alliance between members of the UCR and PJ that eventually sided with the Kirchners' branch of the Peronist Party, Frente para la Victoria (FpV). In more than two decades, the Frente Renovador has yet to lose a gubernatorial election in the province, and its initial governor and current president of the party, Carlos Rovira, is largely perceived to wield the real authority in the province behind the scenes. The rigorous measurement strategies put forth by Gervasoni (2018) and Giraudy (2015) are probably the best place to start for capturing these dynamics, but the question of how the return of dominant parties might affect individuals' attitudes and behaviors is one that remains unanswered.

The possibility that dominant-party tactics can reemerge is one that, in our view, is not confined to Latin America and other developing regions. Gervasoni (2018), in his crossnational analysis of subnational regimes, finds quite a range of subnational regimes across such countries as the United States, Germany, and India (232), suggesting that when moving beyond our "first alternation" rule, both developing and established democracies may have to confront episodes of subnational "dominant-partyism," and the governing tactics often used to keep such machines running as long as possible. From the U.S. case, it seems it is increasingly common to find examples of such tactics in the areas of voter registration, electoral districting, and campaign financing, among others. In the face of such undemocratic governing tactics, our research suggests that either internal conflict within the dominant party must occur or the central government must intervene in order to put an end to such practices. When the Fourth U.S. Circuit Court of Appeals struck down North Carolina's controversial voter ID law in 2016, the decision noted that the law would "target African-Americans with almost surgical precision" (Domonoske 2017). In 2017, a panel of federal judges blocked a bold attempt at gerrymandering by North Carolina Republicans, which was justified by the state legislator who designed the map with the rationale: "I think electing Republicans is better than electing Democrats. So I drew this map to help foster what I think is better for the country" (Liptak and Blinder 2018). The map had produced a substantial winner's bonus for Republicans in North Carolina in the 2016 presidential election, where they garnered 53 percent of the vote statewide, but 10 of the state's 13 seats in the U.S. House of Representatives. Most recently, a sweeping corruption scandal in West Virginia in which state Supreme Court justices were charged with using 3.2 million dollars in public funding to renovate their offices has resulted in an unprecedented situation in which the entire West Virginia Supreme Court could face impeachment (Raby 2018). Shortly after the scandal unfolded and a pair of justices resigned, the Republican governor appointed two Republican legislators with little judicial experience to the court to serve in their stead. While full-blown dominant-party systems similar to those in Argentina and Mexico might not exist in the United States in 2020, clearly undemocratic practices seem to thrive in certain subnational systems more than others, and that could have serious consequences for how citizens of those states understand and participate in politics. Once again, these trends emphasize even more the need for a national government that is willing, and able, to step in with corrective measures for such cases.

One more avenue for future research might explore how politicians from dominant-party systems behave when they gain prominence in national politics. This question clearly lies beyond the individual-level focus of this book, but the presidencies of Carlos Menem, Néstor and Cristina Kirchner in Argentina, and Enrique Peña Nieto, president of Mexico between 2012 and 2018, all of whom hail from dominant-party enclaves, provide grounds for further investigation of the extent to which such presidents take the subnational governing practices that made them successful in dominant-party enclaves with them to the capital (see Gervasoni 2018). Further, this question seems particularly salient given the wide-ranging corruption scandals that have plagued such presidents, with the most notable being an alleged multibillion-dollar scheme to extract bribes in exchange for government construction contracts in Argentina under the Kirchners. It seems possible that dominant-party legislators, too, might utilize less-than-democratic tactics at higher rates than their colleagues from multiparty provinces and states. In sum, the fact that the presidency has so frequently been entrusted in the hands of dominant-party bosses in recent years raises important concerns about the potential impact this might have on national-level politics and democratic consolidation, particularly given the troublesome findings we uncover in such less-than-democratic subnational environs in this book.

Finally, we stop short in examining how dominant-party systems might influence patterns of political representation on key dimensions like race, gender, and socioeconomic status. Our expectation is that women, racial minorities, and the poor are more likely to be left out of the political process in contexts rife with corruption and politicized rule of law, even if those groups receive some degree of political inclusion through clientelism and public sector employment. But for lack of space, we were unable to delve into those vital issues here. Particularly in Argentina, where the rise of the Ni Una Menos feminist movement and the subsequent debate on abortion rights has swept the country, it would be illuminating to investigate how subnational regime differences have manifested in terms of female participation in politics and attention to these important issues. While women have increasingly gained a foothold in national politics in Argentina, from a watershed gender quota system in the Chamber of Deputies to the two-term presidency of Cristina Fernández de Kirchner, those national-level trends might not have trickled down to certain provinces. Indeed, when the abortion law was defeated in the National Senate, many attributed its failure to the votes of senators from conservative provinces in the interior, some of which fall within our category of dominant-party enclaves.

In conclusion, we present abundant evidence in this book to suggest that any effort to empirically evaluate, and understand, the attitudinal consolidation of democracy and patterns of political behavior in emerging regimes needs to account for the distinct subnational political environments found *within* countries, and the many behavioral consequences of this variation. This book represents our effort to push forward understanding of how characteristics of local regimes shape the political attitudes and behaviors of those living within them—what we find here is striking but might only be the tip of the iceberg. It certainly appears to be the case that when it comes to the forces that shape the ways in which individuals perceive and participate in politics, many, if not all of them, are found beneath the national level.

Table A.1. Question Wording and Descriptive Statistics

Variable	Question Wording or Explanation	N	Mean	Min	Max
Dependent Variables					
Corruption Victimization	"Have you used any public health services in the last twelve months? In order to be seen in a hospital or a clinic in the last twelve months, did you have to pay a bribe?" Used the same format for schools, police. 0 if no, 100 if yes for any.	12,103	0.27	0	1
Receipt of Vote-Buying Offer	"In recent years and thinking about election campaigns, has a candidate or someone from a political party offered you something, like a favor, food, or any other benefit or thing in return for your vote or support? Has this happened often, sometimes or never?" 0 never, 1 if often or sometimes.	4,390	0.16	0	1
Perception of Corruption	"Taking into account your own experience or what you have heard, corruption among public officials is: (1) Very common (2) Common (3) Uncommon or (4) Very uncommon?" Recoded 0–100.	11,630	78.22	0	100
Perception of Gov't Efforts to Combat Corruption	"To what extent would you say the current administration combats (fights) government corruption?" 100-point scale; higher values = higher effort to combat corruption.	11,753	36.137	0	100

Continued

Table A.1. *Continued*

Variable	Question Wording or Explanation	N	Mean	Min	Max
Public Contestation	This index gauges support for various forms of political participation, including (a) legal public demonstrations, (b) community activism, and (c) voluntarism in political campaigns. 100-point scale; higher values = more support.	8,827	71.03	0	100
Inclusive Participation	An index that includes whether or not respondents believe citizens who are critical of the regime should be able to (a) vote, (b) conduct peaceful demonstrations, (c) run for office, or (d) appear on television to make speeches. It also includes support for the right of homosexuals to run for public office. 100-point scale; higher values = more support.	10,920	55.75	0	100
Limits on the Executive	An index that includes responses to three questions: (a) whether presidents would be justified in limiting the voice of the opposition for the good of the country, (b) whether people should govern directly and not through elected representatives, and (c) whether those who oppose the majority represent a threat to the country. 100-point scale; higher values = less control. Reverse coding for models.	8,052	34.00	0	100
Institutions and Processes	A single question that asks respondents if the executive would be justified in closing the legislature in the event of a crisis. 100-point scale; higher values = more justified. Reverse coding for models.	8,257	12.73	0	100

Table A.1. *Continued*

Variable	Question Wording or Explanation	N	Mean	Min	Max
Support for Democracy	"Democracy may have problems, but it is better than any other form of government. To what extent do you agree or disagree with this statement?" 100-point scale; higher values = more strongly agree.	11,611	75.05	0	100
Prospective Vote for Incumbent President	"If the next presidential elections were being held this week, what would you do? Wouldn't vote (1); Would vote for the incumbent candidate or party (2); Would vote for a candidate or party different from the current administration (3); Would go to vote but would leave the ballot blank or would purposely cancel my vote (4)." For main analysis, we consider only prospective votes for (1) and against (0) the incumbent. In supplementary models, we consider all respondents who say they would vote, thus including prospective blank votes.	5,269	0.44	0	1
Prospective Vote for Incumbent Governor	"If the next gubernatorial elections were being held this week, what would you do? Wouldn't vote (1); Would vote for the incumbent candidate or party (2); Would vote for a candidate or party different from the current administration (3); Would go to vote but would leave the ballot blank or would purposely cancel my vote (4)." For main analysis, we consider only prospective votes for (1) and against (0) the incumbent. In appendix, we consider all respondents who say they would vote, thus including prospective blank votes.	2,486	0.50	0	1

Continued

Table A.1. *Continued*

Variable	Question Wording or Explanation	N	Mean	Min	Max
Past Turnout	"Did you vote in the last presidential election?" 1 if yes, 0 if no.	12,008	76.02	0	1
Protest Participation	"Have you participated in a street march or demonstration during the past 12 months?" 1 if yes, 0 if no.	9,003	0.08	0	1
Attendance of Party Meetings	Have you attended meetings of a political party or political organization? Do you attend them . . . "once a week," "once or twice a month," "once or twice a year," or "never?" 0 if never, 1 if attended at any point in past year.	12,044	0.06	0	1
Soliciting Help from Local Official	"In order to solve your problems have you ever requested help or cooperation from a local public official or local government: for example, a mayor, municipal council, councilman, provincial official, civil governor or governor?" 0 if no, 1 if yes.	12,059	0.14	0	1
Independent Variables					
Pocketbook Economic Situation	"How would you describe your overall economic situation? Would you say that it is very good, good, neither good nor bad, bad or very bad?" 100-point scale; higher values = good. (Analysis for Chapter 6 2008–2012.)	9,035	50.55	0	100

Table A.1. *Continued*

Variable	Question Wording or Explanation	N	Mean	Min	Max
Sociotropic Economic Situation	"How would you describe the country's economic situation? Would you say that it is very good, good, neither good nor bad, bad or very bad?"	9,013	40.89	0	100
	100-point scale; higher values = good. (Analysis for Chapter 6 2008–2012.)				
Satisfaction with Health Services	"And thinking about this city/area where you live, are you very satisfied, satisfied, dissatisfied, or very dissatisfied with the condition of public health services?"	2,970	51.48	0	100
	100-point scale; higher values = more satisfied. (Analysis for Chapter 6 2008–2012.)				
Government Improves Security	"To what extent would you say the current administration improves citizen safety?"	8,887	41.23	0	100
	100-point scale; higher values = a lot. (Analysis for Chapter 6 2008–2012.)				
Preference for Active State Role in Employment	"Now I am going to read several phrases about the role of the state. Please tell me to what extent you agree or agree with each statement: the state, more than the private sector, should be responsible for creating employment." 100-point scale; higher values = very much agree. (Analysis for Chapter 6 2008–2012.)	8,966	80.01	0	100

Continued

Table A.1. *Continued*

Variable	Question Wording or Explanation	N	Mean	Min	Max
Interest in Politics	"How much interest do you have in politics: a lot, some, little or none?"	12,038	38.60	0	100
	100-point scale; higher values = a lot of interest.				
Age	Respondents' age in years.	12,070	39.71	17	93
Wealth Quintile	A weighted index that measures wealth based on the possession of certain household goods such as televisions, refrigerators, conventional and cellular telephones, vehicles, washing machines, microwave ovens, indoor plumbing, indoor bathrooms and computers.	12,024	2.94	1	5
Education	Level of formal education. 4-point scale; 0=None, 1=Primary, 2=Secondary, 3=Superior	12,110	9.62	0	18
Female	1 if female, 0 if male.	12,137	0.51	0	1
Urban	1 if interview took place in urban setting, 0 if rural.	12,137	0.18	0	1
Church Attendance	Reported attendance of religious organization meetings; 100-point scale; highest values = weekly attendance.	12,092	34.29	0	100
Development	Terciles of per capita *Producto Bruto Interno* (PBG) by province/state.	11,045			
Governor Copartisan	Individual identifies with the same party as the incumbent governor. 1 if yes, 0 if no.	12,137	0.09	0	1

Table A.2: Items for Wealth Index

Could you tell me if you have the following in your house: R3. Refrigerator, R4. Landline/residential telephone (not cellular), R4A. Cellular telephone, R5. Vehicle/car, R6. Washing machine, R7. Microwave oven, R8. Motorcycle, R12. Indoor plumbing, R14. Indoor bathroom, R15. Computer, R18. Internet, R1. Television, R16. Flat panel TV, R26. Is the house connected to the sewage system?

Table A.3. Preference for Active State Role in Employment and Gubernatorial Vote Choice by Subnational Regime Type

VARIABLES	Prospective Vote for Governor
	(1 = Vote for Governor's Party; 0 = Vote for Opposition Party)
Female	0.322***
	(0.103)
Age	0.001
	(0.004)
Wealth (Quintile)	0.023
	(0.040)
Interest in Politics	−0.007***
	(0.002)
Education (Level)	−0.288***
	(0.079)
Urban	−0.046
	(0.143)
Leftist Ideology	0.071***
	(0.024)
Governor Copartisan	1.435***
	(0.162)
President Copartisan	0.094
	(0.181)
Middle Income	0.154
	(0.170)
High Income	−0.573***
	(0.130)
Argentina	0.179
	(0.132)
Pocketbook Economic Evaluation	0.003
	(0.003)
Sociotropic Economic Evaluation	0.014***
	(0.003)
Government Improves Security	0.010***
	(0.002)
Government Should Provide Jobs	0.000
	(0.002)
Dominant-Party System	−0.646
	(0.406)
Dominant-Party*Jobs	0.009*
	(0.005)
Constant	−0.970**
	(0.443)
Observations	1,865

Note: Standard errors in parentheses.
$*p < 0.1; **p < 0.05; ***p < 0.01$

Table A.4. Sociotropic Economic Evaluations and Gubernatorial Vote Choice by Subnational Regime Type (2010–2012)

VARIABLES	Prospective Vote for Governor (Multinomial Logit Models; Reference Category: Vote for Incumbent)		
	Vote for Opposition Party/Candidate	Abstain	Cast Invalid Vote
Female	−0.255***	−0.104	0.019
	(0.098)	(0.129)	(0.147)
Age	0.003	0.016***	−0.004
	(0.003)	(0.004)	(0.005)
Wealth (Quintile)	−0.024	−0.141***	−0.068
	(0.038)	(0.051)	(0.057)
Interest in Politics	0.003*	−0.015***	−0.015***
	(0.002)	(0.002)	(0.003)
Education (Level)	0.292***	0.200**	0.036
	(0.076)	(0.101)	(0.115)
Urban	0.102	−0.084	−0.233
	(0.132)	(0.180)	(0.208)
President Copartisan	0.084	−0.209	−0.716*
	(0.174)	(0.311)	(0.419)
Governor Copartisan	−1.340***	−1.808***	−1.526***
	(0.155)	(0.294)	(0.327)
Voted in Last Election	−0.000	−0.018***	−0.004**
	(0.001)	(0.001)	(0.002)
Indigenous	0.306	0.549	−0.115
	(0.312)	(0.388)	(0.522)
Importance of Religion	−0.005***	−0.006***	−0.009***
	(0.002)	(0.002)	(0.002)
Received Vote-Buying Offer	0.237*	0.350**	0.636***
	(0.134)	(0.175)	(0.186)
Middle Income	−0.053	0.040	−0.079
	(0.163)	(0.209)	(0.230)
High Income	0.499***	0.475***	0.193
	(0.126)	(0.168)	(0.187)
Subnational Democracy Score	0.509***	0.218**	0.238**
	(0.080)	(0.102)	(0.117)
Argentina	0.028	0.646***	0.027
	(0.152)	(0.192)	(0.218)
2012	−0.892***	−1.391***	−1.059***
	(0.141)	(0.186)	(0.213)
Government Security Evaluation	−0.010***	−0.013***	−0.013***
	(0.002)	(0.002)	(0.003)
Government Should Provide Jobs	−0.001	−0.011***	0.000

Table A.4. *Continued*

VARIABLES	Prospective Vote for Governor (Multinomial Logit Models; Reference Category: Vote for Incumbent)		
	Vote for Opposition Party/Candidate	Abstain	Cast Invalid Vote
	(0.002)	(0.002)	(0.003)
Pocketbook Economic Evaluation	0.000	−0.009**	−0.002
	(0.003)	(0.004)	(0.004)
Sociotropic Economic Evaluation	−0.012***	−0.007*	−0.009**
	(0.003)	(0.004)	(0.004)
Dominant Party System	−0.314	−0.395	−0.020
	(0.241)	(0.317)	(0.340)
Dominant Party*Sociotropic	0.010**	0.013*	0.000
	(0.005)	(0.007)	(0.008)
Constant	0.713*	3.001***	2.067***
	(0.407)	(0.515)	(0.599)
Observations	2,880	2,880	2,880

Note: Standard errors in parentheses.
*$p < 0.1$; **$p < 0.05$; ***$p < 0.01$

Table A.5. Pocketbook Economic Evaluations and Gubernatorial Vote Choice by Subnational Regime Type (2010–2012)

VARIABLES	Prospective Vote for Governor (Multinomial Logit Models; Reference Category—Vote for Incumbent)		
	Vote for Opposition Party/Candidate	Abstain	Cast Invalid Vote
Female	−0.256***	−0.110	0.020
	(0.098)	(0.129)	(0.147)
Age	0.003	0.016***	−0.004
	(0.003)	(0.004)	(0.005)
Wealth (Quintile)	−0.024	−0.141***	−0.069
	(0.038)	(0.051)	(0.058)
Interest in Politics	0.003	−0.015***	−0.015***
	(0.002)	(0.002)	(0.003)
Education (Level)	0.293***	0.194*	0.040
	(0.076)	(0.101)	(0.115)
Urban	0.093	−0.088	−0.238
	(0.132)	(0.180)	(0.208)

Continued

Table A.5. *Continued*

VARIABLES	Prospective Vote for Governor (Multinomial Logit Models; Reference Category—Vote for Incumbent)		
	Vote for Opposition Party/Candidate	Abstain	Cast Invalid Vote
President Copartisan	0.093	−0.190	−0.717*
	(0.174)	(0.311)	(0.420)
Governor Copartisan	−1.355***	−1.829***	−1.533***
	(0.155)	(0.294)	(0.327)
Voted in Last Election	0.000	−0.018***	−0.004**
	(0.001)	(0.001)	(0.002)
Indigenous	0.338	0.600	−0.123
	(0.312)	(0.387)	(0.522)
Importance of Religion	−0.005***	−0.006***	−0.009***
	(0.002)	(0.002)	(0.002)
Received Vote-Buying Offer	0.256*	0.348**	0.654***
	(0.134)	(0.175)	(0.186)
Middle Income	−0.082	0.010	−0.084
	(0.162)	(0.209)	(0.229)
High Income	0.479***	0.450***	0.189
	(0.125)	(0.167)	(0.187)
Subnational Democracy Score	0.523***	0.230**	0.242**
	(0.080)	(0.102)	(0.116)
Argentina	0.037	0.647***	0.039
	(0.152)	(0.192)	(0.217)
2012	−0.892***	−1.387***	−1.065***
	(0.141)	(0.187)	(0.213)
Government Security Evaluation	−0.010***	−0.013***	−0.013***
	(0.002)	(0.002)	(0.003)
Sociotropic Economic Evaluation	−0.010***	−0.004	−0.009**
	(0.002)	(0.003)	(0.004)
Government Should Provide Jobs	−0.001	−0.011***	0.000
	(0.002)	(0.002)	(0.003)
Pocketbook Economic Evaluation	0.001	−0.010**	−0.001
	(0.003)	(0.004)	(0.004)
Dominant Party System	0.212	−0.176	0.347
	(0.324)	(0.409)	(0.457)
Dominant Party*Pocketbook	−0.003	0.006	−0.006
	(0.006)	(0.007)	(0.008)
Constant	0.613	2.982***	1.974***
Observations	2,880	2,880	2,880

Note: Standard errors in parentheses.
*$p < 0.1$; **$p < 0.05$; ***$p < 0.01$

Table A.6. Health Service Evaluations and Gubernatorial Vote Choice by Subnational Regime Type (2010–2012)

VARIABLES	Prospective Vote for Governor (Multinomial Logit Models; Reference Category—Vote for Incumbent)		
	Vote for Opposition Party/Candidate	Abstain	Cast Invalid Vote
Female	−0.075	0.318	0.076
	(0.171)	(0.263)	(0.277)
Age	0.006	0.024***	−0.013
	(0.006)	(0.008)	(0.010)
Wealth (Quintile)	−0.043	−0.086	−0.085
	(0.069)	(0.102)	(0.112)
Interest in Politics	0.002	−0.017***	−0.014***
	(0.003)	(0.005)	(0.005)
Education (Level)	0.540***	0.372*	0.008
	(0.135)	(0.210)	(0.219)
Urban	−0.092	−0.088	0.056
	(0.274)	(0.417)	(0.410)
President Copartisan	−0.330	1.108**	−0.520
	(0.336)	(0.495)	(0.672)
Governor Copartisan	−1.121***	−2.252***	−0.477
	(0.334)	(0.612)	(0.597)
Voted in Last Election	−0.001	−0.029***	−0.006
	(0.004)	(0.003)	(0.005)
Indigenous	−0.403	0.366	−14.667
	(0.767)	(1.034)	(1,317.102)
Importance of Religion	−0.003	−0.002	−0.003
	(0.003)	(0.004)	(0.004)
Received Vote-Buying Offer	0.366	−0.027	0.547
	(0.251)	(0.416)	(0.390)
Middle Income	−0.810*	0.020	−1.229
	(0.489)	(0.695)	(1.106)
High Income	0.765***	0.901**	0.814*
	(0.252)	(0.405)	(0.424)
Subnational Democracy Score	0.513***	0.312	0.734***
	(0.148)	(0.225)	(0.263)
Government Security Evaluation	−0.011***	−0.012**	−0.025***
	(0.003)	(0.005)	(0.006)
Sociotropic Economic Evaluation	−0.020***	−0.009	−0.006
	(0.004)	(0.007)	(0.007)
Government Should Provide Jobs	0.002	−0.006	0.002
	(0.004)	(0.006)	(0.006)
Pocketbook Economic Evaluation	0.007	−0.006	−0.003
	(0.005)	(0.007)	(0.008)
Health Services Evaluation	−0.009**	−0.004	−0.001

Continued

Table A.6. *Continued*

| VARIABLES | Prospective Vote for Governor (Multinomial Logit Models; Reference Category—Vote for Incumbent) | | |
	Vote for Opposition Party/Candidate	Abstain	Cast Invalid Vote
	(0.004)	(0.006)	(0.006)
Dominant Party System	−1.465*	1.514	1.645
	(0.829)	(1.089)	(1.495)
Dominant Party*Health	0.031**	−0.011	−0.050
	(0.013)	(0.018)	(0.036)
Constant	−0.580	1.227	0.681
	(0.814)	(1.114)	(1.248)
Observations	967	967	967

Note: Standard errors in parentheses.
*$p < 0.1$; **$p < 0.05$; ***$p < 0.01$

Table A.7. Security Evaluations and Gubernatorial Vote Choice by Subnational Regime Type (2010–2012)

| VARIABLES | Prospective Vote for Governor (Multinomial Logit Models; Reference Category—Vote for Incumbent) | | |
	Vote for Opposition Party/Candidate	Abstain	Cast Invalid Vote
Female	−0.261***	−0.103	0.023
	(0.098)	(0.129)	(0.147)
Age	0.003	0.016***	−0.004
	(0.003)	(0.004)	(0.005)
Wealth (Quintile)	−0.026	−0.142***	−0.068
	(0.038)	(0.051)	(0.057)
Interest in Politics	0.003*	−0.015***	−0.015***
	(0.002)	(0.002)	(0.003)
Education (Level)	0.296***	0.199**	0.035
	(0.076)	(0.101)	(0.115)
Urban	0.098	−0.094	−0.235
	(0.132)	(0.180)	(0.208)
President Copartisan	0.120	−0.212	−0.725*
	(0.174)	(0.311)	(0.420)
Governor Copartisan	−1.357***	−1.825***	−1.526***

Table A.7.   *Continued*

VARIABLES	Prospective Vote for Governor (Multinomial Logit Models; Reference Category—Vote for Incumbent)		
	Vote for Opposition Party/Candidate	Abstain	Cast Invalid Vote
	(0.154)	(0.295)	(0.327)
Voted in Last Election	−0.000	−0.018***	−0.004**
	(0.001)	(0.001)	(0.002)
Indigenous	0.326	0.609	−0.091
	(0.311)	(0.391)	(0.522)
Importance of Religion	−0.005***	−0.006***	−0.009***
	(0.002)	(0.002)	(0.002)
Received Vote-Buying Offer	0.251*	0.352**	0.648***
	(0.134)	(0.175)	(0.186)
Middle Income	−0.052	0.010	−0.089
	(0.162)	(0.210)	(0.230)
High Income	0.473***	0.476***	0.198
	(0.125)	(0.168)	(0.187)
Subnational Democracy Score	0.528***	0.227**	0.239**
	(0.080)	(0.103)	(0.116)
Argentina	0.021	0.655***	0.041
	(0.153)	(0.192)	(0.217)
2012	−0.886***	−1.402***	−1.063***
	(0.142)	(0.187)	(0.213)
Sociotropic Economic Evaluation	−0.009***	−0.004	−0.009**
	(0.002)	(0.003)	(0.004)
Government Should Provide Jobs	−0.001	−0.011***	0.000
	(0.002)	(0.002)	(0.003)
Pocketbook Economic Evaluation	0.000	−0.009**	−0.002
	(0.003)	(0.004)	(0.004)
Government Security Evaluation	−0.012***	−0.012***	−0.013***
	(0.002)	(0.003)	(0.003)
Dominant Party System	−0.308	0.299	0.170
	(0.241)	(0.294)	(0.326)
Dominant Party*Security	0.008**	−0.005	−0.004
	(0.004)	(0.005)	(0.006)
Constant	0.729*	2.840***	2.020***
	(0.408)	(0.518)	(0.600)
Observations	2,880	2,880	2,880

Note: Standard errors in parentheses.
*$p < 0.1$; **$p < 0.05$; ***$p < 0.01$

Table A.8. Sociotropic Economic Evaluations and Presidential Vote Choice by Subnational Regime Type (2008–2012)

VARIABLES	Prospective Vote for President (Multinomial Logit Models; Reference Category—Vote for Incumbent)		
	Vote for Opposition Party/ Candidate	Abstain	Cast Invalid Vote
Female	−0.042	−0.225**	−0.177*
	(0.070)	(0.089)	(0.104)
Age	0.009***	0.001	−0.005
	(0.002)	(0.003)	(0.004)
Wealth (Quintile)	0.096***	−0.110***	0.059
	(0.027)	(0.035)	(0.041)
Interest in Politics	0.003**	−0.018***	−0.015***
	(0.001)	(0.002)	(0.002)
Education (Level)	0.215***	0.070	0.117
	(0.055)	(0.070)	(0.083)
Urban	0.053	−0.017	−0.198
	(0.091)	(0.119)	(0.142)
President Copartisan	−3.248***	−2.316***	−2.886***
	(0.153)	(0.195)	(0.313)
Middle Income	0.376***	0.349**	0.284*
	(0.109)	(0.138)	(0.158)
High Income	0.013	−0.078	−0.143
	(0.087)	(0.111)	(0.130)
Subnational Democracy	0.276***	0.177***	0.076
	(0.055)	(0.068)	(0.081)
Argentina	−0.503***	−0.086	−0.306**
	(0.085)	(0.108)	(0.127)
2010	0.508***	0.579***	0.750***
	(0.090)	(0.111)	(0.128)
2012	0.011	−0.383***	−0.358***
	(0.083)	(0.110)	(0.135)
Government Security Evaluation	−0.017***	−0.020***	−0.019***
	(0.001)	(0.002)	(0.002)
Sociotropic Economic Evaluation	−0.015***	−0.008***	−0.011***
	(0.002)	(0.002)	(0.003)
Dominant-Party Regime	−0.158	−0.193	−0.260
	(0.170)	(0.217)	(0.246)
Dominant-Party*Sociotropic	0.007**	0.004	0.008
	(0.003)	(0.005)	(0.005)
Constant	0.847***	1.651***	1.069***
	(0.249)	(0.312)	(0.369)
Observations	6,107	6,107	6,107

Note: Standard errors in parentheses.
*$p < 0.1$; **$p < 0.05$; ***$p < 0.01$

Table A.9. Security Evaluations and Presidential Vote Choice by Subnational Regime Type (2008–2012)

VARIABLES	*Prospective Vote for President* (Multinomial Logit Models; Reference Category—Vote for Incumbent)		
	Vote for Opposition Party/ Candidate	Abstain	Cast Invalid Vote
Female	−0.047	−0.225**	−0.182*
	(0.070)	(0.089)	(0.104)
Age	0.009***	0.001	−0.005
	(0.002)	(0.003)	(0.004)
Wealth (Quintile)	0.095***	−0.111***	0.058
	(0.027)	(0.035)	(0.041)
Interest in Politics	0.003**	−0.018***	−0.015***
	(0.001)	(0.002)	(0.002)
Education (Level)	0.214***	0.068	0.115
	(0.055)	(0.070)	(0.083)
Urban	0.051	−0.011	−0.199
	(0.091)	(0.119)	(0.142)
President Copartisan	−3.237***	−2.316***	−2.879***
	(0.153)	(0.195)	(0.313)
Middle Income	0.373***	0.341**	0.277*
	(0.109)	(0.138)	(0.158)
High Income	0.000	−0.072	−0.152
	(0.087)	(0.111)	(0.131)
Subnational Democracy	0.283***	0.178***	0.081
	(0.055)	(0.068)	(0.081)
Argentina	−0.515***	−0.074	−0.310**
	(0.086)	(0.108)	(0.127)
2010	0.509***	0.589***	0.757***
	(0.090)	(0.111)	(0.128)
2012	0.014	−0.378***	−0.351***
	(0.083)	(0.110)	(0.135)
Government Security Evaluation	−0.013***	−0.007***	−0.009***
	(0.002)	(0.002)	(0.002)
Sociotropic Economic Evaluation	−0.019***	−0.019***	−0.020***
	(0.002)	(0.002)	(0.002)
Dominant-Party Regime	−0.070	0.114	−0.017
	(0.167)	(0.198)	(0.227)
Dominant-Party*Security	0.004	−0.004	0.001
	(0.003)	(0.004)	(0.004)
Constant	0.839***	1.651***	0.839***
	(0.249)	(0.312)	(0.250)
Observations	6,107	6,107	6,107

Note: Standard errors in parentheses.
$*p < 0.1; **p < 0.05; ***p < 0.01$

Table A.10. Sociotropic Economic Evaluations and Presidential Vote Choice by Subnational Regime Type (2008–2012)

VARIABLES	Prospective Vote for President (Multinomial Logit Models; Reference Category—Vote for Incumbent)		
	Vote for Opposition Party/ Candidate	Abstain	Cast Invalid Vote
Female	−0.042	−0.075	−0.103
	(0.103)	(0.138)	(0.146)
Age	0.009**	0.019***	−0.004
	(0.004)	(0.005)	(0.005)
Wealth (Quintile)	0.151***	−0.056	0.117**
	(0.040)	(0.053)	(0.056)
Interest in Politics	−0.003	−0.022***	−0.021***
	(0.002)	(0.002)	(0.003)
Education (Level)	0.325***	0.224**	0.054
	(0.079)	(0.108)	(0.115)
Urban	0.115	−0.165	−0.244
	(0.142)	(0.196)	(0.205)
President Copartisan	−2.708***	−1.476***	−2.015***
	(0.235)	(0.293)	(0.379)
Voted in Last Election	−0.002	−0.021***	−0.006***
	(0.001)	(0.002)	(0.002)
Indigenous	0.354	0.505	0.388
	(0.348)	(0.439)	(0.461)
Importance of Religion	−0.000	−0.006**	−0.003
	(0.002)	(0.002)	(0.002)
Received Vote-Buying Offer	−0.077	−0.151	0.320*
	(0.140)	(0.191)	(0.185)
Middle Income	0.196	0.239	0.160
	(0.178)	(0.228)	(0.231)
High Income	0.062	0.066	−0.234
	(0.133)	(0.178)	(0.185)
Subnational Democracy Score	0.152*	0.118	0.027
	(0.083)	(0.111)	(0.115)
Argentina	0.066	0.272	−0.059
	(0.163)	(0.208)	(0.217)
2012	−1.162***	−1.445***	−1.371***
	(0.147)	(0.201)	(0.214)
Government Security Evaluation	−0.020***	−0.024***	−0.021***
	(0.002)	(0.003)	(0.003)
Sociotropic Economic Evaluation	−0.018***	−0.011***	−0.013***
	(0.003)	(0.004)	(0.004)
Dominant-Party System	−0.097	−0.088	−0.370
	(0.270)	(0.348)	(0.363)

Table A.10. *Continued*

VARIABLES	Prospective Vote for President (Multinomial Logit Models; Reference Category—Vote for Incumbent)		
	Vote for Opposition Party/ Candidate	Abstain	Cast Invalid Vote
Dominant-Party*Sociotropic	0.009*	0.011	0.012
	(0.005)	(0.007)	(0.008)
Constant	1.191***	2.990***	2.582***
	(0.388)	(0.500)	(0.535)
Observations	2,991	2,991	2,991

Note: Standard errors in parentheses.
*$p < 0.1$; **$p < 0.05$, ***$p < 0.01$

Table A.11. Security Evaluations and Presidential Vote Choice by Subnational Regime Type (2008–2012)

VARIABLES	Prospective Vote for President (Multinomial Logit Models; Reference Category—Vote for Incumbent)		
	Vote for Opposition Party/Candidate	Abstain	Cast Invalid Vote
Female	−0.045	−0.074	−0.109
	(0.103)	(0.138)	(0.146)
Age	0.008**	0.019***	−0.005
	(0.004)	(0.005)	(0.005)
Wealth (Quintile)	0.149***	−0.060	0.115**
	(0.040)	(0.053)	(0.056)
Interest in Politics	−0.003	−0.023***	−0.022***
	(0.002)	(0.002)	(0.003)
Education (Level)	0.329***	0.223**	0.055
	(0.079)	(0.108)	(0.115)
Urban	0.110	−0.175	−0.253
	(0.142)	(0.197)	(0.205)
President Copartisan	−2.678***	−1.493***	−2.000***
	(0.235)	(0.293)	(0.380)
Voted in Last Election	−0.002	−0.021***	−0.006***
	(0.001)	(0.002)	(0.002)
Indigenous	0.364	0.570	0.429
	(0.347)	(0.442)	(0.461)
Importance of Religion	−0.000	−0.006**	−0.002
	(0.002)	(0.002)	(0.002)
Received Vote-Buying Offer	−0.063	−0.145	0.331*

Continued

Table A.11. *Continued*

VARIABLES	Prospective Vote for President (Multinomial Logit Models; Reference Category—Vote for Incumbent)		
	Vote for Opposition Party/Candidate	Abstain	Cast Invalid Vote
	(0.140)	(0.191)	(0.186)
Middle Income	0.187	0.202	0.134
	(0.177)	(0.228)	(0.231)
High Income	0.033	0.079	−0.258
	(0.133)	(0.179)	(0.186)
Subnational Democracy Score	0.169**	0.123	0.045
	(0.082)	(0.111)	(0.115)
Argentina	0.064	0.287	−0.052
	(0.162)	(0.207)	(0.216)
2012	−1.153***	−1.451***	−1.367***
	(0.147)	(0.201)	(0.214)
Government Security Evaluation	−0.016***	−0.009***	−0.010***
	(0.002)	(0.003)	(0.004)
Sociotropic Economic Evaluation	−0.022***	−0.022***	−0.021***
	(0.002)	(0.003)	(0.003)
Dominant-Party System	−0.109	0.562*	−0.053
	(0.272)	(0.330)	(0.351)
Dominant-Party*Security	0.008*	−0.006	0.003
	(0.004)	(0.006)	(0.006)
Constant	1.203***	2.845***	2.524***
	(0.388)	(0.500)	(0.535)
Observations	2,991	2,991	2,991

Note: Standard errors in parentheses.
$*p < 0.1; **p < 0.05; ***p < 0.01$

Table A.12. Models of Prospective Vote Choice in Mexico by Subnational Regime Type

VARIABLES	Models of Prospective Vote Choice in Mexico (0 = Vote for Opposition, 1 = Vote for Incumbent)			
	Vote for Incumbent Governor: Multiparty	Vote for Incumbent Governor: Dominant Party	Vote for Incumbent President: Multiparty	Vote for Incumbent President: Dominant Party
Female	0.669***	0.244	0.255*	0.267*
	(0.209)	(0.249)	(0.132)	(0.151)
Age	−0.006	0.002	−0.012**	−0.010*
	(0.008)	(0.010)	(0.005)	(0.005)

Table A.12. *Continued*

VARIABLES	*Models of Prospective Vote Choice in Mexico* (0 = Vote for Opposition, 1 = Vote for Incumbent)			
	Vote for Incumbent Governor: Multiparty	Vote for Incumbent Governor: Dominant Party	Vote for Incumbent President: Multiparty	Vote for Incumbent President: Dominant Party
Wealth (Quintile)	0.165*	−0.046	0.004	0.037
	(0.086)	(0.099)	(0.054)	(0.058)
Interest in Politics	−0.004	−0.002	−0.006**	−0.005*
	(0.004)	(0.005)	(0.002)	(0.003)
Education (Level)	−0.280	−0.483**	−0.037	−0.013
	(0.173)	(0.215)	(0.108)	(0.126)
Urban	0.113	−0.383	0.075	−0.214
	(0.238)	(0.287)	(0.152)	(0.170)
President Copartisan	−0.202	−0.551	3.496***	3.679***
	(0.327)	(0.474)	(0.251)	(0.364)
Governor Copartisan	0.945***	1.752***		
	(0.308)	(0.378)		
Subnational	−0.436***	0.851	−0.236**	0.025
Democracy	(0.168)	(0.650)	(0.097)	(0.232)
Middle Income	−0.207	0.064	0.180	−0.843***
	(0.336)	(0.283)	(0.198)	(0.183)
High Income	0.007	0.277	0.220	0.011
	(0.246)	(0.417)	(0.154)	(0.200)
Government Security	0.011***	−0.001	0.013***	0.016***
Evaluation	(0.004)	(0.005)	(0.002)	(0.003)
Government Should	−0.007*	0.009*		
Provide Jobs	(0.004)	(0.006)		
Pocketbook Economic	−0.004	0.015**		
Evaluation	(0.006)	(0.007)		
Sociotropic Economic	0.003	0.001	0.005*	0.005
Evaluation	(0.005)	(0.006)	(0.003)	(0.004)
2010			−0.468***	−0.496***
			(0.167)	(0.184)
2012			−0.583***	−0.254
			(0.162)	(0.196)
Constant	−0.182	0.400	−0.857*	−0.619
	(0.830)	(1.127)	(0.461)	(0.544)
Observations	435	343	1,408	1,068

Note: Standard errors in parentheses.
*$p < 0.1$; **$p < 0.05$; ***$p < 0.01$

Table A.13. Models of Prospective Vote Choice in Argentina by Subnational Regime Type

VARIABLES	Models of Prospective Vote Choice in Argentina (0 = Vote for Opposition, 1 = Vote for Incumbent)			
	Vote for Incumbent Governor: Multiparty	Vote for Incumbent Governor: Dominant Party	Vote for Incumbent President: Multiparty	Vote for Incumbent President: Dominant Party
Female	0.287**	0.158	−0.062	−0.297
	(0.133)	(0.391)	(0.117)	(0.354)
Age	0.002	0.029**	−0.005	0.011
	(0.004)	(0.014)	(0.004)	(0.012)
Wealth (Quintile)	−0.013	−0.092	−0.256***	−0.132
	(0.052)	(0.148)	(0.046)	(0.135)
Interest in Politics	−0.005**	−0.012	0.001	−0.002
	(0.002)	(0.009)	(0.002)	(0.007)
Education (Level)	−0.295***	−0.070	−0.483***	−0.080
	(0.099)	(0.298)	(0.089)	(0.266)
Urban	−0.008	0.230	−0.020	0.344
	(0.217)	(0.642)	(0.204)	(0.483)
President Copartisan	0.354	0.666	3.026***	2.036***
	(0.266)	(0.673)	(0.272)	(0.560)
Governor Copartisan	1.075***	1.121*		
	(0.236)	(0.627)		
Subnational Democracy	−0.757***	−0.756***	0.087	−0.637***
	(0.105)	(0.256)	(0.108)	(0.232)
Middle Income	0.220	0.260	−0.229	1.004
	(0.328)	(0.791)	(0.294)	(0.653)
High Income	−0.677***	0.212	−0.263	0.235
	(0.181)	(0.564)	(0.166)	(0.475)
Government Security Evaluation	0.014***	0.010	0.021***	0.024***
	(0.003)	(0.009)	(0.002)	(0.007)
Government Should Provide Jobs	0.004	−0.003		
	(0.003)	(0.008)		
Pocketbook Economic Evaluation	−0.000	−0.008		
	(0.004)	(0.015)		
Sociotropic Economic Evaluation	0.016***	0.021*	0.026***	0.013
	(0.003)	(0.012)	(0.003)	(0.010)
2010			−0.748***	−1.804***
			(0.164)	(0.460)
2012			0.482***	0.633
			(0.147)	(0.456)
Constant	−0.429	−1.517	−0.236	−1.821
	(0.526)	(1.345)	(0.407)	(1.190)
Observations	1,258	152	1,924	248

sNote: Standard errors in parentheses.
*p < 0.1; **p < 0.05; ***p < 0.01

Description of Subnational Democracy Scores

Gervasoni(2010b) proposes an index based on five particular indicators derived from Argentine provincial gubernatorial and legislative elections: *Executive Contestation, Legislative Contestation, Succession Control, Legislature Control,* and *Term Limits.* *Executive Contestation* gauges how competitive elections for the governorship are by subtracting the percentage of the total vote garnered by the winning candidate from one. *Legislative Contestation* does the same, but with the governor's party in provincial legislative elections.[1] *Succession Control* assesses the degree to which incumbent governors are successful in controlling who follows them in office—this variable is coded as high if the governor himself or a close ally achieves reelection (3), medium if someone from the same party as the governor is elected (2), or low if an opposition party captures the provincial executive office (1).

Legislature Control measures congruence between the legislature and the governor in terms of legislative seat shares, operationalized as the percentage of lower house seats won by the governor's party in each election. Finally, *Term Limits* codes whether and to what degree limits exist on the length of a governor's reign in power, coded from 0 (reelection is prohibited) to 3 (indefinite reelection).[2] From these indicators, we follow Gervasoni's lead and create a Subnational Democracy Index using factor analysis, which measures the extent to which provinces hang together across these variables. For the case of Mexico, we calculate a similar measure based on three components of Gervasoni's Subnational Democracy Index: *Executive Contestation, Legislative Contestation,* and *Succession Control* (a simple dummy variable measuring whether the incumbent party retained power). Reelection in Mexico was, until 2018, forbidden at all levels of government, and the *Legislative Contestation* and *Legislature Control* measures are equivalent. Higher values indicate more democratic subnational contexts, whereas lower values correspond to less competitive regimes.

---

[1] In provinces with bicameral legislatures, the measure is calculated for the lower house.

[2] As of 2014, five Argentine provinces allow for indefinite reelection (Formosa, Santa Cruz, San Luis, La Rioja, and Catamarca), and two provinces prohibit reelection for governors altogether (Mendoza and Santa Fé). The rest allow either one or two reelections for governors. Of the five provinces that permit indefinite reelection of governors, four have never experienced a rotation in power since Argentina democratized in 1983, with Catamarca being the only exception.

References

Acemoglu, Daron, and James A. Robinson. (2012). *Why Nations Fail: The Origins of Power, Prosperity, and Poverty*. New York: Crown Publishing.

Acemoglu, Daron, Tristan Reed, and James Robinson. (2014). "Chiefs: Economic Development and Elite Control of Civil Society in Sierra Leone." *Journal of Political Economy* 122(2): 319–368.

Achen, Christopher H., and Larry Bartels. (2017). *Democracy for Realists: Why Elections Do Not Produce Responsive Government*. Vol. 4. Princeton, NJ: Princeton University Press.

Almond, Gabriel, and Sidney Verba. (1963). *The Civic Culture. Political Attitudes and Democracy in Five Nations*. Princeton, NJ: Princeton University Press.

Alonso, Jorge. (1993). *El Rito Electoral en Jalisco (1940–1992)*. Zapopan, Mexico: El Colegio de Jalisco.

Alonso, Jorge. (1995). *El Cambio en Jalisco: Las Elecciones de 1994–1995*. Guadalajara, Mexico: Centro Universitario de Ciencias Sociales y Humanidades, Universidad de Guadalajara.

Alonso, Paula. (1992). The Origins of the Argentine Radical Party, 1889–1898. PhD diss., University of Oxford.

Alonso, Paula. (1993). "Politics and Elections in Buenos Aires, 1890–1898: The Performance of the Radical Party. *Journal of Latin American Studies*, 25(3): 465–487.

Alvarez, Michael, Jose A. Cheibub, Fernando Limongi, and Adam Przeworski. (1996). "Classifying Political Regimes." *Studies in Comparative International Development* 31(2): 3–36.

Alvarez, Michael R., Thad Hall, and Susan Hyde, eds. (2008). *Election Fraud: Detecting and Deterring Electoral Manipulation*. Washington, DC: Brookings Institution Press.

Anderson, Christopher J. (1995). *Blaming the Government: Citizens and the Economy in Five European Democracies*. Armonk, NY: Sharpe.

Anderson, Christopher J. (2000). "Economic Voting and Political Context: A Comparative Perspective." *Electoral Studies* 19: 151–170.

Anderson, Christopher J., Andre Blais, Shaun Bowler, Todd Donovan, and Ola Listhaug. (2005). *Losers' Consent: Elections and Democratic Legitimacy*. Oxford: Oxford University Press.

Anderson, Christopher J., and Christine Guillory. (1997). "Political Institutions and Satisfaction with Democracy: A Cross-National Analysis of Consensus and Majoritarian Systems." *American Political Science Review* 91(1): 66–81.

Ansolabehere, Stephen, and Eitan Hersh. (2012). "Validation: What Big Data Reveal about Survey Misreporting and the Real Electorate." *Political Analysis* 20(4): 437–459.

Arian, Alan, and Samuel Barnes. (1974). "The Dominant Party System: A Neglected Model of Democratic Stability." *Journal of Politics* 36(3): 592–614.

Arias, Mariela. (2017). "Alicia Kirchner continúa atrapada en la gobernación de Santa Cruz por protestas." *La Nación*. May 8, 2017. https://www.lanacion.com.ar/politica/

alicia-kirchner-continua-atrapada-en-la-gobernacion-de-santa-cruz-por-protestas-nid2021915

Arriola, Leonard R. (2005). "Ethnicity, Economic Conditions, and Opposition Support: Evidence from Ethiopia's 2005 Elections." *Northeast African Studies* 10(1): 115–144.

Atkeson, Lonna Rae, and Randall Partin. (1995). "Economic and Referendum Voting: A Comparison of Gubernatorial and Senatorial Elections." *American Political Science Review* 89(1): 99–107.

Auyero, Javier. (1999). "'This Is a Lot Like the Bronx, Isn't It?' Lived Experiences of Marginality in an Argentine Slum." *International Journal of Urban and Regional Research* 23(1): 45–69.

Auyero, Javier. (2000). "The Hyper-Shantytown: Neo-liberal Violence(s) in the Argentine Slum." *Ethnography* 1(1): 93–116.

Auyero, Javier. (2005). "Protest and Politics in Contemporary Argentina," in *Argentine Democracy: The Politics of Institutional Weakness*, ed. Steven Levitsky and Victoria Murillo, 250–268. State College: Penn State University Press.

Auyero, Javier. (2007). *Routine Politics and Violence in Argentina: The Gray Zone of State Power*. New York: Cambridge University Press.

Auyero, Javier, Pablo Lapegna, and Fernanda Poma. (2009). "Patronage Politics and Contentious Collective Action: A Recursive Relationship." *Latin American Politics and Society* 51(3): 1–31.

Bailey, John, and Pablo Paras. (2006). "Perceptions and Attitudes about Corruption and Democracy in Mexico." *Mexican Studies* 22(1): 57–82.

Bailón Corres, Jaime. (1999). "Pueblo Indios, Elites y Territorio: Sistemas de Dominio Regional," in *El Sur de México: Una Historia Politica de Oaxaca*. México, D.F.: El Colegio de México, Centro de Estudios Sociológicos.

Beaulieu, Emily. (2014). *Electoral Protest and Democracy in the Developing World*. New York: Cambridge University Press.

Beck, Hugo. (2012). "Gildo Insfrán, gobernador de Formosa. Clientelismo político y hegemonía peronista." Presented at XXXII Encuentro de Geohistoria Regional. Chaco, Resistencia, Argentina.

Beer, Caroline C. (2006). "Judicial Performance and the Rule of Law in Mexican States." *Latin American Politics and Society* 48(3): 33–61.

Behrend, Jacqueline. (2011). "The Unevenness of Democracy at the Subnational Level: Provincial Closed Games in Argentina." *Latin American Research Review* 46(1): 150–176.

Benton, Allyson L. (2005). "Dissatisfied Democrats or Retrospective Voters? Economic Hardship, Political Institutions, and Voting Behavior in Latin America." *Comparative Political Studies* 38(4): 417–442.

Benton, Allyson L. (2012). "Bottom-up Challenges to National Democracy: Mexico's (Legal) Subnational Authoritarian Enclaves." *Comparative Politics* 44(3): 253–271.

Benton, Allyson L. (2016). "How Participatory Governance Strengthens Authoritarian Regimes: Evidence from Electoral Authoritarian Oaxaca, Mexico." *Journal of Politics in Latin America* 8(2): 37–70.

Berent, Matthew K., Jon Krosnick, and Arthur Lupia. (2016). "Measuring Voter Registration and Turnout in Surveys." *Public Opinion Quarterly* 80(3): 597–621.

Bianchi, Matias. (2013). The Political Economy of Subnational Democracy: Fiscal Rentierism and Geography in Argentina. PhD diss., Institut d'Études Politiques de Paris.

Bingham, Powell, Jr. (2000). *Elections as Instruments of Democracy: Majoritarian and Proportional Visions*. New Haven, CT: Yale University Press.

Bingham, Powell G., and Guy Whitten. (1993). "A Cross-National Analysis of Economic Voting: Taking Account of the Political Context." *American Journal of Political Science* 37(2): 391–414.

Black, Earl, and Merle Black. (1989). *Politics and Society in the South*. Boston: Harvard University Press.

Blake, Charles, and Christopher Martin. (2006). "The Dynamics of Political Corruption: Reexamining the Influence of Democracy." *Democratization* 13(1): 1–14.

Boerr, Martín. (2019). "Un viaje al sistema clientelar que perpetua Insfrán." *La Nación*. June 15, 2019. https://www.lanacion.com.ar/politica/formosa-un-viaje-al-sistema-clientelar-que- perpetua-a-insfran-nid2258231

Bogaards, Matthijs. (2004). "Counting Parties and Identifying Dominant Party Systems in Africa." *European Journal of Political Research* 43: 173–197.

Boulding, Carew. (2014). *NGOs, Political Protest, and Civil Society*. New York: Cambridge University Press.

Brownlee, Jason. (2007). *Authoritarianism in an Age of Democratization*. New York: Cambridge University Press.

Calvo, Ernesto, and Maria Murillo. (2004). "Who Delivers? Partisan Clients in the Argentine Electoral Market." *American Journal of Political Science* 48(4): 742–757.

Camp, Roderic Ai. (2013). *Politics in Mexico: Consolidation or Decline?* New York: Oxford University Press.

Camp, Roderic Ai. (2017). *Mexico: What Everyone Needs to Know*. New York: Oxford University Press.

Campbell, James E., Helmut Norpoth, Alan Abramowitz, Michael Lewis-Beck, Charles Tien, Robert Erikson, Christopher Wlezien, et al. (2017). "A Recap of the 2016 Election Forecasts." *PS: Political Science & Politics* 50(2): 331–338.

Carlin, Ryan E., and Mason Moseley. (2015). "Good Democrats, Bad Targets: Democratic Values and Clientelistic Vote Buying." *Journal of Politics* 77(1): 14–26.

Carlin, Ryan E., and Matthew Singer. (2011). "Support for Polyarchy in the Americas." *Comparative Political Studies* 44(11): 1500–1526.

Carlin, Ryan E., Matthew Singer, and Elizabeth Zechmeister, eds. (2015). *The Latin American Voter: Pursuing Representation and Accountability in Challenging Contexts*. Ann Arbor: University of Michigan Press.

Carlin, Ryan E., and Shane Singh. (2015). "Executive Power and Economic Accountability." *Journal of Politics* 77(4): 1031–1044.

Carrión, Julio F. (2008). "Illiberal Democracy and Normative Democracy: How Is Democracy Defined in the Americas?," in *Challenges to Democracy in Latin America and the Caribbean*, ed. Mitchell Seligson, 21–46. Nashville, TN: Vanderbilt University.

Catterberg, Gabriela, and Alejandro Moreno. (2006). "The Individual Bases of Political Trust: Trends in New and Established Democracies." *International Journal of Public Opinion Research* 18: 31–48.

Chavez, Rebecca B. (2004). *The Rule of Law in Nascent Democracies*. Palo Alto, CA: Stanford University Press.

Chubb, Judith. (1982). *Patronage, Power and Poverty in Southern Italy: A Tale of Two Cities*. New York: Cambridge University Press.

Clarín.(2017)."Enunaudio,AdolfoRodríguezSaápromete'limpiaralostraidores.'"August16, 2017. https://www.clarin.com/politica/audio-adolfo-rodriguez-saa-promete-limpiar-traidores_0_S1_i8QzuZ.html

Cleary, Matthew R., and Susan Stokes. (2006). *Democracy and the Culture of Skepticism: Political Trust in Argentina and Mexico*. New York: Russell Sage Foundation.

CNN. (2017). "99.97% of North Koreans Turn Out for Local Elections." Accessed March 2017. http://www.cnn.com/2015/07/21/asia/north-korea-election-result/

Cohen, Mollie J., Noam Lupu, and Elizabeth. J. Zechmeister, eds. (2016). *The Political Culture of Democracy in the Americas, 2016/17*. Nashville, TN: Latin American Public Opinion Project, Vanderbilt University.

Cohen, Mollie J., Elizabeth J. Zechmeister, and Eui Young Noh. (n.d.). "Vote Buying and Trust in Elections in the Americas." Unpublished manuscript. Vanderbilt University.

Collier, David, and Levitsky Steven. (1997). "Democracy with Adjectives: Conceptual Innovation in Comparative Research." *World Politics* 49(3): 430–451.

Córdova, Abby. (2009). "Methodological Note: Measuring Relative Wealth Using Household Asset Indicators." *AmericasBarometer Insights* 6: 1–9.

Cornelius, Wayne A., Todd Eisenstadt, and Jane Hindley, eds. (1999). *Subnational Politics and Democratization in Mexico*. La Jolla: Center for U.S.-Mexican Studies, University of California, San Diego.

Croke, Kevin, Guy Grossman, Horacio Larreguy, and John Marshall. (2016). "Deliberate Disengagement: How Education Can Decrease Political Participation in Electoral Authoritarian Regimes." *American Political Science Review* 110(3): 579–600.

Cruz, José M. (2008). "The Impact of Violent Crime on the Political Culture of Latin America: The Special Case of Central America," in *Challenges to Democracy in Latin America and the Caribbean: Evidence from the AmericasBarometer 2006–07*, ed. Mitchell A. Seligson, 219–250. Nashville, TN: Vanderbilt University.

Dahl, Robert A. (1971). *Polyarchy: Participation and Opposition*. New Haven, CT: Yale University Press.

Dahlum, Sirianne. (2018). "Students in the Streets: Education and Nonviolent Protest." *Comparative Political Studies*. doi: 10.1177/0010414018758761.

Dahlum, Sirianne, and Carl Knutsen. (2017). "Democracy by Demand? Reinvestigating the Effect of Self-expression Values on Political Regime Type." *British Journal of Political Science* 47(2): 437 461

de Remes, Alain. (2000). *Municipal Electoral Processes in Latin America and Mexico*. Mexico, D.F.: Centro de Invesitgación y Docencia Económicas.

Diamond, Larry. (2015). "Facing Up to the Democratic Recession." *Journal of Democracy* 26(1): 141–155.

Diamond, Larry, and Marc F. Plattner, eds. (2006). *Electoral Systems and Democracy*. Baltimore: JHU Press.

Díaz-Cayeros, Alberto, Federico Estévez, and Beatriz Magaloni. (2009). "Welfare Benefits, Canvassing, and Campaign Handouts," in *Consolidating Mexico's Democracy: The 2006 Presidential Campaign in Comparative Perspective*, eds. Jorge I Domínguez, Chappell Lawson, and Alejandro Moreno. 229–245. Baltimore: Johns Hopkins University Press.

Diaz-Cayeros, A., and Beatriz Magaloni. (2001). "Party Dominance and the Logic of Electoral Design in Mexico's Transition to Democracy." *Journal of Theoretical Politics* 13(3): 271–293.

Domonoske, Camila. (2017). "Supreme Court Declines Republican Bid to Revive North Carolina Voter ID Law." NPR, May 15.

Downs, Anthony. (1957). "An Economic Theory of Political Action in a Democracy." *Journal of Political Economy* 65(2): 135–150.

Duch, Raymond M. (2001). "A Developmental Model of Heterogeneous Economic Voting in New Democracies." *American Political Science Review* 95: 895–910.

Duch, Raymond, and Randy Stevenson. (2008). *The Economic Vote*. New York: Cambridge University Press.

Eaton, Kent. (2004). *Politics beyond the Capital: The Design of Subnational Institutions in South America*. Palo Alto, CA: Stanford University Press.

Eaton, Kent. (2013). "Recentralization and the Left Turn in Latin America: Diverging Outcomes in Bolivia, Ecuador, and Venezuela." *Comparative Political Studies* 47(8): 1130–1157.

Echeverri-Gent, John. (1992), "Popular Participation and Poverty Alleviation: The Experience of Reform Communists in India's West Bengal," *World Development* 20(10): 1401–1422.

Eckstein, Harry. (1975). "Case Study and Theory in Political Science," in *Handbook of Political Science*, eds. Fred I. Greenstein and Nelson W. Polsby, 79–138. Reading, MA: Addison-Wesley.

Eisenstadt, Todd. (2004). *Courting Democracy in Mexico: Party Strategies and Electoral Institutions*. New York: Cambridge University Press.

El Puntano. (2017). " 'Quieren formar merenderos para conseguir 150 mil votos', el repudiable relato de un dirigente." *El Puntano*. August 20, 2017. https://elpuntano. com/2017/08/20/quieren-formar-merenderos-para-conseguir-150-mil-votos-el-repudiable-relato-de-un-dirigente/

Evans, Geoffrey and Mark Pickup. (2010). "Reversing the Causal Arrow: The Political Conditioning of Economic Perceptions in the 2000-2004 U.S. Presidential Election Cycle." *Journal of Politics* 72(4): 1236-1251.

Fagen, Richard R. and William S. Tuohy. (1972). Stanford: Stanford University Press.

Falleti, Tulia. (2010). *Decentralization and Subnational Politics in Latin America*. New York: Cambridge University Press.

Finkel, Steven E. (1985). "Reciprocal Effects of Participation and Political Efficacy: A Panel Analysis." *American Journal of Political Science* 29(4): 891–913.

Fiorina, Morris. (1981). *Retrospective Voting in American National Elections*. New Haven, CT: Yale University Press.

Flores, Oscar. (2017). "Resultados en San Luis: Adolfo Rodríguez Saá se adjudica el triunfo y ya habla de 'epopeya.'" *Clarín*. October 22, 2017. https://www.clarin.com/politica/ elecciones-2017-adolfo-rodriguez-saa-adjudica-triunfo-san-luis-habla-epopeya_0_ HJ5hsoc6b.html

Foweraker, Joe, and Roman Krznaric. (2002). "The Uneven Performance of Third Wave Democracies: Electoral Politics and the Imperfect Rule of Law in Latin America." *Latin American Politics and Society* 44(3): 29–60.

Fox, Jonathan. (1994). "Latin America's Emerging Local Politics." *Journal of Democracy* 5(2): 105–116.

Freedom House. (2017). *Freedom in the World 2017*. Available at: https://freedomhouse. org/sites/default/files/FH_FIW_2017_Report_Final.pdf (last accessed December, 2019)

Freedom House. (2018). *Freedom in the World, 2018: Democracy in Crisis*. https:// freedomhouse.org/report/freedom-world/freedom-world-2018

Freedom House. (2019). "Freedom in the World, 2019: Democracy in Retreat." https:// freedomhouse.org/report/freedom-world/freedom-world-2019/democracy-in-retreat(last accessed March 26, 2020)

Gandhi, Jennifer. (2008). *Political Institutions under Dictatorships*. New York: Cambridge University Press.

Gandhi, Jennifer, and Ellen Lust-Okar. (2009). "Elections under Authoritarianism." *Annual Review of Political Science* 12: 403–422.

Gannett, Robert, T. (2005). "Tocqueville and Local Government: Distinguishing Democracy's Second Track." *The Review of Politics* 67(4): 721–736.

Gans-Morse, Jordan, Sebastian Mazzuca, and Simeon Nichter. (2014). "Varieties of Clientelism: Machine Politics during Elections." *American Journal of Political Science* 58(2): 415–432.

Geddes, Barbara. (1991). "A Game Theoretic Model of Reform in Latin American Democracies." *American Political Science Review* 85(2): 371–392.

Gélineau, Francois, and Matthew Singer. (2015). "The Economy and Incumbent Support in Latin America," in *The Latin American Voter: Pursuing Representation and Accountability in Challenging Contexts*, ed. Ryan E. Carlin, Matthew Singer, and Elizabeth Zechmeister, 281–299. Ann Arbor: University of Michigan Press.

Gerring, John. (2004). "What Is a Case Study and What Is It Good for?" *American Political Science Review* 98(2): 341–354.

Gerring, John, and Strom C. Thacker. (2004). "Political Institutions and Corruption: The Role of Unitarism and Parliamentarism." *British Journal of Political Science* 34: 295–330.

Gervasoni, Carlos. (2010a). "Measuring Variance in Subnational Regimes: Results from an Expert-Based Operationalization of Democracy in the Argentine Provinces." *Journal of Politics in Latin America* 2. doi: 10.1177/1866802X1000200202

Gervasoni, Carlos. (2010b). "A Rentier Theory of Subnational Regimes: Fiscal Federalism, Democracy, and Authoritarianism in the Argentine Provinces." *World Politics* 62(2): 302–340.

Gervasoni, Carlos. (2015). "The Dimensions of Democratic and Hybrid Subnational Regimes: Evidence from an Expert Survey in Argentina," in *Illiberal Practices*, ed. Jacqueline Behrend and Laurence Whitehead, 67–108. Baltimore: Johns Hopkins University Press.

Gervasoni, Carlos. (2018). *Hybrid Regimes within Democracies: Fiscal Federalism and Subnational Rentier States*. New York: Cambridge University Press.

Gibson, Edward L. (2005). "Boundary Control: Subnational Authoritarianism in Democratic Countries." *World Politics* 58(1): 101–132.

Gibson, Edward L. (2013). *Boundary Control: Subnational Authoritarianism in Federal Democracies*. New York: Cambridge University Press.

Gibson, Edward L., and Ernesto Calvo. (2000). "Federalism and Low-Maintenance Constituencies: Territorial Dimensions of Economic Reform in Argentina." *Studies in Comparative International Development* 35(3): 32–55.

Giraudy, Agustina. (2009). Subnational Undemocratic Regime Continuity after Democratization: Argentina and Mexico in Comparative Perspective. PhD diss., Department of Political Science, University of North Carolina at Chapel Hill.

Giraudy, Agustina. (2011). "La Política Territorial de la Democracia Subnacional." *Journal of Democracy en Español* 3(Julio): 42–57.

Giraudy, Agustina. (2013). "Varieties of Subnational Undemocratic Regimes: Evidence from Argentina and Mexico." *Studies in Comparative International Development* 48(1): 51–80.

Giraudy, Agustina. (2015). *Democrats and Autocrats: Pathways of Subnational Undemocratic Regime Continuity within Democratic Countries*. New York: Oxford University Press.

Gomez, Brad T., and Wilson, Mathew. (2001). "Political Sophistication and Economic Voting in the American Electorate: A Theory of Heterogeneous Attribution." *American Journal of Political Science* 45(4): 899–914.

Gomez-Tagle, Silvia. (1997). *La transición inconclusa: Treinta años de Elecciones en México.* México, D.F.: El Colegio de México.

Gosnell, H. F. (1933). "The Political Party versus the Political Machine." *The Annals of the American Academy of Political and Social Science* 169(1): 21–28.

Granato, Jim, Ronald Inglehart, and David Leblang. (1996). "The Effect of Cultural Values on Economic Development: Theory, Hypotheses, and Some Empirical Tests." *American Journal of Political Science* 40(3): 607–631.

Greene, Kenneth F. (2007). *Why Dominant Parties Lose: Mexico's Democratization in Comparative Perspective.* New York: Cambridge University Press.

Grzymala-Busse, Anna. (2007). *Rebuilding Leviathan: Party Competition and State Exploitation in Post-Communist Democracies.* Cambridge: Cambridge University Press.

Guillén Lopéz, Tonatiuh. (1996). *Gobiernos Municipales en México: Entre la Modernizacion y la Tradicion Politica.* Tijuana, Mexico: El Colegio de la Frontera Norte.

Guiñazú, María C. (2003). *The Subnational Politics of Structured Adjustment in Argentina: The Case of San Luis.* PhD diss., Massachusetts Institute of Technology, Cambridge, MA.

Guiso, Luigi, Paola Sapienza, and Luigi Zingales. (2006). "Does Culture Affect Economic Outcomes?" *Journal of Economic Perspectives* 20(2): 23–48.

Gutiérrez Rodríguez, and José Javier. (2015). "Elecciones en Colima: del partido hegemónico al bipartidismo competitivo." *El Cotidiano* 193: 107–120.

Hayes, Danny, and Seth C. McKee (2008). "Toward a One-party South?" *American Politics Research* 36(1): 3–32.

Herrmann, Julian D. (2010). "Neo-Patrimonialism and Subnational Authoritarianism in Mexico: The Case of Oaxaca." *Journal of Politics in Latin America* 2: 85–112.

Hillygus, Sunshine. (2005). "The Missing Link: Exploring the Relationship between Higher Education and Political Engagement." *Political Behavior* 27(1): 25–47.

Hiskey, Jonathan T., and Shaun Bowler. (2005). "Local Context and Democratization in Mexico." *American Journal of Political Science* 49(1): 57–71.

Hiskey, Jonathan T., and Mitchell A. Seligson. (2003). "Pitfalls of Power to the People: Decentralization, Local Government Performance, and System Support in Bolivia." *Studies in Comparative International Development* 37(4): 64–88.

Iglesia, Maria. (2019). "En tres años de gestión de Macri, solo tres provincias mejoraron su economía." *El Cronista.* February 3, 2019. https://www.cronista.com/economiapolitica/En-tres-anos-de-la-gestion-de-Macri-solo-tres-provincias-mejoraron-su-economia-20190201-0036.html

Inglehart, Ronald. (1988). "The Renaissance of Political Culture." *American Political Science Review* 82(4): 1203–1230.

Inglehart, Ronald. (1990). *Culture Shift in Advanced Society.* Princeton, NJ: Princeton University Press.

Inglehart, Ronald. (1999). "Postmodernization Brings Declining Respect for Authority but Rising Support for Democracy," in *Critical Citizens: Global Support for Democratic Government,* ed. Pippa Norris. Oxford: Oxford University Press.

Inglehart, Ronald, and Christian Welzel. (2005). *Modernization, Cultural Change, and Democracy: The Human Development Sequence.* New York: Cambridge University Press.

Instituto Nacional de Estadística y Geografía (INEGI). (2017). *Anuario estadístico y geográfico por entidad federativa 2017.* Aguascalientes, Mexico: Instituto Nacional de Estadística y Geografía.

Instituto Nacional de Estadística y Geografía. (2019). "México en Cifras." https://www. inegi.org.mx/app/areasgeograficas/?ag=00(last accessed March 26, 2020)

Jackman, Robert W., and Ross Miller. (1996). "A Renaissance of Political Culture?" *American Journal of Political Science* 40(3): 632–659.

Kam, Cindy D., and Carl Palmer. (2008). "Reconsidering the Effects of Education on Political Participation." *Journal of Politics* 70(3): 612–631.

Karklins, Rasma. (1986). "Soviet Elections Revisited: Voter Abstention in Noncompetitive Voting." *American Political Science Review* 80(2): 449–469.

Karp, Jeffrey A., and Susan A. Banducci. (2008). "Political Efficacy and Participation in Twenty-Seven Democracies: How Electoral Systems Shape Political Behaviour." *British Journal of Political Science* 38: 311–334.

Keefer, Philip. (2006). Programmatic Parties: Where Do They Come from and Do They Matter? Paper presented at the Annual Meeting of the American Political Science Association, Philadelpia, PA, August–September 2006.

Key, Valdimer O. (1949). *Southern Politics in State and Nation.* New York: Vintage Books.

Key, Valdimer O. (1966). *The Responsible Electorate.* New York: Vintage Books.

Kiewiet, Roderick. (1983). *Macroeconomics and Micropolitics: The Electoral Effects of Economic Issues.* Chicago: University of Chicago Press.

Kiewiet de Jonge, Chad P. (2016). "Should Researchers Abandon Questions about Democracy? Evidence from Latin America." *Public Opinion Quarterly* 80(3): 694–716.

Kinder, Donald R., and Roderick Kiewiet. (1981). "Sociotropic Politics: The American Case." *British Journal of Political Science* 11(2): 129–161.

Kitschelt, Herbert, Kirk Hawkins, Juan Luna, Guillermo Rosas, and Elizabeth Zechmeister. (2010). *Latin American Party Systems.* New York: Cambridge University Press.

Kitschelt, Herbert, and Steven Wilkinson, eds. (2007). *Patrons, Clients and Policies: Patterns of Democratic Accountability and Political Competition.* New York: Cambridge University Press.

Klesner, Joseph L. (2001). "Adios to the PRI? Changing Voter Turnout in Mexico's Political Transition." *Mexican Studies/Estudios Mexicanos* 17(1): 17–39.

Kousser, Thad. B. (2010). "Does Partisan Polarization Lead To Policy Gridlock in California?" *California Journal of Politics and Policy* 2(2): 1–23.

Kramer, Gerald H. (1971). "Short-Term Fluctuations in U.S. Voting Behavior, 1896–1964." *American Political Science Review* 65: 131–143.

Lakhani, Nina. (2017). "Mexico State Election Heads to Court amid Allegations of Intimidation and Vote-Buying." *The Guardian.* June 5, 2017. https://www. theguardian.com/world/2017/jun/05/mexico-state-election-court-alfredo-del-mazo-maza-delfina-gomez

La Nación. (2003). "Formosa: los constituyentes aprobaron la reelección indefinida." *La Nación.*July1,2003.https://www.lanacion.com.ar/politica/formosa-los-constituyentes-aprobaron-la-reeleccion-indefinida-nid508034

La Nación. (2017a). "Elecciones 2017 - San Luis: por primera vez en 34 años perdieron los Rodríguez Saá." *La Nación.* August 14, 2017. https://www.lanacion.com.ar/2052873-elecciones-2017-san-luis-por-primera-vez-en-34-anos-perdieron-los-rodriguez-saa.

La Nación. (2017b). "Francisco Nazar: Formosa es una pequeña Venezuela." *La Nación.*July 23, 2017. https://www.lanacion.com.ar/politica/francisco-nazar-formosa-hoy-es-una-pequena-venezuela-nid2046257

Langston, Joy K. (2017). *Democratization and Authoritarian Party Survival*. New York: Oxford University Press.

Lasswell, Harold. (1936). *Who Gets What, When, How*. New York/London: Whittlesey House.

La Tinta. (2019, December 31). "No fue magia: la Victoria de los Rodríguez Saá en San Luis." *La Tinta*. October 27, 2017. https://latinta.com.ar/2017/10/victoria-rodriguez-saa-san-luis-latinta/ (last accessed March 26, 2020)

Latin American Public Opinion Project. (2004). "AmericasBarometer 2004." https://www.vanderbilt.edu/lapop/ab2004.php

Latin American Public Opinion Project. (2006). "AmericasBarometer 2006." https://www.vanderbilt.edu/lapop/ab2006.php

Latin American Public Opinion Project. (2008). "AmericasBarometer 2008." https://www.vanderbilt.edu/lapop/ab2008.php

Latin American Public Opinion Project. (2012). "AmericasBarometer 2012." https://www.vanderbilt.edu/lapop/ab2012.php

Latin American Public Opinion Project. (2016/2017). "AmericasBarometer 2016/17." https://www.vanderbilt.edu/lapop/ab2016.php

Lawson, Chappell. (2000). "Mexico's Unfinished Transition: Democratization and Authoritarian Enclaves." *Mexican Studies/Estudios Mexicanos* 16(2): 267–287.

Lawson, Chappell, and Kenneth F. Greene. (2014). "Making Clientelism Work: How Norms of Reciprocity Increase Voter Compliance." *Comparative Politics* 47(1): 61–77.

Levitsky, Steven, and Maria Murillo. (2005). *Argentine Democracy: The Politics of Institutional Weakness*. University Park: Penn State University Press.

Levitsky, Steven, and Lucan A. Way. (2010). *Competitive Authoritarianism: Hybrid Regimes after the Cold War*. New York: Cambridge University Press.

Lewis-Beck, Michael. (1988). *Economics and Elections: The Major Western Democracies*. Ann Arbor: University of Michigan Press.

Lijphart, Arend. (1999). *Patterns of Democracy: Government Forms and Performance in Thirty-Six Countries*. New Haven, CT: Yale University Press.

Linz, Juan J., and Amando De Miguel. (1966). *Within-Nation Differences and Comparisons: The Eight Spains*. New Haven, CT: Yale University Press.

Lipset, Seymour M. (1959). Some Social Requisites of Democracy: Economic Development and Political Legitimacy. *American Political Science Review* 53(1): 69–105.

Liptak, Alan., and Adam Blinder. (2018). "Supreme Court Temporarily Blocks North Carolina Gerrymandering Ruling." *The New York Times*. January 8, 2018. Retrieved from https://www.nytimes.com/2018/01/18/us/politics/supreme-court-north-carolina-gerrymandering.html

Lisoni, Carlos M. (2018). "Persuasion and Coercion in the Clientelistic Exchange: A Survey of Four Argentine Provinces." *Journal of Politics in Latin America* 10(1): 133–156.

Loaza, Soledad. (2000). *El Partido Acción Nacional, La Larga Marcha, 1939–1994: Oposición Leal y Partido de Protesta* México, D.F.: Fondo de Cultura Económica.

Lust-Okar, Ellen. (2005). *Structuring Conflict in the Arab World: Incumbents, Opponents, and Institutions*. New York: Cambridge University Press.

Lust-Okar, Ellen. (2006). "Elections under Authoritarianism: Preliminary Lessons from Jordan." *Democratization* 13(3): 456–471.

Machado, Fabiana, Carlos Scartascini, and Mariano Tommasi. (2011). "Political Institutions and Street Protests in Latin America." *Journal of Conflict Resolution* 55(3): 340–365.

Magaloni, Beatriz. (2006). *Voting for Autocracy: Hegemonic Party Survival and Its Demise in Mexico*. New York: Cambridge University Press.

Magaloni, B. (2008). Credible Power-sharing and the Longevity of Authoritarian Rule. *Comparative Political Studies* 41(4–5): 715–741.

Magaloni, Beatriz, and Kricheli, Ruth. (2010). Political Order and One-Party Rule. *Annual Review of Political Science* 13: 123–143.

Mainwaring, Scott, and Aníbal Pérez Liñán. (2014). *Democracies and Dictatorships in Latin America: Emergence, Survival, and Fall.* New York: Cambridge University Press.

Malkin, Elisabeth. (2011). "A Departing Governor Looks Ahead to a Bigger Prize in Mexico." *New York Times.* July 2, 2011. https://www.nytimes.com/2011/07/03/world/americas/03mexico.html

Markus, Gregory B. (1998). "The Impact of Personal and National Economic Conditions on the Presidential Vote: A Pooled Cross-Sectional Analysis." *American Journal of Political Science* 32: 137–154.

Mattes, Robert, and Michael Bratton. (2007). "Learning about Democracy in Africa: Awareness, Performance, and Experience." *American Journal of Political Science* 51(1): 192–217.

Mattingly, Daniel. (2016). "Elite Capture: How Decentralization and Informal Institutions Weaken Property Rights in China." *World Politics* 68(3): 383–412.

Mayor, Santiago. (2017). "No fue magia: la victoria de los Rodríguez Saá en San Luis." *La Tinta.* October 27, 2017. https://latinta.com.ar/2017/10/victoria-rodriguez-saa-san-luis-latinta/

McMann, Kelly. (2005, September). "The Impact of Neoliberal Reforms on State-Society Relations: Coping without Communism in Central Asia," American Political Science Association, Washington, DC.

McMann, Kelly. (2006). *Economic Autonomy and Democracy: Hybrid Regimes in Russia and Kyrgyzstan.* New York: Cambridge University Press.

Mickey, Robert. (2015). *Paths out of Dixie: The Democratization of Authoritarian Enclaves in America's Deep South, 1944–1972.* Princeton, NJ: Princeton University Press.

Molzahn, Cory, Octavio Ferreira, and David Shirk. (2013). *Drug Violence in Mexico: Data and Analysis through 2012.* San Diego, CA: Trans-Border Institute, University of San Diego.

Montes, Juan, and José de Córdoba. (2017). "The Town Where Mexico's Political Machine, and Six Governors, Were Born." June 2, 2017. *The Wall Street Journal.* https://www.wsj.com/articles/the-town-where-mexicos-political-machine-and-six-governors-were-born-1496395801

Montinola, Gabriela R., and Robert W. Jackman. (2002). "Sources of Corruption: A Cross-Country Study." *British Journal of Political Science* 32(1): 147–170.

Moreno, Alejandro. (2011). "ENVUD-Apéndice Metodológico." *EstePaís.* May 19. https://archivo.estepais.com/site/2011/envud-apendice-metodologico/

Morgenstern, Scott, and Elizabeth Zechmeister. (2001). "Better the Devil You Know than the Saint You Don't? Risk Propensity and Vote Choice in Mexico." *Journal of Politics* 63(1): 93–119.

Morris, Stephen D. (2003). "Corruption and Mexican Political Culture." *Journal of the Southwest* 45(4): 671–708.

Morris, Stephen D. (2008). "Disaggregating Corruption: A Comparison of Participation and Perceptions in Latin American with a Focus on Mexico." *Bulletin of Latin American Research* 27(3): 388–409.

Morris, Stephen D. (2009). *Political Corruption in Mexico: The Impact of Democratization.* Boulder, CO: Lynne Reinner.

Morris, Stephen D., and Charles H. Blake. (2010a). "Corruption and Politics in Latin America," in *Corruption and Politics in Latin America: National and Regional Dynamics*, ed. Stephen D. Morris and Charles H. Blake, 1–28. Boulder, CO: Lynne Reinner.

Morris, Stephen D., and Charles H. Blake, eds. (2010b). *Corruption and Politics in Latin America: National and Regional Dynamics*. Boulder, CO: Lynne Reinner.

Moseley, Mason W. (2018). *Protest State: The Rise of Everyday Contention in Latin America*. New York: Oxford University Press.

Muller, Edward N. (1988). "Democracy, Economic Development, and Income Inequality." *American Sociological Review* 53: 50–68.

Muller, Edward N., and Mitchell A. Seligson. (1994). "Civic Culture and Democracy: The Question of Causal Relationships." *American Political Science Review* 88(3): 635–652.

Nazar, Francisco. (2004). "Formosa, un pueblo cautivo." *Criterio* 2291(March). 70-77.

Nickson, Andrew. (1995). *Local Government in Latin America*. Boulder, CO: Lynne Rienner Publishers.

Nichter, Simeon. (2008). "Vote Buying or Turnout Buying? Machine Politics and the Secret Ballot." *American Political Science Review* 102(1): 19–31.

Nichter, Simeon. (2018). *Votes for Survival: Relational Clientelism in Latin America*. New York: Cambridge University Press.

Nichter, Simeon, and Michael Peress. (2017). "Request Fulfilling: When Citizens Demand Clientelist Benefits." *Comparative Political Studies* 50(8): 1086–1117.

Niemi, Richard G., Stephen C. Craig, and Franco Mattei. (1991). "Measuring Internal Political Efficacy in the 1988 National Election Study." *American Political Science Review* 85(4): 1407–1413.

Norris, Pippa. (1997). "Choosing Electoral Systems: Proportional, Majoritarian and Mixed Systems." *International Political Science Review* 18(3): 297–312.

Observatorio #NiUnFraudeMas. (2017). "Informe final sobre las elecciones para gobernador del estado de México del 2017." *El Pais*. June 7, 2017. http://niunfraudemas. org/documentos/informe_final.pdf

O'Donnell, Guillermo. A. (1993). "On the State, Democratization and Some Conceptual Problems: A Latin American View with Glances at Some Postcommunist Countries." *World Development* 21(8): 1355–1369.

O'Donnell, Guillermo. A. (1998). "Horizontal Accountability in New Democracies." *Journal of Democracy* 9(3): 112–126.

O'Donnell, Guillermo. A. (1999). *Counterpoints: Selected Essays on Authoritarianism and Democratization*. Notre Dame, IN: Notre Dame University Press.

OECD. (2015). *Measuring Well-Being in Mexican States*. Paris: OECD Publishing.

Olson, Mancur. (1982). *The Rise and Decline of Nations: Economic Growth, Stagflation, and Social Rigidities*. New Haven, CT: Yale University Press.

O'Neill, Thomas P., and Gary Hymel. (1993). *All Politics Is Local: And Other Rules of the Game*. New York: Times Books.

Peffley, Mark, and Robert Rohrschneider. (2003). "Democratization and Political Tolerance in Seventeen Countries: A Multi-Level Model of Democratic Learning." *Political Research Quarterly* 56(3): 243–257.

Pérez, Orlando J. (2015). "The Impact of Crime on Voter Choice in Latin America," in *The Latin American Voter: Pursuing Representation and Accountability in Challenging Contexts*, ed. Ryan E. Carlin, Matthew Singer, and Elizabeth Zechmeister, 324–345. Ann Arbor: University of Michigan Press.

Perfil. (2019). "Alberto Rodríguez Saá pide echar a empleados públicos de la oposición." *Perfil*. March 29, 2019. https://www.perfil.com/noticias/politica/audio-alberto-rodriguez-saa-pide-echar-empleados-publicos-de-la-oposicion.phtml

Petersen, German. (2018). "Elites and Turnovers in Authoritarian Enclaves: Evidence from Mexico." *Latin American Politics and Society* 60(2): 23–40.

Pickup, Mark, and Geoffrey Evans. (2013). "Addressing the Endogeneity of Economic Evaluations in Models of Political Choice." *Public Opinion Quarterly*, 77(3): 735–754.

Pop-Eleches, George, and Joshua Tucker. (2011). "Communism's Shadow: Postcommunist Legacies, Values, and Behavior." *Comparative Politics* 43(4): 379–408.

Posner, Daniel N., and David Simon. (2002). "Economic Conditions and Incumbent Support in Africa's New Democracies: Evidence from Zambia." *Comparative Political Studies* 35(3): 313–336.

Powell, Bingham, Jr. (2000). *Elections as Instruments of Democracy*. New Haven, CT: Yale University Press.

Powell, G. Bingham, Jr., and Guy D. Whitten. (1993). "A Cross-National Analysis of Economic Voting: Taking Account of the Political Context." *American Journal of Political Science* 37(2): 391–414.

Preston, Julia. (1999). "PRI Shows It Can Win." *The New York Times*. July 6, 1999. https://archive.nytimes.com/www.nytimes.com/library/world/americas/070699mexico-assess.html

Przeworski, Adam. (1991). *Democracy and the Market: Political and Economic Reforms in Eastern Europe and Latin America*. New York: Cambridge University Press.

Przeworski, Adam. (2015). "Acquiring the Habit of Changing Governments through Elections." *Comparative Political Studies* 48(1): 101–129.

Przeworski, Adam, Mike Alvarez, José A. Cheihub, and Fernando Limongi. (2000). *Democracy and Development: Political Institutions and Well-Being in the World, 1950–1990*. Cambridge: Cambridge University Press.

Przeworski, Adam, and Henry Teune. (1970). *The Logic of Comparative Social Inquiry*. New York: Wiley-Interscience.

Putnam, Robert D. (1993). *Making Democracy Work: Civic Traditions in Modern Italy*. Princeton, NJ: Princeton University Press.

Quiñones, Sam. (2017). "A Discouraging Day for Mexico." Dreamland, a Reporter's Blog from Author/Journalist Sam Quinones. June 5, 2017. http://samquinones.com/reporters-blog/2017/06/05/discouraging-day-mexico/

Raby, John. (2018). "Supreme Court, Teachers' Strike Dominated Headlines in W. Va." December 21, 2018. *AP News*. https://apnews.com/06f14c504cca48e79f78556955e9b466

Rauschenbach, Mascha, and Katrin Paula. (2019). "Intimidating Voters with Violence and Mobilizing Them with Clientelism." *Journal of Peace Research* 56(5): 682–696.

Remmer, Karen, and Gélineau, Francois. (2003). "Subnational Electoral Choice Economic and Referendum Voting in Argentina, 1983–1999." *Comparative Political Studies* 36(7): 801–821.

Roberts, Carlos Reymundo. (2017). "Formosa: El reino implacable del todopoderoso Gildo Insfrán." *La Nación*. July 23, 2017. https://www.lanacion.com.ar/politica/formosa-el-reino-implacable-del-todopoderoso-gildo-insfran-nid2046357

Robertson, Graeham B. (2007). "Strikes and Labor Organization in Hybrid Regimes." *American Political Science Review* 101(4): 781–798.

Rock, M. (2009). "Corruption and Democracy." *Journal of Development Studies* 45(1): 55–75.

Rodríguez, Flavia. (2012). *Evolución y Prospectiva del PIB Regional y Estatal de México, 2005–2014*. Distrito Federal, Mexico: Aregional.

Rodríguez, Victoria E. (1997). *Decentralization in Mexico from Reforma Municipal to Solidaridad to Nuevo Federalism*. Boulder, CO: Westview Press.

Rodríguez, Victoria E., and Peter M. Ward. (1995). *Opposition Government in Mexico*. Albuquerque: University of New Mexico Press.

Rohrschneider, Robert. (1994). "Report from the Laboratory: The Influence of Institutions on Political Elites' Democratic Values in Germany." *American Political Science Review* 88(9): 27–41.

Rohrschneider, Robert. (1996). "Institutional Learning versus Value Diffusion: The Evolution of Democratic Values among Parliamentarians in Eastern and Western Germany." *Journal of Politics* 58(2): 422–446.

Rohrschneider, Robert. (1999). *Learning Democracy: Democratic and Economic Values in Unified Germany*. New York: Oxford University Press.

Rokkan, Stein. (1970). *Citizens, Elections, Parties*. New York: McKay.

Rose-Ackerman, Susan. (1999). "Political Corruption and Democracy." *Connecticut Journal of International Law* 14: 363–378.

Salinas, Eduardo, and John A. Booth. (2011). "Micro-Social and Contextual Sources of Democratic Attitudes in Latin America." *Journal of Politics in Latin America* 3(1): 29–64.

Samper, José. (2006). *Entre el atraso y el autoritarismo*. Buenos Aires: Editorial Dunken.

Samuels, David. (2004). "Presidentialism and Accountability for the Economy in Comparative Perspective." *American Political Science Review* 98(3): 425–436.

Samuels, David, and Richard Snyder. (2001). "The Value of a Vote: Malapportionment in Comparative Perspective." *British Journal of Political Science* 31(4): 651–671.

Sartori, Giovanni. (1976). *Parties and Party Systems: A Framework for Analysis*. Cambridge: Cambridge University Press.

Scartascini, Carlos, and Mariano Tommasi. (2012). "The Making of Policy: Institutionalized or Not?" *American Journal of Political Science* 56(4): 787–801.

Schaffer, Joby, and Andy Baker. (2015). "Clientelism as Persuasion-Buying: Evidence from Latin America." *Comparative Political Studies* 48(9): 1093–1126.

Schedler, Andreas. (2006). Electoral Authoritarianism: The Dynamics of Unfree Elections. Boulder, CO: Lynne Rienner.

Schedler, Andreas. (2013). *The Politics of Uncertainty: Sustaining and Subverting Electoral Authoritarianism*. Oxford: Oxford University Press.

Schedler, Andreas, and Rodolfo Sarsfield. (2009). "Demócratas iliberales: Configuraciones contradictorias de apoyo a la democracia en México." *Espiral (Guadalajara)* 15(44): 123–159.

Scott, James C. (1972). *Comparative Political Corruption*. Englewood Cliffs, NJ: Prentice-Hall.

Scott, James C. (1969). "Corruption, Machine Politics, and Political Change." *American Political Science Review* 63(4): 1142–1158.

Seligson, Mitchell A. (2001). "Corruption and Democratization." *Public Integrity* 3 (Summer): 221–241.

Seligson, Mitchell A. (2002). "The Impact of Corruption on Regime Legitimacy: A Comparative Study of Four Latin American Countries." *Journal of Politics* 64(2): 408–433.

Seligson, Mitchell A. (2006). "The Measurement and Impact of Victimization: Survey Evidence from Latin America." *World Development* 34(2): 381–404.

Semple, Kirk. (2017). "P.R.I. closes in on narrow victory in state of Mexico governor's race." *New York Times,* 5 June. Last accessed on March 9, 2020 at: [https://www.nytimes.com/2017/06/05/world/americas/mexico-pri-party-state-election.html]

Sharafutdinova, Gulnaz. (2010). "What Explains Corruption Perceptions? The Dark Side of Political Competition in Russia's Regions." *Comparative Politics* 42(2): 147–166.

Shi, Tianjian. (1997). *Political Participation in Beijing.* London/Cambridge, MA: Harvard University Press.

Silva, Eduardo. (2009). *Challenging Neoliberalism in Latin America.* New York: Cambridge University Press.

Silver, B. D., B. A. Anderson, and P. R. Abramson. (1986). "Who Overreports Voting?" *American Political Science Review* 80(2): 613–624.

Simpser, Alberto. (2005). "Strategic Incentives for Electoral Corruption." Unpublished manuscript, University of Chicago.

Singer, Matthew M. (2009, September). "Buying Voters with Dirty Money: The Relationship between Clientelism and Corruption." Presented at the American Political Science Association 2009 Annual Meeting, Toronto, Canada.

Singer, Matthew M. (2011). "Who Says It's the Economy? Cross-National and Cross-Individual Variation in the Salience of Economic Performance." *Comparative Political Studies* 44(3): 284–312.

Singer, Matthew M., and Ryan Carlin. (2013). "Context Counts: The Election Cycle, Development and the Nature of Economic Voting." *Journal of Politics* 75(3): 730–742.

Singer, Mathew. M., Ryan Carlin, and Roland Love. (2014). "Corruption in the Americas," in *The Political Culture of Democracy in the Americas: Democratic Governance across 10 Years of the AmericasBarometer,* ed. Elizabeth J. Zechmeister, 143–163. Nashville, TN: Vanderbilt University.

Smets, Kaat, and Carolien van Ham. (2013). "The Embarrassment of Riches? A Meta-Analysis of Individual-Level Research on Voter Turnout." *Electoral Studies* 32: 344–359.

Snyder, Richard. (2001). "Scaling Down: Subnational Approaches to Comparative Politics." *Studies in Comparative International Development* 36(1): 93–110.

Sobel, Michael. E. (1982). "Asymptotic Confidence Intervals for Indirect Effects in Structural Equation Models." *Sociological Methodology* 13: 290–312.

Spiller, Pablo, and Mariano Tommasi. (2009). *The Institutional Foundations of Public Policy in Argentina.* New York: Cambridge University Press.

Sticco, Daniel. (2015). "Santa Cruz tiene la mayor cantidad de empleos públicos." *Infobae.* July 20, 2015. https://www.infobae.com/2015/07/20/1742453-santa-cruz-tiene-la-mayor-cantidad-empleados-publicos/

Stokes, Susan. C. (1996). "Public Opinion and Market Reforms:: The Limits of Economic Voting." *Comparative Political Studies,* 29(5), 499–519. https://doi.org/10.1177/0010414096029005001

Stokes, Susan. C. (2001). *Mandates and Democracy: Neoliberalism by Surprise in Latin America.* New York: Cambridge University Press.

Stokes, Susan C. (2005). "Perverse Accountability: A Formal Model of Machine Politics with Evidence from Argentina." *American Political Science Review* 99(3): 315–325.

Stokes, Susan C. (2007). "Political Clientelism." In *Oxford Handbook of Comparative Politics,* eds. Carles Boix and Susan C. Stokes, pp. 604-627

Stokes, Susan. C., T. Dunning, M. Nazareno, and V. Brusco. (2013). *Brokers, Voters, and Clientelism: The Puzzle of Distributive Politics.* New York: Cambridge University Press.

Stoyan, Alissandra T., and Sara Niedzwiecki. (2018). "Decentralization and Democratic Participation: The Effect of Subnational Self-Rule on Voting in Latin America and the Caribbean." *Electoral Studies* 52: 26–35.

Szwarcberg, Mariela. (2015). *Mobilizing Poor Voters: Machine Politics, Clientelism, and Social Networks in Argentina*. New York: Cambridge University Press.

Teune, Henry, and Adam Przeworski. (1970). *The Logic of Comparative Social Inquiry*. New York: Wiley-Interscience.

Thornton, Christy. (2017). "Cracks in the Fortress." *NACLA*. June 6, 2017. https://nacla. org/news/2017/06/06/cracks-fortress(last accessed March 26, 2020)

Tolbert, Caroline J., Ramona McNeal, and Daniel Smith. (2003). "Enhancing Civic Engagement: The Effect of Direct Democracy on Political Participation and Knowledge." *State Politics & Policy Quarterly* 3(1): 23–41.

Torrez, Juan Manuel. (2017). "Alberto Rodríguez Saá negó clientelismo político en plena campaña y confía en una victoria." *Los Andes*. October 22, 2017. https://www.losandes. com.ar/article/alberto-rodriguez-saa-nego-clientelismo-politico-en-plena-campana-y-confia-en-una-victoria

Triesman, Daniel. (2007). "What Have We Learned about the Causes of Corruption from Ten Years of Cross-National Empirical Research?" *Annual Review of Political Science* 10: 211–244.

Tucker, Joshua A. (2006). *Regional Economic Voting: Russia, Poland, Hungary, Slovakia, and the Czech Republic, 1990–1999*. New York: Cambridge University Press.

Varieties of Democracy. (2017). https://www.v-dem.net/en/reference/version-7-may-2017/ (last accessed March 26, 2020)

Veneranda, Marcelo. (2017). "Denunciaron Penalmente a los Hermanos Rodríguez Saá por un subsidio millonario." *La Nación*. October 2, 2017. https://www.lanacion. com.ar/2068489-denunciaron-penalmente-a-los-hermanos-rodriguez-saa-por-un-subsidio-millonario

Verba, Sidney, and Norman Nie. (1972). *Participation in America: Social Equality and Political Democracy*. New York: Harper & Row.

Vetter, Angelika. (2002). "Local Political Competence in Europe: A Resource of Legitimacy for Higher Levels of Government." *International Journal of Public Opinion Research* 14(1): 3–18.

Watkins, Kevin. (2006). *Human Development Report 2006 Beyond Scarcity: Power, Poverty and the Global Water Crisis*. New York: United Nations Development Programme.

Weitz-Shapiro, Rebecca. (2014). *Curbing Clientelism in Argentina: Politics, Poverty, and Social Policy*. New York: Cambridge University Press.

Whitten, Guy D., and Harvey Palmer. (1999). "Cross-National Analyses of Economic Voting." *Electoral Studies* 18(1): 49–67.

Wiarda, Howard J. (1971). "Toward a Framework for Analysis." *The American Journal of Comparative Law* 19(3): 434–463.

Wiarda, Howard J. (1973). "Toward a Framework for the Study of Political Change in the Iberic-Latin Tradition: The Corporative Model." *World Politics* 25(2): 206–235.

Wibbels, Erik. (2005). *Federalism and the Market: Intergovernmental Conflict and Economic Reform in the Developing World*. New York: Cambridge University Press.

Wilson, James Q., and Edward C. Banfield. (1965). "Voting Behavior on Municipal Public Expenditures: A Study in Rationality and Self-Interest," in *The Public Economy of Urban Communities*, ed. Julius Margolis, 74-91. Washington, DC: Resources for the Future.

Wiñazki, Miguel. (1995). *El último feudo. San Luis y el caudillismo de los Rodríguez Saá* [The Last Fiefdom: San Luis and the Bossism of the Rodríguez Saá]. Buenos Aires: Ediciones Temas de Hoy.

Wrong, Michaela. (2009). *It's Our Turn to Eat: A Story of a Kenyan Whistle Blower.* London: Fourth Estate.

Ybarra, Gustavo. (2017). "Elecciones 2017: La avalancha de fondos públicos con la que Rodríguez Saá dio vuelta la elección en San Luis." *La Nación.* October 23, 2017. https://www.lanacion.com.ar/2075517elecciones-2017-la-avalancha-de-fondos-publicos-con-la-que-rodriguez-saa-dio-vuelta-la-eleccion-en-san-luis

Ziccardi, Alicia, ed. (1995). *La tarea de gobernar: Gobiernos locales y demandas ciudadanas* ("The task of governing: Local Governments and Citizen Demands"). México, D.F.: Instituto de Investigaciones Sociales, UNAM.

Index

For the benefit of digital users, indexed terms that span two pages (e.g., 52–53) may, on occasion, appear on only one of those pages.

Note: Tables and figures are indicated by *t* and *f* following the page number